*CAROLINA*
*CRADLE*

*Settlement of the*
*Northwest Carolina*
*Frontier, 1747-1762*

On the eve of All-Souls' Day
I heard the dead men say
Who lie by the tottering tower,
To the dark and doubling wind
At the midnight's turning hour,
When other speech had thinned:
  "What of the world now?"
The wind whiffed back: "Men still
Who are born, do good, do ill
Here, just as in your time:
Till their years the locust hath eaten,
Leaving them bare, downbeaten;
Somewhiles in Springtide rime,
Somewhiles in summer glow,
Somewhiles in winter snow:—
  No more I know."

—*Thomas Hardy*

# CAROLINA CRADLE

*Settlement of the Northwest Carolina Frontier, 1747-1762*

## ROBERT W. RAMSEY

*The University of North Carolina Press*
*Chapel Hill*

© 1964 by the University of North Carolina Press
All rights reserved
Manufactured in the United States of America
ISBN 978-0-8078-0934-1
ISBN 978-0-8078-4189-1 (pbk.)
Library of Congress Catalog Card Number 64-22530

12  11  10  09  08      15  14  13  12  11

To my father,
whose profound understanding of the history and people
of piedmont Carolina helped make this work possible

# INTRODUCTION

The records of Rowan County, North Carolina, date as far back as 1752. These ancient land grants, deeds, wills, marriages, and church and cemetery records contain the history of the northwest Carolina frontier, the doorway to the South and West. Rowan County originally included practically all of central and northwestern North Carolina and extended westward to the Mississippi River, having no western boundary line.

While the vast amount of public and other records are in existence in this region, there is no information here to indicate whence these settlers came and why they came. From a historical standpoint, these facts are vital and badly needed. No one has ever taken the time and made the effort to dig out the facts contained in thousands of pages of courthouse and other pertinent records. No historian has ever gone back into the records at both ends—at the source and here in the area between the Yadkin and the Catawba rivers. As a beginning, a deep and intensive study would need to be made of the courthouse and other records in the states of Pennsylvania, Maryland, New Jersey, Delaware, and Virginia to ascertain when these early settlers arrived from Europe, where they settled, what they did, and what became of them.

Their story has been hidden in the many church, state, and county records from New Jersey to North Carolina. Over two hundred years have passed since these settlers began their journey to the south. The records that they left have never before been explored by a skilled and resourceful historian and researcher who knew how to find the records and how to arrange and evaluate them. Great skill, patience, perservance, knowledge, and intelligence, coupled with a deep personal interest, were necessary to present the facts and to establish them by documentary evidence. After two hundred years, this volume will now record for all time the needed facts that persons of this and later generations will need and want to know. Dr. Robert Ramsey has done a magnificent service to North Carolina and to the nation. The work represents many years of hard labor, study, travel, and research in those places where the facts were recorded. Only by the wide use of actual records can the historical accuracy of such a volume be achieved. Dr. Ramsey has done what was needed and what was necessary in this respect. Since his family background is here in the land of the "Carolina Cradle," he has a deep personal interest in his subject. As a result of Dr. Ramsey's years of effort, it is now possible for the student, the historian, the librarian, and the genealogist to read the story of the evolution of the northwest Carolina frontier.

In a speech at the Rowan Public Library, at Salisbury, N. C., in April 1964, Dr. Hugh Lefler, a native of the area and one of the outstanding historians of the United States, paid a high tribute to the work of Dr. Ramsey. Dr. Lefler stated that the research for the volume *Carolina Cradle* was of the highest order. He said that Dr. Ramsey's book was one of the really outstanding works on North Carolina that had been written.

The appendices and bibliography to the volume consist of 34 pages of material that are filled with a wealth of information, giving actual records or abstracts of data used in the volume. Many names of Quakers, Presbyterians, Baptists, and other denominations, both in North Carolina and those colonies that furnished the early settlers, are given. Passenger lists from ships with origins of sailings, destinations, and dates are listed in detail. Difficult names spelled in many various ways are made clear. North Carolina courthouse records are, in an understanding way, tied in with the records from those colonies in which the settlers of the northwest Carolina frontier originated.

The volume includes fully and completely the names of the early families that settled between the Yadkin and the Catawba, with maps showing the exact places where they settled on the frontier. These maps show the streams, churches, and landmarks of the frontier area.

There are eighteen chapters in Dr. Ramsey's volume. Each deals with some vital aspect of the northwest Carolina frontier and its settlement. For instance, in chapter three there is a list of the first settlers in the area between the Yadkin and the Catawba that includes such names as James Carter, Morgan Bryan, Edward

Hughes, Samuel Davis, Robert Gamble, John Dunn, George Forbush, William Linville, Thomas Gillespie, John Holmes, Thomas Bell, James Cathey, George Cathey, John Cathey, James Graham, Richard Graham, John Graham, Felix Kennedy, John Withrow, John Brandon (senior and junior), Richard Brandon, William Brandon, John Lock, Matthew Lock, John Davidson, George Davidson (senior and junior), David Templeton, James Templeton, John Sill, Alexander Osborne, Walter Carruth, Jane Carruth, Adam Carruth, James Marlin, James Mackilwean, John Brevard, Robert Brevard, William Sherrill, Abenton Sherrill, and Adam Sherrill. There are forty others whose names should probably be included in the above, but no evidence has been discovered to show that they were in North Carolina before June, 1749. The names of Cowan and Barkley would be among these.

Historians, genealogists, libraries, schools, and colleges as well as the general public will find this volume an invaluable source of information. They will find it a reference work that will give facts that will be found in no other work. The index makes it easy to locate any given item. The maps and charts giving the names and places of settlement of the early families is a most valuable part of the work. Among the valuable and interesting chapters of the book are those which tell about "The Forks of the Yadkin," "The First Settlements," "The Germans of Present Rowan County," "The Western Settlements, 1752-1762," "The Irish Settlement," "The Scotch-Irish Migration," "The German Migration," "The Establishment of Salisbury," "The French and Indian War," and other pertinent information.

In order for the reader of the volume to easily understand the text, Dr. Ramsey has included many pages of maps, old documents, and charts which give a clear picture of the meaning of each subject covered in the book.

One of the outstanding features of this volume is the inclusion of great numbers of notes, gathered from countless original sources as well as other sources where advisable. These notes give details and list the sources of the information given, enabling those who desire more about any given subject to know exactly where to look for additional information.

This volume by Dr. Ramsey will give a new conception to the history of North Carolina. It shows the importance and the great influence of the North Carolina frontier upon the growth and development of our nation. The records of the early settlers who came here and then moved on to the west will remain here in the "Carolina Cradle" and in those states that gave these settlers to the northwest Carolina frontier. Dr. Ramsey has made a great and lasting contribution to history by gathering these records and including them in this volume. Its importance extends far beyond the borders of North Carolina.

William D. Kizziah

# PREFACE

Historians have long been fascinated by the concept of the American frontier. Countless books and monographs have been written in an effort to explain, define, justify, or otherwise expound upon the term. Notable among these efforts have been Frederick Jackson Turner's *The Frontier in American History,* Frederick L. Paxson's *History of the American Frontier,* G. P. Garrison's *Westward Extension,* Thomas D. Clark's *Frontier America,* and Ray A. Billington's *Westward Expansion.*

Many able historians have recognized in their works that the frontier was really synonymous with the people who occupied it. Chief among these have been M. L. Hansen's *The Immigrant in American History,* H. J. Ford's *The Scotch-Irish in America,* A. B. Faust's *The German Element in the United States,* Louis B. Wright's *Culture on the Moving Frontier,* W. P. Webb's *The Great Plains,* and Lois Kimball Mathews' *The Expansion of New England.*

Clearly, much has been written about the frontier. And yet, the writing has been largely general in nature, particularly with regard to the colonial period. With the exception of great land speculators and other key figures in the development of land companies, remarkably few individuals are identified and assessed. This represents a serious weakness in our knowledge of the colonial frontier, for the population was quite small prior to 1720 and the role of each individual was necessarily of greater significance than was the case during the nineteenth century.

American historians have erred grievously in emphasizing the westward movement after the Revolution, while virtually ignoring the vital population shifts before 1754. Lois Kimball Mathews made an important contribution with her books on the movement westward from seventeenth-century New England, but virtually nothing has been done to trace the southward migration of thousands of persons from the Chesapeake Bay–Delaware River region during the second quarter of the eighteenth century. During the century prior to 1830, the entire piedmont South was settled by those who took part in this migration or by their sons and grandsons. Thus, an adequate comprehension of the cultural, political, and economic realities of the ante-bellum South is impossible without a knowledge of this settlement process and of the individuals who participated in it.

This study represents an attempt to trace the process by which a part of the piedmont South was populated. Eighteenth-century Rowan County embraced the entire northwestern quarter of North Carolina prior to 1770; however, only that portion lying between the Yadkin and Catawba rivers is considered in this study. Primary emphasis is placed upon the identity, origin, and location of the original settlers, although considerable attention is also given to those factors which most strongly influenced the settlement process. Geography, economic conditions in England and the colonies, social and religious motivation, the abundance of cheap land, and international conflict are among the determinants considered. Finally, an attempt is made to indicate the character of the initial settlers, as well as how and to what extent the frontier community was organized and supervised.

It was Frederick Jackson Turner's thesis that the frontier was instrumental in forming the American character. But until we learn who the frontiersmen were, where they came from, and what their motives were, we shall merely be guessing about much that is fundamental in the evolving history of this nation.

The author wishes to express his indebtedness to William D. Kizziah, David Randleman, Miss Edith Clark, and Joseph Frick of Salisbury, North Carolina, for their invaluable advice and technical assistance. Thanks are also extended to Dr. Morris L. Radoff and Guy Weatherly of the Hall of Records, Annapolis, Maryland; Dr. G. S. Klett of the Department of History of the Presbyterian General Assembly, Philadelphia; Miss Dorothy B. Lapp, Corresponding Secretary of the Chester County Historical Society, West Chester, Pennsylvania; Dr. Fletcher M. Green of the Department of History of the University of North Carolina at Chapel Hill; Dr. Frederick B. Tolles of the Friends Historical Library, Swarthmore, Pennsylvania; Dr. Leroy Corbit and Dr. Christopher Crittenden of the Department of Archives and History, Raleigh, North Carolina; Dr. James Patton and his staff of the Southern Historical Collection, The University of North Carolina at Chapel Hill; H. W. Bisbee of Burlington, New Jersey; and the clerks and registrars of two dozen county courthouses in six states.

Robert W. Ramsey

Hollins College, Virginia
Spring, 1964

# CONTENTS

# LIST OF
# ILLUSTRATIONS

# CAROLINA
# CRADLE

*Settlement of the
Northwest Carolina
Frontier, 1747-1762*

# I

## THE SETTING

Ulrich Bonnell Phillips opened his famous *Life and Labor in the Old South* with the suggestion, "Let us begin by discussing the weather, for that has been the chief agency in making the South distinctive." He went on to observe that "The climate has been responsible . . . in a measure also for the quality of the soil."[1] Whether or not the weather was "the chief agency," there can be little doubt that the soil—or, more properly, the land—played a vital role in the settlement of the southern frontier.

Until Governor Alexander Spotswood's expedition to the Shenandoah Valley in 1716, inland America lying southeast of the Susquehanna River—a vast, rolling, thinly-forested region rising gradually toward the long, dim line of the distant Alleghenies—was virtually unexplored and inhabited only by Indians. A century of English settlement had ended in 1707 with the Anglicans, Quakers, and Puritans clinging resolutely to the coastal plain and venturing but seldom from the friendly bays and broad rivers which insured contact with the mother country. A few intrepid explorers and Indian traders[2] penetrated the interior, but others

1. (Boston: Little, Brown, and Co., 1948), p. 5.
2. Among the more important were John Lederer, who explored the Virginia and Carolina piedmont in the 1670's; John Lawson, who traveled extensively in the back country of Carolina in 1709; Louis Michel, a Pennsylvania Swiss believed to have been the first man to explore the Shenandoah Valley (1706-7); and William Sherrill, a Conestoga Pennsylvania trader in 1712. Hugh T. Lefler and Albert R. Newsome, *North Carolina: The History of a Southern State* (Chapel Hill: University of North Carolina Press, 1954), pp. 11, 20; Charles E. Kemper, "Historical Notes from the Records of Augusta County, Virginia, Part Two," *Papers and Addresses of the Lancaster County Historical Society*, 65 vols. (Lancaster, Pa: published by the Society, 1897-1961), XXV, 89; Charles A. Hanna, *The Wilderness Trail; Or, The Ventures and Adventures of the Pennsylvania Traders on the Allegheny Path With Some New Annals of the Old West, and the Records of Some Strong Men and Some Bad Ones*, 2 vols. (New York: G. P. Putnam's Sons, Knickerbocker Press, 1911), II, 341.

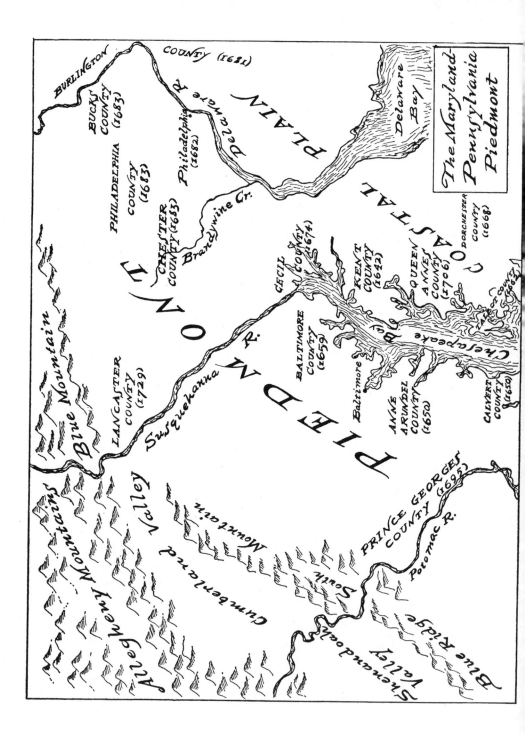

The Maryland-Pennsylvania Piedmont

could find little reason to follow them into the uncharted, Indian-infested west.

What was the nature of this vast territory so long and so steadfastly ignored? What were the geographic features of the Pennsylvania interior and the piedmont south which were to prove so important in determining the course and scope of the southwestward movement after 1707?

To the observer traveling west from Philadelphia, the Pennsylvania countryside very quickly and emphatically loses its coastal characteristics. By the time the traveler reaches Brandywine Creek, he finds himself in an exceedingly fertile, gently undulating region possessing the chief physical qualities of the Virginia and Carolina piedmont.[3] William Penn, in a letter to the Committee of the Free Society of Traders, observed that

The Country itself in its Soyl, Air, Water, Seasons and Produce both Natural and Artificial is not to be despised. The land containeth divers sorts of Earth, as sand Yellow and Black, Poor and Rich: also gravel both Loomy and Dusty; and in some places a fast fat Earth, like to our best Vales in England, especially by Inland Brooks and Rivers . . . the Advantages of the Country are divided, the Black-lands being generally three to one Richer than those that lie by Navigable Waters.[4]

Indeed, virtually all of Pennsylvania east of South Mountain and southeast of the Blue Mountain ridges could be described as a piedmont region. Beyond South Mountain, the beautiful Cumberland Valley, in actuality a northeastern extension of the Shenandoah, provides the westward traveler with a pleasant vista before he finds himself confronted by the forbidding heights of the Alleghenies.

In Maryland, the same geographical phenomenon may be observed. Anne Arundel, Calvert, and Prince Georges counties,[5] far from comprising a flat plain, manifest a piedmont character even more sharply defined than that of southeastern Pennslyvania. It would be no exaggeration to say that virtually the entire region

3. Raymond E. Murphy and Marion Murphy, *Pennsylvania: A Regional Geography* (Harrisburg: Pennsylvania Book Service, 1937), pp. 18, 20, 70-73.

4. *Narratives of Early Pennsylvania, West New Jersey and Delaware, 1630-1707*, ed. Albert Cook Myers (New York: Barnes and Noble, Inc., 1959 [reprint] ), pp. 225-26.

5. Geographically, this area of Maryland strikingly resembles parts of west-central North Carolina.

north and west of Chesapeake Bay is an extension of the piedmont[6] rather than part of the eastern Virginia–Eastern Shore–
New Jersey coastal plain.

It is this piedmont country then, much of it extending to within a few miles of Chesapeake Bay and the Delaware River, which
formed a broad, fertile, grassy, unsettled belt[7] stretching from the
Delaware westward and southward along both sides of the Blue
Ridge and into the Yadkin-Catawba basin of west-central North
Carolina. John Lederer, in August, 1670, passed through Manas-
sas Gap in the Blue Ridge and "descended into broad savannas,
flowery meads, where herds of red deer were feeding. The grass
which sprang from the limestone soil was so high they could tie it
across their saddles. Since the Indians burned their land over
every autumn to make their game preserve, it was only lightly
wooded with occasional groves of oak or maple."[8]

In 1728, seven of the eight Lords Proprietors of Carolina sold
their lands to the crown; only John Carteret, Earl of Granville,
kept his share, consisting of the country lying south of the
Virginia border to 35° 34' north latitude. The southern boundary
was surveyed from the coast to Bath in 1743, and then to the
corner of what is now Chatham County, on Deep River.[9] In
1746, the line was extended westward to Coldwater Creek at a
point approximately fourteen miles southwest of the present site
of Salisbury.[10]

That section of the Granville district lying between the Yadkin
and Catawba rivers consisted of a fertile, well-watered, virtually
treeless meadow land. John Lawson left the following interesting
account of the territory embraced within what was to become
Rowan County:

6. This phenomenon is due largely to the fact that the Alleghenies extended
from the western Carolinas in a northeasterly direction, bringing them much
closer to the coast in Maryland and Pennsylvania.

7. In 1721, the only organized Virginia county west of the coastal plain
was Spotsylvania. Hugh Jones, *The Present State of Virginia, From Whence
Is Inferred a Short View of Maryland and North Carolina*, ed. Richard L.
Morton (Chapel Hill: University of North Carolina Press, 1956), pp. 194, 216.

8. Julia Davis, *The Shenandoah* (New York and Toronto: Farrar and Rinehart, Inc., 1945), pp. 24-25.

9. John Preston Arthur, *Western North Carolina, A History* (Raleigh,
N.C.: Edwards and Broughton Printing Co., 1914), p. 83.

10. James S. Brawley, *The Rowan Story, 1753-1953: A Narrative History of
Rowan County, North Carolina* (Salisbury, N.C.: Rowan Printing Co., 1953),
p. 11.

We traveled this day about twenty-five miles over pleasant savanna ground, high and dry, having very few trees upon it, and those standing at a great distance. The land was very good and free from grubs and underwood. A man near Sapona may more easily clear ten acres of ground than in some places he can one; there being much loose stone upon the land, being very convenient for making of dry walls or other sort of durable fence. . . . That day we passed through a delicious country—none that I ever saw exceeds it. We saw fine bladed grass six feet high along the banks of these pleasant rivulets. . . . We reached the fertile and pleasant banks of Sapona River. . . . This most pleasant river is beautified with a numerous train of swans and other sorts of water fowl, not common though extraordinary to the eye.[11]

Jethro Rumple felt that the Sapona River was in actuality the Yadkin and that the Sapona town mentioned elsewhere in Lawson's account was an Indian village near the trading ford.[12]

In enlarging upon Lawson's description, Rumple recorded the statement of a resident of Rowan to the effect that the region was destitute of forest and that one eighteenth-century settler was obliged to haul the logs for his house more than a mile. Another inhabitant told Rumple that he could remember when the land between Third and Fourth creeks was open prairie in which wild deer mingled with the horses and cattle as they grazed.[13] It is probable, judging from the creeks so named, that numbers of buffalo shared the veldt-like terrain with less celebrated animals.

The region extending westward from Haw River was of characteristic piedmont quality, but was less fertile and well-

11. *The History of North Carolina, Containing the Exact Description and Natural History of that Country, Together with the Present State Thereof and a Journal of a Thousand Miles Traveled Through Several Nations of Indians, Giving a Particular Account of their Customs, Manners, etc.* (London: printed for W. Taylor at the Ship, and F. Baker at the Black Boy, in Pater Noster Row, 1714; and Raleigh, N.C.: printed by Strother and Marcom at their Book and Job Office, 1860), pp. 80-81.

12. *A History of Rowan County, North Carolina, Containing Sketches of Prominent Families and Distinguished Men* (Salisbury, N.C.: J. J. Bruner, 1881), p. 28. The names of places (and distances to them) mentioned by Lawson beyond the Sapona which accurately correspond to places known today (Eno, Heighwarrie, Sissipahaw, Neuse) confirm Rumple's analysis. The trading ford referred to here was located approximately seven miles northeast of present-day Salisbury. An old Indian path, the most important road in piedmont North Carolina in that day, crossed the Yadkin at this ford. The great trading path, as it was called, connected the Catawbas and Cherokees with the tribes along the James River in Virginia.

13. *Ibid*, p. 29.

watered than the land in southeastern Pennslyvania.[14] It was not until the traveler approached the Yadkin from the east that one small stream after another flowed southwestward across his path. Indeed, the country between the Yadkin and Catawba formed a kind of depression,[15] bisected by a triangular-shaped ridge extending first from northeast to southwest, then curving sharply southeastward to the Granville line. Myriads of little rivulets, combining to form large creeks,[16] flowed from countless sequestered springs along the watershed formed by the ridge and poured into the two great rivers.

Thus, it can be seen that vast prairies covered with pea-vine grass and canebrake stretched across western Virginia and Carolina in the early eighteenth century. Game abounded, and the rolling land supplied the numerous Indian tribes with a good livelihood.

In describing the Indians of Pennsylvania the Reverend Israel Acrelius stated in 1759 that

The land on the west side of the river, which the Swedes had purchased of the heathen . . . stretched from Cape Hinlopen to the Falls of the Delaware, and thence westward to the Great Fall on the river Susquehanna, near the mouth of the Conewaga [sic] Creek. These Indians were called by Europeans, in general, Delawares, but within a circle of eighteen miles (118 English miles) around the Swedes there were ten or eleven separate tribes.[17]

Among these tribes were the "Minquas," of Iroquoian stock, who lived in the lower Susquehanna Valley. They often traveled eastward to the Delaware River for hunting, trading, fishing, or war against the whites.[18] The warlike nature of the numerous Pennsylvania tribes, together with the fact that many of the western Indians were partly under French Catholic influence,[19] were important reasons for the development of a peace policy by the Quakers. Conditions in West Jersey were somewhat different.

14. Myers, ed., *Narratives*, p. 382.
15. The author's grandmother, who spent her early life on the upper waters of Third Creek, stated that the land in places was so marshy and damp that the people suffered much from malaria.
16. The larger creek beds are in many places ten to fifteen feet deep, indicating that they flow today exactly where they did two centuries ago.
17. Myers, ed., *Narratives*, pp. 69-70.
18. *Ibid.*, p. 70.
19. Marcus W. Jernegan, *The American Colonies, 1492-1750* (New York: Frederick Ungar Publishing Co., 1959), p. 37.

The natives there were described in 1681 as "Peaceable, Useful, and Serviceable to the English Inhabitants."[20]

West of the Blue Ridge, in Maryland and Virginia, were to be found Delawares from the Susquehanna and Catawbas from the Carolinas. The Shawnees had several villages in the northern portion of the Shenandoah Valley, and the Tuscaroras occupied the area of present-day Berkeley County, West Virginia.[21] In North Carolina, the Tutelo, Saponi, and Keyauwee Indians inhabited the region between the Yadkin and Catawba rivers, while the Waxhaws and Catawbas lived to the south on the vast up-country west of the Catawba River.[22]

Of great importance in the geographical configuration of the region involved in this study was the Delaware Valley. It has been correctly stated that the Delaware River "united West Jersey, Pennsylvania, and the lower counties (which eventually became the state of Delaware) into a single economic province, and. . . . unified the valley into a single 'cultural area.' "[23] There can be little question that the peculiarly uniform quality of the piedmont, doubtless contributing to the close interrelationshp among its aboriginal inhabitants, played a fundamental role in extending the "cultural unity" of the Delaware Valley to include the piedmont portions of Maryland, Virginia, and the Carolinas.

20. Myers, ed., *Narratives*, p. 192.
21. Davis, *The Shenandoah*, p. 18.
22. Lefler and Newsome, *North Carolina*, pp. 24-25.
23. Frederick B. Tolles, *Quakers and the Atlantic Culture* (New York: Macmillan Co., 1960), p. 117.

# II

## GENERAL CAUSES
## OF THE
## SOUTHWARD MIGRATION

The movement of large numbers of people westward and southward from the Delaware Valley and Chesapeake Bay should be considered as two distinct yet interrelated migrations. The first began about 1710 and developed into the second, which continued steadily from 1725 until 1744. The fundamental cause of the earlier movement was unquestionably pressure arising from a natural increase in population. This natural growth was also an important cause of the second wave of migration. In Maryland, especially on the Eastern Shore, this pressure developed because the land was rapidly becoming impoverished[1] and because there was not a sufficient amount of land to support the steadily increasing population.

By 1733, according to Greene and Harrington, the small Maryland counties of Talbot, Queen Annes, and Kent contained 6,825 taxable persons.[2] At the same time, the combined area of Chester, Lancaster, and Philadelphia counties in Pennsylvania contained an estimated 7,600 taxables.[3] Although historians have accepted the fact that "thousands" of Scotch-Irish and Germans entered Penn's colony after 1720, little attention has been paid to the significant population trends on Maryland's Eastern Shore.

Of the early pioneers who settled on the Susquehanna River prior to 1725, a majority were Quakers from the lower Delaware

1. George Johnston, *History of Cecil County, Maryland and the Early Settlements Around the Head of Chesapeake Bay and on the Delaware River With Sketches of Some of the Old Families of Cecil County* (Elkton, Md.: published by the author, 1881), p. 291. According to Cunz, settlement of the western parts of Maryland came to be encouraged in an effort to develop a grain industry to counterbalance the decline in tobacco. Dieter Cunz, *The Maryland Germans, A History* (Princeton, N.J.: Princeton University Press, 1948), p. 47.

2. E. B. Greene and Virginia D. Harrington, *American Population Before the Census of 1790* (New York: Columbia University Press, 1932), pp. 129-30.

3. *Ibid.*, p. 117.

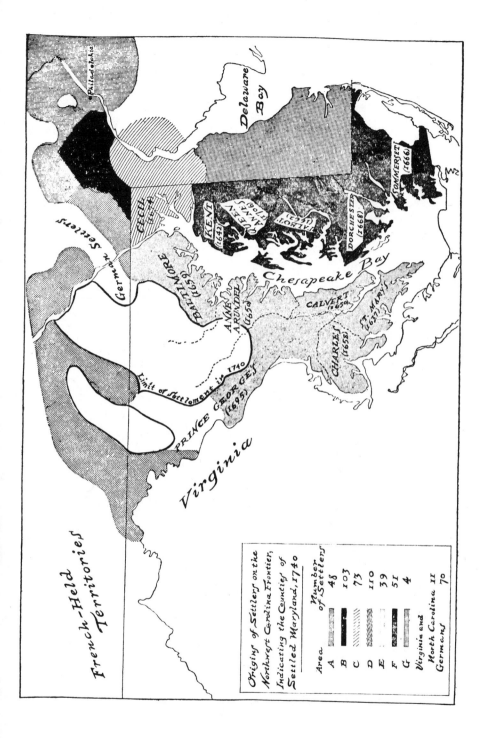

French-Held Territories

Philadelphia

Delaware Bay

German Settlers

CECIL (1674)

KENT (1642)

QUEEN ANNE (1706)

TALBOT (1662)

DORCHESTER (1668)

SOMERSET (1666)

BALTIMORE (1659)

Chesapeake Bay

ANNE ARUNDEL (1650)

CALVERT (1650)

Limit of Settlement in 1740

ST. MARY'S (1637)

CHARLES (1658)

PRINCE GEORGES (1695)

Virginia

Origins of Settlers on the
Northwest Carolina Frontier,
Indicating the Counties of
Settled Maryland, 1740

| Area | | Number of Settlers |
|------|---|---|
| A | | 48 |
| B | | 103 |
| C | | 73 |
| D | | 110 |
| E | | 39 |
| F | | 51 |
| G | | 4 |
| Virginia and | | |
| North Carolina 11 | | |
| Germany | | 70 |

Valley; that is to say, from the east.[4] On the other hand, the first settlements in Maryland were made in the southern part of the colony on both sides of Chesapeake Bay. Consequently, the principal movement of population in Baltimore's colony was northward rather than westward. This movement became a migration with the beginning of the eighteenth century.[5]

After 1700, large numbers of Ulster Scots, Welshmen, Huguenots, and Germans streamed across the Atlantic and into the colonies. A majority of these landed at Philadelphia or New Castle,[6] where they immediately found themselves in an unfamiliar Quaker environment or caught up in the wave of Marylanders advancing northward up the shores of the Chesapeake. It was for this reason that the New Castle–Cecil–Chester area became a crossroad used alike by Pennsylvania Quakers and Germans moving southwestward, Marylanders migrating northward, and the new Scotch-Irish and Welsh immigrants willing to go wherever cheap land could be had.

The Germans and Scotch-Irish streamed into Lancaster County after 1723.[7] At the same time, Marylanders reached the head of the Chesapeake only to find hundreds of new immigrants entering the region. They then joined the movement into Lancaster.

By 1730, Lancaster County was filling rapidly.[8] The Germans settled in the center of the county along a fertile belt extending from the Susquehanna River northeastward. The Scotch-Irish and Welsh occupied the land to the north and south.

Geography played a key role in the subsequent chain of events. Because of the high bluffs on the broad Susquehanna, there was no way that wagons could cross the river except at Harris' Ferry,[9] located in the northern, or Scotch-Irish, portion of the

4. See p. 31n; also Appendix B.
5. James G. Leyburn, *The Scotch-Irish: A Social History* (Chapel Hill: University of North Carolina Press, 1962), pp. 248-49.
6. Henry J. Ford, *The Scotch-Irish in America* (Princeton, N.J.: Princeton University Press, 1915), p. 261.
7. *Ibid.*, pp. 261-65.
8. In 1725 there were approximately 2,660 persons in the region which became Lancaster County (1729). There were nearly 300 taxables in the Pequea-Conestoga area and 56 in Donegal. *Lancaster County, Pennsylvania: A History*, 3 vols., ed. H. M. J. Klein (New York and Chicago: Lewis Historical Publishing Co., Inc., 1924), I, 17.
9. Leyburn, *Scotch-Irish*, pp. 197-98. Harris' Ferry is now Harrisburg, Pennsylvania.

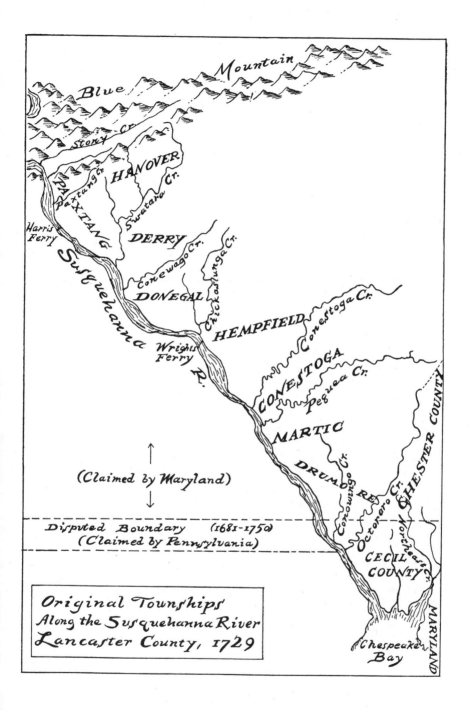

Blue Mountain

Stony Cr.

Paxtang Cr.

HANOVER

Swatara Cr.

Harris Ferry

Susquehanna

PAXTANG

DERRY

Conewago Cr.

Chickasalunga Cr.

DONEGAL

HEMPFIELD

Conestoga Cr.

Wrights Ferry

R.

CONESTOGA

Pequea Cr.

MARTIC

DRUMORE

Conowingo Cr.

CHESTER COUNTY

(Claimed by Maryland)

Octoraro Cr.

Disputed Boundary     (1681-1750)
(Claimed by Pennsylvania)

Northeast Cr.

CECIL COUNTY

Original Townships
Along the Susquehanna River
Lancaster County, 1729

Chesapeake Bay

MARYLAND

county, and at Wright's Ferry, thirty miles downstream.[10] Rhoda Barber, a descendant of one of the early settlers on the Susquehanna, wrote that

[Wright's Ferry] appears to have been early set up. It was very imperfect at first two large canoes lash'd together was us'd to take over a waggon which had to be unloded before it could be taken over. I find in 1750 it was in a better way. At that time it rented for £100 per annum with the ground alloted to it. 60 years ago the idea of a bridge across the Susquehanna was laughed at even by intelligent persons as a thing impossible.[11]

The Penn heirs refused to permit the issuance of grants to land lying west of the Susquehanna and south of Harris' Ferry pending settlement of the boundary dispute with Maryland and legal purchase of the western land from the Indians.[12] On July 2, 1722, Pennsylvania's Governor William Keith wrote the provincial council that

Finding the Indians since I came last here, to be very much alarmed with the noise of an intended survey from Maryland upon the banks of Sasquehanna [sic], I held a council with them at Conestogoe . . . wherein I proposed to them to cause a large tract of land to be surveyed on the side of that river for the Proprietor.[13]

It was the established policy of Penn and his heirs to obtain Indian lands only by purchase or treaty, thereby avoiding violence and discouraging Indian alliances with the French.

By 1734, so many Scotch-Irish had crossed the river into the Cumberland Valley that Samuel Blunston of Wright's Ferry was given authority to sell to trans-Susquehanna pioneers a limited number of licenses to settle.[14] This policy was abandoned follow-

10. Located at the present site of Columbia, Pennsylvania.
11. Journal of Rhoda Barber, 1726-82, Historical Society of Pennsylvania, Philadelphia.
12. William H. Egle, *History of the Commonwealth of Pennsylvania, Civil, Political and Military, From Its Earliest Settlement to the Present Time, Including Historical Descriptions of Each County in the State, Their Towns, and Industrial Resources* (Philadelphia: E. M. Gardner, 1883), pp. 821-24; George P. Donehoo, *A History of the Cumberland Valley in Pennsylvania*, 2 vols. (Harrisburg, Pa.: Susquehanna History Association, 1930), I, 39.
13. Letter in *Minutes of the Provincial Council of Pennsylvania, From the Organization to the Termination of the Proprietary Government*, 16 vols. (Philadelphia: Jo. Severns and Co. [and other printers], 1851-53), III, 178 (hereafter cited as *Pennsylvania Council Minutes*).
14. Donehoo, *Cumberland Valley*, I, 39.

ing the settlement of large numbers of Germans along Codorus Creek[15] and the renegotiation of the Maryland boundary dispute.[16]

The controversy concerning the border between Pennsylvania and Maryland must be regarded as an important factor in causing people to seek new homes to the west and south. The dispute was at its height between 1732 and 1737, during which time large numbers of persons abandoned the region most seriously affected.[17] Many of these people migrated to the Cumberland Valley, the "back parts" of Prince Georges County, the Shenandoah Valley, and subsequently to the Carolina frontier.

The boundary dispute was essentially a struggle for control of a strip of territory extending from the New Castle circle westward beyond the Susquehanna.[18] Lord Baltimore selected Thomas Cresap as his agent, and violence marked most of the decade after 1730. On August 17, 1733, the Pennsylvania House found itself "obliged at this time to represent to the governor the hardships which many of our peaceable inhabitants living near the borders of Maryland have suffered from that government."[19] Two years later, the House advised the governor that success by Baltimore in his efforts to obtain the disputed territory "would be attended with consequences truly unhappy . . . depriving many of us of our properties and destroying those religious and civil liberties which were one of the chief inducements to the first planting of this colony."[20] The struggle reached its height in the summer of 1736. The Pennsylvania legislature recorded on September 8 that the sheriff of Baltimore County had invaded Lancaster County with two hundred men.

The Sheriff of Lancaster had got about a hundred and fifty people together at John Wright's, Junior, where they have continued since Sunday evening, that no hostilities had been yet committed . . . but that . . . the inhabitants tho' unprovided with arms and ammunition,

15. Cunz, *Maryland Germans*, p. 49. Codorus Creek flows in a northeasterly direction, through present York, Pennsylvania, and enters the Susquehanna approximately nine miles above Wright's Ferry.

16. Hugh Jones, *The Present State of Virginia, From Whence Is Inferred a Short View of Maryland and North Carolina*, ed., Richard L. Morton (Chapel Hill: University of North Carolina Press, 1956), pp. 27-30; *Pennsylvania Council Minutes*, III, 485, 347.

17. Egle, *History of Pennsylvania*, pp. 821-24; *Pennsylvania Council Minutes*, III, 471.

18. Egle, *History of Pennsylvania*, p. 821.

19. *Pennsylvania Council Minutes*, III, 566.

20. *Ibid.*, III, 596-97.

yet endeavored to defend themselves and such of his majesties peaceable subjects as fled from their houses to them for refuge.[21]

Meanwhile, in 1735, the Penns brought suit against Baltimore which dragged on for fifteen years.[22] Hostilities were suspended in 1737 pending the outcome of the suit, and a temporary boundary was surveyed in 1739, probably by William Rumsey of Bohemia, Maryland.[23]

Violation of the Asiento contract by England, coupled with Spanish concern over the settlement of Georgia in 1732, led to the outbreak of war in Europe after twenty-seven years of uneasy peace.[24] The "War of Jenkins Ear" became King George's War with the entry of France on the side of Spain in 1744.

There can be little doubt that the prospect of war with France in Canada and the Ohio Valley caused many people to leave New Jersey and Pennsylvania. The frontier settlements grew particularly apprehensive because of their exposure to attack by Indian allies of the French. On June 18, 1743, Governor George Thomas of Pennsylvania informed the council that

. . . one James Hendricks, servant to an Indian Trader at Alligheny [sic] who had deposed that he had seen the Indians there in pursuit of some of the traders . . . declared his apprehensions that the Indians designed to cut off all the traders in those parts, which had alarmed the inhabitants of Lancaster county to that degree that several had left their habitations . . . likewise . . . two other Indian traders, who deposed that they were desired by some Indian friends of theirs to make the best of their way out of the Indian country, to avoid their being murdered by the Indians, who were come to a Resolution to cut off all the white people.[25]

In December, 1745, Governor Thomas notified the "back inhabitants" of Lancaster County that "the French and Indians were preparing . . . to march in the winter time to the frontiers of Pennsylvania."[26] One month later, the inhabitants of Lancaster

21. Ibid., IV, 63-64.
22. Jones, Present State of Virginia, p. 30.
23. Johnston, Cecil County, p. 508
24. Marcus W. Jernegan, The American Colonies, 1492-1750 (New York: Frederick Ungar Publishing Co., 1959), p. 327.
25. Pennsylvania Council Minutes, IV, 655-56.
26. Ibid., V, 1-2.

County notified the governor that they were short of arms and ammunition and were unable to purchase any "from their having expended what little substance they had in clearing and improving their lands."[27]

In June, 1746, Governor Thomas issued a proclamation to the effect that

... His Majesty has been pleased to order a considerable body of his troops from England under the command of Lt. Gen. St. Clair . . . for the immediate reduction of Canada, and that I should forthwith make the necessary dispositions for raising as many men as the shortness of the time will permit within my government. . . . the troops to be raised should consist of companies of one hundred men each; and that those that shall be raised in the several provinces of New York, New Jersey, Pennsylvania, Maryland and Virginia . . . should rendezvous at Albany . . . in order to proceed . . . into the southern parts of Canada; whilst those to be raised in the provinces of Massachusetts Bay, New Hampshire, Rhode Island and Connecticut are to rendezvous at Louisburg, and to proceed with the forces sent from England . . . to Quebec.[28]

It will at once be observed that the Carolinas were excluded from this levy. Within a year of this proclamation, the first settlers entered the Yadkin Valley from New Jersey, Pennsylvania, Maryland, and Virginia.

Perhaps the most important single cause of the southward movement was the land problem which developed in Pennsylvania after 1725. Bishop Spangenberg and Governor Gabriel Johnston of North Carolina stated that the high price of land in Pennsylvania was the cause of the southward migration.[29] According to Carl Hammer, Jr., the principal reason for the movement was the scarcity of good land on the Pennsylvania frontier and the prohibitive cost of farms farther east.[30]

27. *Ibid.,* V, 26.
28. *Ibid.,* V, 39-40.
29. R. D. W. Connor, "Race Elements in the White Population of North Carolina," *North Carolina State Normal and Industrial College Historical Publications,* No. 1 (Raleigh, N.C.: Edwards and Broughton Printing Co., 1920), p. 83. Spangenberg also expressed the opinion that many people removed to Carolina because they had been told (erroneously, so he said) that it would be unnecessary to feed their stock in the winter.
30. *Rhinelanders on the Yadkin: The Story of the Pennsylvania Germans in Rowan and Cabarrus* (Salisbury, N.C.: Rowan Printing Co., 1943), p. 25.

Before 1713, the price of land in Pennsylvania was £2 per hundred acres and 1s. quit-rent.[31] In 1713, the price was raised to £10 and in 1732 to £15.[32] Also in 1732, the quit-rent was increased from 2s. to 4s. 2d. sterling.[33]

As may readily be seen from the accompanying list of taxables in Salsbury township, Lancaster County, for the year 1750, the average size of a farm there was approximately fifty acres. On the basis of the price established in 1732, such a farm would cost £7 10s. In the Granville district of North Carolina, land was selling in 1753 at the rate of 5s. per hundred acres regardless of acreage.[34]

William Penn died in 1718, and control of his colony devolved upon his grandsons, Richard and Thomas, both minors. The proprietary land office was closed from 1718 to 1732, during which period the Penn heirs refused to issue land patents or clear title to the land.[35] The council noted on February 2, 1726/7, that "in remote parts of this province where lands have not been regularly surveyed or granted, divers persons not only enter and settle the proprietor's lands without any grant or permission, but sometimes have proceeded to acts of violence in forcibly ousting of others."[36] James Logan wrote to John Penn in 1727 that both the Germans ("many of them surly people, divers Papists among them and the men generally well-armed"[37]) and the Scots "frequently sit down on any spot of vacant land they can find, without asking question."[38] Logan went on to say that "both groups pretend that they will buy, not one in twenty has anything to

31. S. H. Sutherland, *Population Distribution in Colonial America* (New York: Columbia University Press, 1936), p. 143.

32. Sutherland, *Population Distribution,* p. 143; The Taylor Papers: Being a Collection of Warrants, Surveys, Letters, &C. Relating to the Early Settlement of Pennsylvania (including correspondence for the period 1723-50 and scattered miscellaneous items for the period 1672-1775 in unmarked volumes), 10 vols. (vols. I, II, and III: Chester County Warrants, 1682-1742), Historical Society of Pennsylvania, Philadelphia, I, 171, II, 251.

33. Sutherland, *Population Distribution,* p. 143.

34. Rowan County Deed Books, Office of Registrar of Deeds, Rowan County Courthouse, Salisbury, N.C., I, 30, 58, 181. Lord Granville rented his lands upon payment of three shillings sterling followed by an annual rent of three shillings sterling or four shillings proclamation money for each hundred acres.

35. Egle, *History of Pennsylvania,* pp. 75, 820.

36. *Pennsylvania Council Minutes,* III, 266.

37. Charles A. Hanna, *The Scotch-Irish, Or the Scot in North Britain, North Ireland, and North America,* 2 vols. (New York: Knickerbocker Press, 1902), II, 62-63.

38. *Ibid.*

| Name | | | | | | | | |
|---|---|---|---|---|---|---|---|---|
| James Mooer | 50 | 8 | 2 | 2 | 1 | 0 | 0 | 0 |
| Thomas Green | 50 | 5 | 3 | 2 | 0 | 0 | 0 | |
| Jason Cookson | 50 | 4 | 3 | 2 | 1 | 0 | 0 | |
| George Douglass | 50 | 5 | 2 | 2 | 1 | 6 | 0 | |
| Edward Douglass | 50 | 6 | 3 | 3 | 1 | 0 | 0 | |
| Thomas Climson | 100 | 10 | 1 | 3 | 0 | 6 | 0 | |
| Pattrick Reede | 100 | 6 | 2 | 2 | 0 | 0 | 0 | |
| Thomas Johnston | 50 | 5 | 2 | 3 | 0 | 6 | 0 | |
| Andrew Caldwel | 50 | 5 | 2 | 3 | 1 | 3 | 0 | |
| Sara Hoar | 1 | 1 | 1 | 1 | 0 | 0 | 0 | |
| Benjamen Hoar | 50 | 2 | 1 | 0 | 0 | 0 | 0 | |
| William Posfiel | 50 | 6 | 2 | 1 | 01 | 2 | 0 | |
| Daniel Afton | 50 | 10 | 4 | 4 | 2 | 10 | 0 | |
| James Keefs | 60 | 6 | 2 | 2 | 0 | 4 | 0 | |
| John Hostins | 50 | 5 | 2 | 1 | 0 | 6 | | |
| George Dosffiel | 50 | 7 | 3 | 4 | 0 | 6 | | |
| George Boyde | 50 | 10 | 2 | 4 | 0 | 6 | | |
| Isabell Griffeth | 50 | 5 | 2 | 4 | 1 | 6 | | |
| Isac Tayeler | 25 | 3 | 2 | 2 | 1 | 6 | | |
| James Johnston | 200 | 10 | 2 | 5 | 1 | 0 | | |
| Thomas Hostins | 100 | 6 | 3 | 2 | 1 | | | |

pay with."[39] He pointed out that the Scotch-Irish settled "generally toward the Maryland line, where no lands can honestly be sold
until the dispute with Lord Baltimore is settled."[40]

These land problems played a key role in producing the southward migration. In August, 1755, the Pennsylvania Provincial
Council called attention to the steady flow of settlers out of the
colony by asking

> . . . was it ever known that any people came from Virginia to purchase
> here on account of the superior goodness or convenience of our Land?
> On the contrary, have not many thousands of families gone from hence
> thither . . . ? Have not thousands likewise left us to settle in Carolina?
> Has not the exorbitant price at which the proprietors held their lands,
> and their neglect of Indian purchasing in order to keep up that price,
> driven these people from us? . . . But they are gone and gone forever,
> and numbers are going after them![41]

Two additional causes for emigration from Pennsylvania—
distaste for authority and the high cost of consumer goods—are
hinted at in two items gleaned from the records of Penn's colony.
In 1734, a number of the inhabitants of Ridley township, Chester
County, signed their names in support of a tavern petition—with
the reservation that "we agree to the matter but object somewhat
against the form viz the word worships."[42]

In 1725, one Robert Parke, a Quaker immigrant living in
Chester township, wrote a lengthy and extremely informative
letter to his sister Mary Valentine, a resident of Ireland. In call-
ing attention to economic conditions in Chester County, Parke
advised his sister to "have brother Thomas to bring a good new
saddle with proper housin to it for they are very dear here a
saddle that will cost 18 or 20 shills in Ireland will cost 50 shills or
3 pounds & not so good neither."[43] Despite the high price of saddles, however, it seems clear that scarcity of cheap land, a disputed boundary, the rapidly growing population, and fear of

39. *Ibid.*
40. *Ibid.*
41. *Pennsylvania Council Minutes,* VI, 574.
42. In the text of the formal petition the justices of the peace are referred
to as "your Worships." Chester County Tavern License Papers, 10 vols. (1700-
54), Chester County Historical Society, West Chester, Pennsylvania, II (1729-
36), 114.
43. Chester County Miscellaneous Papers, 1684-1847, Historical Society of
Pennsylvania, Philadelphia, p. 87.

armed conflict provided the chief stimuli for emigration southward from the middle colonies.

Why, then, having once reached the Shenandoah Valley, did
erstwhile Marylanders and Pennsylvanians move on to the northwest Carolina frontier? The answer would seem to be provided
by geography and arithmetic. The first settlers entered the valley
of Virginia between 1725 and 1730.[44] By 1749, there were an
estimated 4,102 taxables in Augusta and Orange counties.[45] A
cursory glance at Lyman Chalkley's three-volume abridgment of
the Augusta County court records is sufficient to indicate the
extraordinary number of people who settled in the valley between
1726 and 1749. As the total area of the valley is approximately
7,500 square miles,[46] it is evident that the choice land was taken up
during this period.

A second cause of emigration from the Shenandoah was
provided by the Indians, who had long considered the valley their
private preserve. The Virginia governors rarely adopted the
lenient Indian policy of the Penns, with the result that frontier
settlers were constantly being attacked. Resumption of the southward march was undoubtedly stimulated by the heavy losses
(particularly in goods) suffered by the settlers during severe
Indian attacks in Augusta County in 1745.[47]

The reasons for migration thus far discussed may be described
as fundamental causes. Investigation of the origins of the
pioneers quickly reveals a less apparent but equally important and
much more immediate cause. Perusal of county records, especially
will books, makes it clear that movement of families often
occurred immediately after the death of the father or family
patriarch. The deaths of John Cathey, William Brandon, John
Frohock, Thomas Parker, Archibald Little, Robert Luckie,
Alexander and John McConnell, Alexander McCulloch, John
Mordah, John McKee, John McQuown, Henry Schiles, William

44. Howard McKnight Wilson, *The Tinkling Spring, Headwater of
Freedom: A Study of the Church and Her People* (Richmond, Va.: Garrett
and Massie, Inc., 1954), pp. 10-16.

45. Greene and Harrington, *American Population*, pp. 150-51.

46. A. B. Faust, *The German Element in the United States, With Special
Reference to Its Political, Moral, Social and Educational Influence,* 2 vols.
(New York: Steuben Society of America, 1927), I, 187.

47. *Chronicles of the Scotch-Irish Settlements in Virginia, Extracted from
the Original Court Records of Augusta County, 1745-1800,* 3 vols., compiled and
edited by Lyman Chalkley (Rosslyn, Va.: Commonwealth Printing Co., 1912),
I, 15.

Tate, John Reed, John Strain, Hugh McWhorter, John McManus, John and Gideon Howard, and Richard Lewis were among those resulting in an exodus of sons or nephews to the Shenandoah Valley and Carolina. In such cases, the patriarch was often unable or unwilling to leave the land he had acquired in America. Even though his sons may have desired to leave sooner, they postponed their departure until after his death. In some cases, this was evidence of filial affection; in others, it sprang from necessity, for the father customarily disposed of his lands among his faithful sons. Only by remaining until after probation of the will or other disposal of the estate could the sons obtain the shillings necessary for the acquisition of cheaper land to the south. There can be no doubt that the patriarchal position of the father in colonial America was a powerful controlling factor in the westward—and southward—movement of population.

# III

# *THE FIRST*
# *SETTLEMENTS,*
# *1747-1751*

By 1747, a few intrepid adventurers had entered the country west of the Yadkin. Memoranda preserved by the Clark family, which settled along the upper Cape Fear River before 1740, clearly indicated that a family or company of emigrants moved west across the Yadkin as early as 1746 to join "some families that were living sequestered in that fertile region."[1] That their numbers were few may be inferred from the fact that the commissioners engaged in running the line between the king's lands and the Granville district were obliged to discontinue their work in 1746 because the country was very thinly populated, and they could not obtain sufficient corn for their horses or provisions for themselves.[2] In 1755, Governor Arthur Dobbs, in a report to the Board of Trade in London stated that seventy-five Scotch-Irish and twenty-two German families had been settled on his western lands for seven or eight years.[3] Gehrke concluded that in 1747 there were not more than one hundred fighting men in the entire region west of Hillsboro.[4]

By the fall of 1748, however, there was a sufficient number of settlers to warrant the formation of a new political unit out of the old county of Bladen. Accordingly, on September 29, 1748, Governor Gabriel Johnston declared that the county of Anson was

1. William Henry Foote, *Sketches of North Carolina, Historical and Biographical, Illustrative of the Principles of a Portion of Her Early Settlers* (New York: Robert Carter, 58 Canal Street, 1846), pp. 187-88. These settlers probably crossed over into present-day Stanly and Anson counties.

2. William Herman Gehrke, "The German Element in Rowan and Cabarrus Counties" (unpublished master's thesis, University of North Carolina, 1934), p. 8.

3. *The Colonial Records of North Carolina,* 10 vols., ed., William L. Saunders (Raleigh, N.C.: Printers to the State, 1886-90), V, 355 (hereafter cited as *NCCR*).

4. "The German Element," p. 29. Adolf Nüssmann, a Lutheran pastor, declared that in 1747 there were few if any inhabitants (except Indians) in the district around what is now Salisbury.

in existence and accompanied his proclamation with the following statement:

> . . . that by the great distance of that settlement (settlers along the Yadkin) from the county court of Bladen, and the badness of the ways they were in a manner excluded from all benefits of the said court, to which, by reason of the bad behavior of many amongst them, they have frequent occasions of recourse. Wherefore they pray for a division, and to be made a separate county, when (tho' now but few) they doubt not to increase to a competent number. . . . And it appearing to the satisfaction of his excellency and the council that the number of white tithables upon Peedee (Yadkin) River and near the same is between two and three hundred, and that the courthouse of Bladen County (in which county they have been hitherto included) is above one hundred miles distant from the nearest inhabitants of Peedee; and that at some seasons of the year the roads between are very bad, if not impracticable.[5]

Thus, in 1749, western North Carolina was formed into Anson County. The bill providing for the creation of Anson stipulated

> . . . That Bladen County be divided by a line, beginning at the Place where the South Line of this Province crosseth the Westernmost Branch of Little Pee-Dee River, then by a straight line to a place where the Commissioners for running the Southern Boundary of this Province crosseth that Branch of Little Pee-Dee River, called Drowning Creek, thence up that Branch to the Head thereof; then by a Line, to run, as near as may be, equidistant from Saxapahaw River, and the Great Pee-Dee River; and that the upper Part of the Said County and Parish so laid off and undivided, be erected into a County and Parish by the Name of Anson County . . .[6]

Who were the first settlers in that part of Lord Granville's domain lying west of the Yadkin? Where did they come from? Precisely where on the northwestern frontier did they locate? Although the sources are inadequate and widely scattered, it is possible to identify many—possibly even a majority—of these initial immigrants.

In 1749, the governor in council considered and granted peti-

5. *NCCR*, IV, 889.
6. David Leroy Corbitt, *The Formation of the North Carolina Counties, 1663-1943* (Raleigh, N.C.,: State Department of Archives and History, 1950), pp. 8-9. The new county was named for George, Lord Anson, an English admiral who sailed around the world.

tions from 80 different persons for land warrants in the new county of Anson.[7] The following year, 88 additional applications for land warrants were made.[8] As Hanna has pointed out,[9] there is no way of determining from the warrants exactly when the land in question was actually entered upon. The dates of the warrants (or land grants) do not mark the time of immigration, because in most cases the lands were occupied long before the grants were made. In other cases, the patents were granted to individuals who obtained them for speculative purposes and never actually resided on the land. Of these 168 petitions, 30 were made by known inhabitants of that part of Anson considered in this study. An additional 8 persons may have resided in the area,[10] but the author has no conclusive evidence of the fact.

In the spring and fall of 1751, the Governor's Council considered other petitions for land warrants, at least twelve of them from persons then living on Lord Granville's lands between the Yadkin and Catawba.[11] The court records of Anson and Rowan counties, the colonial land grant records of North Carolina, and the court records of Augusta County, Virginia, provide evidence sufficient to identify forty additional persons living on the northwestern frontier prior to 1752. Thus, before the end of 1751, the total number of identifiable inhabitants (most of them heads of families) of Granville's domain between the Yadkin and Catawba rivers may be conservatively placed at eighty-two.

It is impossible to determine which among these settlers were the initial arrivals. However, there is reason to believe that James Carter, Morgan Bryan, Edward Hughes, Samuel Davis, Robert Gamble, John Dunn, George Forbush, William Linville, Thomas Gillespie, John Holmes, Thomas Bell, James Cathey, George Cathey, John Cathey, James Graham, Richard Graham, John Graham, Felix Kennedy, John Withrow, John Brandon, John Brandon, Jr., Richard Brandon, William Brandon, John Lock, Matthew Lock, John Davidson, George Davidson, George Davidson, Jr., David Templeton, James Templeton, John Sill, Alex-

7. *NCCR*, IV, 946, 949, 950, 959, 961, 965.
8. *Ibid.*, IV, 952, 1037, 1039, 1046, 1047.
9. Charles A. Hanna, *The Scotch-Irish, or the Scot in North Britain, North Ireland, and North America,* 2 vols. (New York: Knickerbocker Press, 1902), II, 33.
10. They were James McKee, William Burnett, Robert Jennings, Francis Mackilwean, James Gillespie, Bostian Best, John Docherty, and Daniel McFeeters.
11. *NCCR*, IV, 1238-55.

ander Osborne, Walter Carruth, Jane Carruth, Adam Carruth, James Marlin, James Mackilwean, John Brevard, Robert Brevard, William Sherrill, Abenton Sherrill, and Adam Sherrill were among them. A number of the remaining forty should in all likelihood be included with these, but no evidence has been discovered to show that they were in North Carolina before June, 1749.

James Carter was probably the son of James and Susannah Carter of Southampton Township, Bucks County, Pennsylvania.[12] Sometime prior to 1736, he made his way into the Appoquinimink Creek district on the border between Pennsylvania (now Delaware) and Maryland. A certain William Williams, then living in the area, made the following statement on April 28, 1739, when interrogated regarding the boundary controversy between Maryland and Pennsylvania: ". . . about two years ago and since, part of the said land within the fork of the main branch of Appoquinak [sic] Creek has been entered on by one Mathew Donohoe, James Carter, Augustine Noland, and James Poor, pretending to be tenants of one Mr. James Paul Heath of Cecil County and Province of Maryland."[13] The deposition of Thomas Rothwell,

12. Abstracts of Bucks County Wills, 1685-1795, in Collections of the Genealogical Society of Pennsylvania, Historical Society of Pennsylvania, Philadelphia, p. 19 (hereafter cited as Bucks County Abstracts) ; Alfred R. Justice Collection (ca to clarl), in Collections of the Genealogical Society of Pennsylvania, Historical Society of Pennsylvania, Philadelphia, p. 29 ; Calendar of New Jersey Wills, in Documents Relating to the Colonial History of the State of New Jersey, First Series, vols. XXX and XXXIII, ed. by A. Van Doren Honeyman (vol. XXX) and William Nelson (vol. XXXIII) (Somerville, N.J.: Unionist Gazette Association, 1918 [vol. XXX], and Patterson, N.J.: Press Printing and Publishing Co., 1901 [vol. XXXIII]) XXXIII, 461, XXX, 47, 184 (hereafter cited as New Jersey Wills) ; Minutes of Rowan County Court of Pleas and Quarterly Sessions, 1753-1869, typed copy in 3 vols. (part of the original manuscript, torn, faded, and very difficult to read, is in the State Department of Archives and History, Raleigh, N.C.), Salisbury Public Library, Salisbury, N.C., I, 32 (hereafter cited as Rowan Court Minutes) ; Rowan County Will Books, Clerk's Office, Rowan County Courthouse, Salisbury, N.C., A, 43 (hereafter cited as Rowan Wills) ; Record of Removals of Middletown Monthly Meeting of Friends, Bucks County, Pennsylvania, 1682-99, Friends Library, Swarthmore College, Swarthmore, Pennsylvania, p. 2; Bucks County, Pennsylvania, Miscellaneous Papers, 1682-1850, 2 vols., Historical Society of Pennsylvania, Philadelphia, I, 135. Carter had many close relatives in eastern and western New Jersey, in Chester County (Bradford Township), and on the Eastern Shore of Maryland.

13. Pennsylvania Archives, First Series, 12 vols., selected and arranged from original documents in the Office of the Secretary of the Commonwealth, conformably to Acts of the General Assembly, Feb. 15, 1851, and March 1, 1852, ed. Samuel Hazard (Philadelphia: printed by Joseph Severns and Co., 1852-56), I, 563-64 (hereafter cited as Pennsylvania Archives, First Series).

living in the same area, was to the effect that "a certain James Carter, also pretending to be a tenant of the aforesaid James Heath, entered on the aforesaid tract of land (though often required to forbear) and built a house about 200 yards within the line and cleared some of the said land, and after left it when said small settlement was entered on about four months ago by one James Poor."[14]

James Paul Heath was a staunch Catholic[15] and violently opposed any encroachments made by Anglicans, Quakers, or Presbyterians. Cecil County in 1739 was a veritable hotbed of religious conflict, and the bitterness arising out of the clash of four or five antithetical beliefs combined with the boundary controversy to produce considerable unrest at the "head of Chesapeake." Hugh Jones, the famous Anglican rector of St. Stephen's Parish at Bohemia Manor, wrote in 1739 to the Society for the Propagation of the Gospel that

. . . 'tis hoped you will be so good as to contribute your extensive charitable benevolence, by a set of books . . . as you shall judge . . . the best answer to Barclay's apology, the independent whig, and all the other favorite books of the Quakers, Deists, Presbyterians, Anabaptists and Papists, with books of piety and devotion and vindication of the doctrines and discipline of our established church against all sorts of adversaries.[16]

In 1740, James Carter was caught in the midst of this turmoil and found himself "a languishing prisoner [for debt] in the Cecil County Gaol."[17] Late the same year, due largely to the influence of William Rumsey,[18] Carter was released. The association between the two men was very close; indeed, the prominent Marylander may be regarded as Carter's patron. Rumsey loaned considerable sums of money to the vigorous millwright and taught

14. *Ibid.*, I, 564.

15. *The Woodstock Letters: A Record of Current Events and Historical Notes Connected with the Colleges and Missions of the Society of Jesus in North and South America*, 90 vols. (Woodstock, Md.: published by Woodstock College, 1872-1961), XIV, 351-54. John Carroll (later Archbishop of Baltimore) was among the first students at the Jesuit classical school, which Heath helped establish at Bohemia in 1745 or 1746.

16. *Ibid.*, XV, 103-4.

17. *Proceedings and Acts of The General Assembly of Maryland, 1737-1744*, in the *Archives of Maryland*, vols. XL and XLII, ed. Bernard C. Steiner (Baltimore: Maryland Historical Society, 1921 and 1923), XLII, 146.

18. *Ibid.*, XLII, 146-50.

him the secrets of surveying.[19] Moreover, Carter witnessed Rumsey's will, which was probated in 1743.[20]

Bereft of his patron, Carter moved to Augusta County, Virginia, in 1744 and settled in the Shenandoah Valley on the Great Calfpasture River.[21] He built a mill and apparently prospered before moving on to the Yadkin in 1747.[22] Carter seems to have located at first on the river itself,[23] but obtained a 350-acre tract on the future site of Salisbury in 1753.[24] He spent the remainder of his life in Rowan County and died there in 1765.[25]

Of the other initial settlers, at least seven were close friends of Carter and had known him for many years before moving to North Carolina. They were Gamble, Dunn, Bryan, Davis, Hughes, Forbush, and Linville.

Robert Gamble, originally from Bucks County, Pennsylvania, was James Carter's son-in-law.[26] He was in Augusta County in 1746 and removed to North Carolina in 1747 or 1748,[27] undoubtedly with Carter. Gamble settled on the west bank of the Yadkin near the trading ford, but moved to South Carolina sometime between 1756 and 1765.[28]

John Dunn, a lawyer, was registrar of deeds for Anson County and first clerk of the court for Rowan.[29] It is evident that

19. Rowan Court Minutes, I, 11; Rowan County Deed Books, Office of Registrar of Deeds, Rowan County Courthouse, Salisbury, N.C., II, 255 (hereafter cited as Rowan Deeds); Testamentary Proceedings of Maryland, 1657-1777, Maryland Hall of Records, Annapolis, Md., XXXIV, 120.

20. *Maryland Calendar of Wills,* 8 vols., comp. and ed. Jane [Baldwin] Cotton (Baltimore: Kohn and Pollock, Inc., 1904-28), VIII, 200 (hereafter cited as *Maryland Calendar of Wills*).

21. "A Plan of 16,500 Acres of Land Lying on the Great or West River of the Calfpasture," in *The Preston and Virginia Papers of the Draper Collection of Manuscripts,* Publications of the State Historical Society of Wisconsin, Calendar Series, I (Madison, Wis.: published by the Society, 1915), 3. Carter obtained Tract No. 22, located seventeen miles west of present-day Staunton.

22. *Chronicles of The Scotch-Irish Settlements in Virginia, Extracted From the Original Court Records of Augusta County, 1745-1800,* 3 vols., comp. and ed. Lyman Chalkley (Rosslyn, Va.: Commonwealth Printing Co., 1912), I, 32; II, 413 (hereafter cited as *Records of Augusta County*).

23. Rowan Deeds, VI, 294.

24. *Ibid.,* I, 72. As Carter became a trustee for the town land in 1755, it seems probable that he lived on this tract at the time. Rumple, writing in 1881, expressed the same opinion.

25. Rowan Wills, A, 43.

26. *Records of Augusta County,* I, 300; Rowan Wills, A, 43.

27. *Records of Augusta County,* II, 413.

28. Rowan Deeds, III, 5, 527; Rowan Wills, A, 43.

29. "Anson County, North Carolina, Abstracts of Early Records," *The May Wilson McBee Collection,* ed. May Wilson McBee (Greenwood, Miss.: May

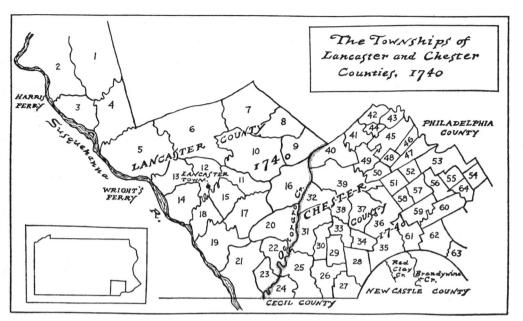

The Townships of Lancaster and Chester Counties, 1740

| Lancaster County | Chester County | |
|---|---|---|
| | 22. Colerain | 42. North Coventry |
| | 23. Little Britain | 43. East Coventry |
| 1. Hanover | | 44. South Coventry |
| 2. Paxtang | | 45. West Vincent |
| 3. Swatara | Chester County | 46. East Pikeland |
| 4. Derry | | 47. Charlestown |
| 5. Donegal | 24. West Nottingham | 48. West Pikeland |
| 6. Warwick | 25. East Nottingham | 49. Upper Uwchlan |
| 7. Cocalico | 26. New London | 50. Uwchlan |
| 8. Brecknock | 27. London Britain | 51. West Whiteland |
| 9. Caernarvon | 28. New Garden | 52. East Whiteland |
| 10. Earl | 29. London Grove | 53. Tredyffrin |
| 11. Leacock | 30. Londonderry | 54. Radnor |
| 12. Manheim | 31. West Fallowfield | 55. Easttown |
| 13. Hempfield | 32. Sadsbury | 56. Willistown |
| 14. Manor | 33. West Marlboro | 57. East Goshen |
| 15. Lampeter | 34. East Marlboro | 58. West Goshen |
| 16. Salsbury | 35. Kennet | 59. Westtown |
| 17. Strasburg | 36. East Bradford | 60. Edgmont |
| 18. Conestoga | 37. West Bradford | 61. Birmingham |
| 19. Martic | 38. East Fallowfield | 62. Concord |
| 20. Sadsbury | 39. Caln | 63. Chichester |
| 21. Drumore | 40. West Nantmeal | 64. Newtown |
| | 41. East Nantmeal | |

he originated among the numerous Dunns of Kent and Queen Annes counties in Maryland.[30] He was a member of the Cecil County colonial militia in 1740,[31] and, like his friend James Carter, was a tenant or servant of William Rumsey of Bohemia.[32] After Rumsey's death in 1743, Dunn accompanied Carter as far west as Prince Georges County, Maryland, where he remained until 1747.[33] He moved to the Yadkin Valley before the summer of 1748 and settled near a commanding eminence four miles south of the site of Salisbury.[34] After the town's establishment in 1755, Dunn established a law practice which he maintained until the Revolution.[35]

The most prominent of the settlers in northwestern Carolina before 1752 was Morgan Bryan. He was a member of the New Garden Quaker community in Chester County, Pennsylvania, in 1719,[36] and, accompanied by his brother William, he moved westward into the Pequea Creek district by 1724.[37] Bryan evidently prospered through the Indian trade, for in October, 1730, he and

Wilson McBee, 1950), pp. 30, 118 (hereafter cited as "Anson Abstracts") ; Rowan Deeds, I, 74; Anson County Deed Books, Office of Registrar of Deeds, Anson County Courthouse, Wadesboro, N.C., book 1, p. 272 (hereafter cited as Anson Deeds).

30. Rowan Deeds, IV, 351; Delaware Land Records, Hall of Records, Dover, Del.: New Castle County Reference, p³, No. 36; Maryland Wills, 1635-1777, Maryland Hall of Records, Annapolis, Md., XXV, 73, 105, XXI (Part One), 346 (hereafter cited as *Maryland Wills*).

31. "Colonial Militia, 1740, 1748," *Maryland Historical Magazine,* 56 vols. (Baltimore: published under authority of the Maryland Historical Society, 1906-61), VI, 51 (hereafter cited as "Colonial Militia").

32. Letter from William Rumsey to Sabinah Rumsey, dated May 26, 1739, in Papers of the Rumsey Family of Bohemia Manor, Cecil County, Maryland, 1662-1870 (approximately 1,250 items in seven boxes, Library of Congress Box No. 2) ; *Maryland Calendar of Wills,* VIII, 200.

33. Prince Georges County Judgments (1731, 1732, 1738-40, 1747), Hall of Records, Annapolis, Md., volume of 1738 judgments, p. 63 (hereafter cited as Prince Georges County Judgments).

34. Anson Deeds, Book 1, p. 240; Rowan Deeds, VII, 4; Jethro Rumple, *A History of Rowan County, North Carolina, Containing Sketches of Prominent Families and Distinguished Men* (Salisbury, N.C.: J. J. Bruner, 1881), p. 165.

35. Rumple, *Rowan County,* pp. 68-69.

36. Mary J. Heitman, "The Bryan Family of Rowan Prominent in Early Days," *The Mocksville Enterprise* (Feb. 10, 1938), p. 4; Record of Marriages of New Garden Monthly Meeting of Friends, 1704-65, Friends Library, Swarthmore College, Swarthmore, Pa., p. 73.

37. "Assessment Lists and Other Manuscript Documents of Lancaster County Prior to 1729," compiled by H. Frank Eshleman, *Papers and Addresses of the Lancaster County Historical Society,* 65 vols. (Lancaster, Pa., 1897-1961), XX, 176, 181 (hereafter cited as "Lancaster Assessment Lists"). Pequea Creek is in present-day Lancaster County.

Alexander Ross, another Quaker from New Garden, purchased from Virginia's Governor Gooch one hundred thousand acres of land on the waters of Opequon Creek[38] upon which they settled a colony of Friends.[39] Bryan himself purchased a tract (in present-day Berkeley County, West Virginia) on a branch of Opequon Creek and settled there in 1734.[40] Fourteen years later, he removed with his large family[41] to North Carolina, making his home on the south bank of Deep Creek four or five miles above "shallow ford" on the Yadkin.[42]

Sometime prior to 1746, Bryan was joined in the valley of Virginia by John, Thomas, and William Linville, three Quakers originally from Chichester township, Chester County,[43] with whom he had been intimately acquainted for twenty-five years. Thomas and John were associates of Bryan in the Conestoga Indian trade in 1724.[44] All three Linvilles were in the Susque-

38. Opequon Creek rises ten miles south of modern Winchester and flows into the Potomac five miles northwest of Shepherdstown.

39. Frederick B. Kegley, *Kegley's Virginia Frontier: The Beginning of the Southwest, the Roanoke of Colonial Days, 1740-1783* (Roanoke, Va.: Southwest Virginia Historical Society, 1938), pp. 33-34.

40. *Records of Augusta County*, II, 109.

41. *Records of Augusta County*, I, 469; III, 285. Bryan's will, dated 1763, mentions sons Morgan, Jr.; William; James; Samuel; John; Joseph; and Thomas (all adults). The daughters were Eleanor Linville and Mary Forbush. Rowan Wills, A, 13; Anson Deeds, book 1, pp. 327, 329, 330, 332; Rowan Deeds, V, 148, 335; Colonial Land Grant Records of North Carolina, State Library, Raleigh, N.C., VI, 98 (hereafter cited as N.C. Land Grants).

42. Rowan Deeds, I, 178.

43. The Taylor Papers: Being a Collection of Warrants, Surveys, Letters &C. Relating to the Early Settlement of Pennsylvania (including correspondence for the period 1723-50 and scattered miscellaneous items for the period 1672-1775 in unnumbered volumes), 10 vols. (vols. VII and VIII: Delaware County Land Warrants and Surveys), Historical Society of Pennsylvania, Philadelphia, VII, 1345. John Linville became one of the first settlers on the Tyger River in South Carolina. R. L. Meriwether, *The Expansion of South Carolina, 1728-1765* (Kingsport, Tenn.: Southern Publishers, Inc., 1940), p. 150.

44. "Lancaster Assessment Lists," pp. 177, 180. Among others engaged in the trans-Susquehanna Indian trade were William Sherrill (1712); Richard Carter, probably the uncle or elder brother of James Carter (Bucks County Abstracts, p. 14); and Charles A. Hanna, *The Wilderness Trail: Or, the Ventures and Adventures of the Pennsylvania Traders on the Allegheny Path, With Some New Annals of the Old West, and the Records of Some Strong Men and Some Bad Ones*, 2 vols. (New York and London: G. P. Putnam's Sons, 1911), I, 163; Thomas Cresap, a leading figure in the border war between Pennsylvania and Maryland; John and Edmund Cartledge (the Cartledges, from Reddings, County Derby, England, were prominent Quaker merchants in Chester and Philadelphia before 1700; Edmund Cartledge removed to Anson [then Bladen] County, N.C., before the spring of 1745), N.C. Land Grants, V, 323; Samuel Blunston (trustee for the famous Blunston licenses, issued to early

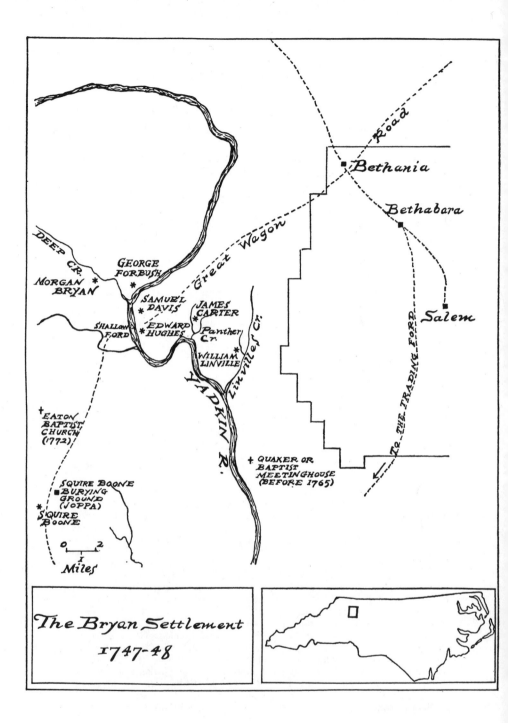

Bethania

Bethabara

Road

Great Wagon

Salem

To the Trading Ford

DEEP CR.

GEORGE
FORBUSH

MORGAN
BRYAN

SAMUE'L
DAVIS

JAMES
CARTER

SHALLOW
FORD

EDWARD
HUGHES

Panther
Cr.

WILLIAM
LINVILLE

Linville's Cr.

YADKIN R.

†EATON
BAPTIST
CHURCH
(1772)

†QUAKER OR
BAPTIST
MEETINGHOUSE
(BEFORE 1765)

SQUIRE BOONE
■BURYING
GROUND
(JOPPA)

*SQUIRE
BOONE

0        2
    1
Miles

The Bryan Settlement
1747-48

hanna Valley by 1730,[45] whence they moved on to the Shenandoah.[46] It is probable that Bryan and William Linville, his son-in-law,[47] traveled together to the Yadkin, where they settled within ten miles of each other.[48] In 1766, William and his son John were killed by the Indians while hunting in the Blue Ridge.[49]

In addition to Carter, Bryan, and Linville, the original "Bryan settlement"[50] included George Forbush, Samuel Davis (or Davies), and Edward Hughes. Forbush seems to have moved northward from Somerset or St. Marys County, Maryland.[51] He was in Lancaster County, Pennsylvania, in 1735,[52] and in the "back parts" of Prince Georges County, Maryland, four years later.[53] Before the summer of 1743, he settled in the Shenandoah Valley, where his daughter Mary evidently married one of the sons of Morgan Bryan.[54] Forbush moved to North Carolina in

settlers across the Susquehanna in 1734); John Wright; John Hendricks; Joshua Minshall; John Harris (who established the first ferry across the Susquehanna); and John Ross (brother of Alexander Ross). The Historical Society of Pennsylvania possesses an interesting contemporary map showing the locations of most of these early settlers on the Susquehanna in 1722.

45. Lancaster County Common Pleas Dockets, 1729-51, Office of County Commissioner, Lancaster, Pa., vol. I (1729-31) (hereafter cited as Lancaster Common Pleas). These documents are collected in twenty-three chronological listings of cases in pamphlet form (for the most part unpaginated), each one containing cases for approximately two years. In this study, reference is made by volume (pamphlet) and year.

46. Records of Augusta County, I, 298.

47. Rowan Wills, A, 13; Hazel A. Spraker, *The Boone Family: A Genealogical History of the Descendants of George and Mary Boone, who came to America in 1717, Containing Many Unpublished Bits of Early Kentucky History, Also a Biographical Sketch of Daniel Boone, the Pioneer, By One of His Descendants* (Rutland, Vt.: Tuttle Co., 1922), p. 538.

48. N.C. Land Grants, VI, 171, 180; Rowan Deeds, I, 178.

49. Spraker, *Boone Family*, p. 538.

50. *Records of the Moravians in North Carolina*, 7 vols., ed. Adelaide Fries (Raleigh, N.C.: Edwards and Broughton Printing Co., 1922-47), I, 289.

51. *Maryland Calendar of Wills*, VIII, 49.

52. Lancaster Common Pleas, VIII (1735).

53. *The Black Books: Calendar of Maryland State Papers* (Annapolis, Md.: Hall of Records Commission, 1943), No. 1, pp. 60-61. Forbush was one of a group of settlers on the Prince Georges County frontier who drew up a petition to Governor Samuel Ogle sometime after May, 1739, to the effect that "the court of judicature . . . [being] . . . from 120 to 200 miles away . . . the petitioners . . . pray that the county may be divided and that the courthouse may be erected at Salsbury Plain." Others joining in the petition included John Heller, Adam Sherrill, George Parker, William and Elesiah [sic] Alexander, and John, Thomas, and David Jones. Montgomery (1776) and Frederick (1748) counties were formed from Prince Georges.

54. *Records of Augusta County*, I, 33; Rowan Wills, A, 58; John W. Wayland, *The German Element of the Shenandoah Valley of Virginia* (Charlot-

the fall of 1748 and established his residence overlooking a beautiful, mile-long meadow on the west (or south) bank of the Yadkin two miles north of the shallow ford.[55]

Although inconclusive, the evidence strongly suggests that Samuel Davis migrated from Cecil or Kent County, Maryland,[56] to the "back parts" of Prince Georges County in 1738 or earlier.[57] He was still there in 1747[58] and, like John Dunn, seems to have proceeded directly from western Maryland to North Carolina. His 579-acre tract (lying directly opposite that of George Forbush) in the bend of the Yadkin passed into the hands of Edward Hughes in 1752,[59] and Davis moved out of the region.[60]

Perhaps the most interesting of the early inhabitants of the Bryan settlement, and the only one still there at the time of the Revolution, was Edward Hughes. This extraordinary man may well have been the first one actually on the ground, for his land was advantageously situated on both sides of the trail which wound through a broad, gradually-descending meadow to the eastern end of the shallow ford.[61] This trail was to become a road traversed by countless wagons[62] in the years that followed. In 1753, Hughes established a tavern at the ford.[63] It must have proven highly profitable, for he continued to live at the ford for over fifty years.

Hughes was from Philadelphia County, Pennsylvania, where

tesville, Va.: published by the author, 1907), p. 70. Forbush's land was probably located in Brock's Gap in the northwestern portion of present-day Rockingham County.

55. *Records of Augusta County*, II, 414, III, 269; N.C. Land Grants, VI, 147.

56. Rowan Wills, A, 33; "Colonial Militia," pp. 47, 51; "Lancaster Assessment Lists," p. 177; *Maryland Calendar of Wills*, VIII, 71, 91; *Records of Augusta County*, I, 27, 35, 294; Maryland Wills, XXVIII, 41; Anson Deeds, Book 1, p. 338.

57. Prince Georges County Judgments volume for 1738, p. 154.

58. *Ibid.*, volume for 1747, pp. 113-14.

59. Rowan Deeds, II, 321. Davis' deed, bearing date 20 September 1748, refers to him as "Samuel Davis, Esquire," indicating that he was probably a man of means. He was made a justice of the peace for Anson County on Sept., 29, 1748. *NCCR*, IV, 889.

60. It is possible that Davis operated a mill for some time prior to 1758 on Dutch (lower) Second Creek, nine miles southeast of Salisbury. Rowan Deeds, V, 529.

61. Rowan Deeds, VI, 382.

62. Except for the trading ford, this was the only spot at which wagons could cross the river.

63. Rowan Court Minutes, I, 15.

he married Ann Zanes in 1730.[64] The Hughes family was closely affiliated with the Boones of Exeter township. Edward, John, George, and Jane Hughes appeared in the will (dated 1753) of George Boone.[65]

In December, 1746, Edward Hughes purchased a tract of land in the valley of Virginia (for £25 Pennsylvania money) on Wallings Creek, a branch of the North Shenandoah.[66] He was still there in the fall of 1747,[67] but removed to the Yadkin (probably with the Bryans) in 1748.[68]

Hughes lived on and on. A Rowan County deed dated 7 November, 1802, informs us that Edward Hughes sold fifty acres, "part of a tract . . . conveyed to said Edward Hughes by Henry McCulloh . . . in the Third year of the reign of George III."[69] Hughes left no will, but, as he married in 1730, he may well have been one hundred years old before he died.

Any description of the early Bryan Settlement would hardly be complete without reference to Squire Boone, father of Daniel, who settled near the Yadkin with his family in 1750.[70] Boone, born in Devonshire, England, was brought to Pennsylvania by his father, George, in 1713.[71] The family settled first in Bucks County, residing most of the time prior to 1729 in New Britain township.[72] It was probably during this period that an association with the Carter family was established.[73] Squire Boone sold his land in Bucks County to Edward Milnor in 1730 and settled in

64. Gilbert Cope Collection (hope to hum), Collections of the Genealogical Society of Pennsylvania, Historical Society of Pennsylvania, Philadelphia, p. 121 (hereafter cited as Cope Collection) ; Rowan Deeds, II, 321.

65. Spraker, *Boone Family*, pp. 29-30.

66. *Records of Augusta County*, III, 258. Witnesses to this transaction were Samuel Bryan, Morgan Bryan, Jr., and John Ellis.

67. *Ibid.*, I, 469.

68. *Records of Augusta County*, I, 469; III, 258, 263. Hughes disappeared from the Augusta records in October, 1747.

69. Rowan Deeds, XVIII, 324.

70. John J. Stoudt, "Daniel and Squire Boone," *The Historical Review of Berks County*, 27 vols. (Reading, Pa.: published quarterly by the Society, 1935-61), I (No. 4), 108.

71. Spraker, *Boone Family*, p. 32; Stoudt, "The Boones," p. 108.

72. George McReynolds, *Place Names in Bucks County, Pennsylvania, Alphabetically Arranged in an Historical Narrative* (Doylestown, Pa.: Bucks County Historical Society, 1955), pp. 263-64; Stoudt, "The Boones," p. 108.

73. Squire Boone's son Jonathan (according to Stoudt, born in Bucks County) married James Carter's daughter Mary (Rowan Deeds, III, 367). The Boone farm (near modern Chalfont) was approximately twelve miles from the Carter place in Southampton township.

The Irish Settlement
1747-49

| Map Number | Name | Map Number | Name |
|---|---|---|---|
| 1 | James Cathey | 12 | Richard Brandon |
| 2 | George Cathey | 13 | Matthew Lock |
| 3 | George Cathey, Jr. | 14 | John Lock |
| 4 | Alexander Cathey | 15 | George Lock |
| 5 | Andrew Cathey | 16 | Thomas Gillespie |
| 6 | Richard Graham | 17 | John Sill |
| 7 | James Graham (younger) | 18 | James Marlin |
| 7a | James Graham (older) | 19 | Thomas Bell |
| 8 | John Graham | 20 | John Holmes |
| 9 | John Brandon | 21 | Felix Kennedy |
| 10 | John Brandon, Jr. | 22 | Alexander Dobbin |
| 11 | William Brandon | 23 | John Withrow |

Oley township, Philadelphia County.[74] In 1750 the family moved to the Yadkin River, following a short sojourn in the Shenandoah Valley,[75] and settled on Bear Creek twelve miles south of the shallow ford.[76]

In addition to the Bryan settlement, two other centers of population developed before 1752 on the northwestern Carolina frontier. The first of these was the so-called "Irish settlement,"[77] located in the headwaters of Second Creek thirty miles southwest of the shallow ford. The second evolved in the vicinity of Davidson's Creek, with its center near the Catawba River approximately twelve miles southwest of the Irish settlement.

By the spring of 1749, the Irish settlement consisted of at least fourteen families, including those of James Cathey, George Cathey, George Cathey, Jr., Richard Graham, John Brandon, Thomas Gillespie, John Sill, James Marlin, John Holmes, Thomas Bell, Felix Kennedy, Alexander Dobbin, and John Withrow. In addition (because of the close family relationships involved), it seems highly probable that the settlement included Alexander Cathey, Andrew Cathey, James Graham, James Graham, Jr., and John Graham, bringing the total number of families to twenty.

With respect to the settlement process, few names carry greater significance than that of James Cathey. He and his son George were the leaders in the organization of what was probably the first English-speaking settlement to be established in North Carolina (or, indeed, in the entire South, exclusive of Virginia) so far from a navigable river. Moreover, it was on George Cathey's land that the settlers constructed the earliest known religious edifice west of the Yadkin—Thyatira Presbyterian Church.[78]

James Cathey's first place of residence seems to have been Cecil County, where he purchased a tract of land from one James Scott sometime between 1719 and 1724.[79] In the latter year he was referred to as James Cathey "of Chester County, Pennsyl-

---

74. McReynolds, *Bucks County,* pp. 263-64.

75. Stoudt, "The Boones," p. 108.

76. N.C. Land Grants, VI, 114. Boone's sons were Israel, John, Jonathan, Squire, Jr., Daniel, and George. All were adults by 1762. Rowan Deeds, VII, 202, IV, 196, V, 450; N.C. Land Grants, VI, 103, 118; Stoudt, "The Boones," p. 108.

77. Also known as the "Cathey settlement."

78. Anson Deeds, Book 1, p. 272; Rowan Court Minutes, I, 2.

79. Cecil County Deed Books, Office of the Registrar of Deeds, Cecil County Courthouse, Elkton, Md., IV, 128 (hereafter cited as Cecil Deeds).

vania,"[80] but his son George was living in Cecil County as late as 1734.[81] By 1736, James and George were in Lancaster County, the home of John Cathey.[82] Accompained by his sons George, William, and Andrew, James Cathey removed to the Shenandoah Valley in 1738, where the family settled on a tract of land adjoining the northern boundary of the Beverly Patent.[83] John Cathey died in Lancaster County in 1743, whereupon his son Alexander joined the other Cathey's in Virginia.[84]

Sometime prior to 1751, William Cathey died, leaving his land in the Shenandoah Valley to an older brother (John) still living in Ireland. The latter came to America to claim the land, but moved to North Carolina upon discovering that the rest of the family had done so.[85]

Richard Graham married Hanna Cathey in 1736[86] and was a resident of Cecil County, Maryland, seven years later.[87] He was closely related to the numerous Grahams in the northern part of the adjoining Delaware County of New Castle,[88] and at least

80. *Ibid.*

81. Surveying Report, "Part of Rumsey's Ramble to John McFarland," 1734, in Papers of the Rumsey Family of Bohemia Manor, Cecil County, Maryland, 1662-1870 (approximately 1,250 items in seven boxes, Library of Congress).

82. John Cathey, brother of James and father of Alexander Cathey, was a resident of Paxtang (Paxton) Township. Lancaster Common Pleas, vol. II (1731-32); Lancaster County Will Books, Clerks Office, Lancaster County Courthouse, Lancaster, Pa., A-1, 77 (hereafter cited as Lancaster Wills).

83. Orange County Deed Books, Office of Registrar of Deeds, Orange County Courthouse, Orange, Va., III, 7 (hereafter cited as Orange County Deeds), *Records of Augusta County*, III, 302.

84. Lancaster Wills, A-1, 77; Howard M. Wilson, *The Tinkling Spring, Headwater of Freedom: A Study of the Church and Her People* (Richmond, Va.: Garrett and Massie, Inc., 1954), p. 472.

85. *Records of Augusta County*, III, 302. John Cathey made his home on the east bank of the Catawba (in present-day Mecklenburg County) near the mouth of Davidson's Creek.

86. "Records of Holy Trinity (Old Swedes) Church, Wilmington, Delaware, From 1697 to 1773," translated from the original Swedish by Horace Burr, with an abstract of the English records from 1773 to 1810, in *Papers of the Historical Society of Delaware*, 67 volumes (Wilmington, Del.: Delaware Printing Company, 1890), IX, 365 (hereafter cited as "Records of Old Swedes Church"). Hanna died subsequently, for Graham refers to his wife Agnes in his will.

87. Cecil County Judgments, S.K. No. 3 (1723-30) and S.K. No. 4 (1730-32, 1736-41, 1741-43, 1746-47), Hall of Records, Annapolis, Md., S.K. No. 4 (1741-43), p. 204 (hereafter cited as Cecil Judgments).

88. New Castle County Assessment Lists (Brandywine Hundred, 1739), Hall of Records, Dover, Del., unpaginated folder (hereafter cited as New Castle Assessments, unpaginated). New Castle County Court of Common Pleas, 1703-17, 1727-40 (the original lists are in folders undesignated save by a penciled number on the outside cover), Hall of Records, Dover, Del., Folder XIV (1727-

three of them accompanied him to North Carolina. On April 11, 1749, Richard Graham petitioned for a tract of land in Anson County and nine years later received a 567-acre tract "on each side of Second Creek, commonly called Withrow's Creek."[89] James and John Graham, brothers or cousins of Richard, probably took up residence in the "Irish settlement" at the same time as he, though proof of their presence in 1749 is lacking. John Graham resided on a branch of the South Yadkin eleven miles north of George Cathey.[90] James Graham's grant, dated 24 June 1751, was described as being "on the headwaters of cold water joining a branch of cane [sic] Creek about two miles from his own house southeast between him and the trading path."[91] Graham thus lived six miles southeast of George Cathey and (as the above description indicates) might well have been there in the spring of 1749.[92]

John Brandon, a widower with three sons, was living in Lancaster County in 1733.[93] He may have resided at the "head of Chesapeake" before that, for he removed to Brandywine Hundred, New Castle County, in 1739.[94] His twenty–two–year–old son, John, Jr., married Maley (or Mary) Cathy in that year;[95] and, about the same time, John, senior, married the widow Elizabeth Lock, a tavern-keeper in Middletown township, Chester County.[96] Brandon returned to Hanover township, Lancaster County, in 1740 or 1741, where he joined his kinsmen William,

30), 7, 9; XXVIII (1733), 34, 46; XXI (1731-36), 5; XXV (1732-40), 2, 48, 50; XXVI (1738-41), 11 (hereafter cited as New Castle Common Pleas). Rowan Wills, B, 27, 89; G, 66, 67, 86, 87.

89. *NCCR*, IV, 949-50; Rowan Deeds, II, 253.

90. Rowan Deeds, XXIII, 645.

91. N.C. Land Grants, XI, 10.

92. A tombstone in Thyatira Cemetery bears the inscription "James Graham, died January 1, 1758, aged 88." This aged patriarch, who was born before any of the other settlers considered in this study (as far as the author has been able to determine), was evidently the father or uncle of these early Grahams of North Carolina.

93. Records of the Donegal Presbytery [typed copy], vols. 1A and 1B (Philadelphia: Presbyterian Historical Society, 1937), 1A, 12-13 (hereafter cited as Donegal Presbytery); Commissioner's Minute Book, 1729-70, Office of County Commissioner, Lancaster, Pa., pp. 39, 41 (hereafter cited as Lancaster Minute Book.)

94. New Castle Assessments, unpaginated.

95. "Records of Old Swedes Church," XI, 367.

96. Chester County Tavern License Papers, 10 vols. (1700-54), Chester County Historical Society, West Chester, Pa., III (1736-41), 41 (hereafter cited as Chester Tavern Petitions).

George, and James Brandon.[97] A husbandman,[98] John Brandon prospered in Lancaster County, where he was tax collector for Hanover township in 1736, 1737, and 1744, and constable in 1745.[99]

In 1748 (or early spring 1749), Brandon took his leave of the rolling hills of the Susquehanna Valley and conducted his small army of Locks and Brandons along the wagon road[100] to the fertile fields beyond the Yadkin. There, Brandon made his home on Grants Creek six miles east of James Cathey's house.[101]

Although it cannot be proved that the sons of John Brandon and Elizabeth Lock settled in Carolina as early as 1749, it is difficult to conceive otherwise. In any event, land grants were issued to Brandon's three sons as follows: John, Jr., 640 acres "on Buffalo Creek between the western path and John Nesbit's place" (November 26, 1753); Richard, 480 acres on a branch of Grants Creek a mile from Alexander Cathey's place (March 25, 1752); and William, 350 acres adjoining James Cathey's land.[102] As for the Locks, John received 415 acres adjoining the land of John Brandon, senior (August 14, 1756); Matthew, 620 acres adjoining Brandon on the south side (March 25, 1752); and George, 450 acres approximately three miles northeast of the senior Brandon's house.[103]

Thomas Gillespie was born in 1719, either in Cecil County or in New London township, Chester County.[104] The Gillespies, like

97. Lancaster Minute Book, 53, 66; Lancaster Wills, B-1, 7; Lancaster Common Pleas, vol. XII (1739-44).

98. Lancaster County Miscellaneous Papers, 1724-1816, Historical Society of Pennsylvania, Philadelphia, I (1724-70), 15 (hereafter cited as Lancaster Miscellaneous Papers).

99. Lancaster Minute Book, 39, 41, 66; Lancaster Miscellaneous Papers, I (1724-70), 15.

100. The "Old Carolina Road," extending from Lancaster, Pennsylvania, to the Yadkin Valley, was one of the most heavily traveled highways in eighteenth-century America.

101. N.C. Land Grants, XI, 4.

102. Ibid., VI, 113; XI, 2, 4.

103. Ibid., VI, 176, XI, 16; Rowan Deeds, I, 199.

104. Cecil Deeds, X, 468; Wilson, Tinkling Spring, p. 475; "Colonial Militia," VI, 50; Rowan Deeds, XII, 188-90; Chester County Will Books, Clerks Office, Chester County Courthouse, West Chester, Pa., IV, 223 (hereafter cited as Chester Wills.); The Taylor Papers: Being a Collection of Warrants, Surveys, Letters, &C. Relating to the Early Settlement of Pennsylvania (including correspondence for the period 1723-50 and scattered miscellaneous items for the period 1672-1775 in unnumbered volumes), 8 vols., Historical Society of Pennsylvania, Philadelphia, volume of miscellaneous items, p. 3351 (hereafter cited as Taylor Papers); tombstone of Thomas Gillespie, Thyatira Presbyterian Church.

so many other families at the "head of Chesapeake," moved west-ward after 1730, first into Lancaster County and then through the Cumberland Valley into the Shenandoah.[105]  Thomas Gillespie's eldest son, James, was baptised in the valley of Virginia by the Reverend John Craig in 1741, and his son William in 1747,[106] shortly before Gillespie departed for Carolina.

The late Professor Walter L. Lingle, in his book on Thyatira Church, included an item gleaned from the *North Carolina Journal* (January 9, 1797) to the effect that Thomas Gillespie and his wife, Naomi, were the first people to settle in Rowan County west of the Yadkin River;[107] but the date of their arrival in Rowan was not given.  There seems little doubt that Gillespie was among the earliest settlers, for it is recorded in the Augusta County, Virginia, court proceedings for September, 1747, that "Thomas Gillespie, about to remove an orphan boy of William Humphrey's, deceased, out of the Colony, is ordered to deliver said orphan to the church wardens."[108]  The first record of Gillespie's presence in North Carolina is a land grant dated June 24, 1751;[109] but it is clear that he was there before the summer of 1749—and possibly before the winter of 1747-48.  The Gillespie homeplace was located on Sill's Creek, approximately one mile west of James Cathey's house.[110]

Between April 27 and December 3, 1751, a certain James McManus of Northampton County, North Carolina, acquired 4,480 acres of desirable land lying north and west of William Brandon and George Cathey.[111]  McManus purchased the land in seven 640-acre sections, one of them being "between Sills Creek and Third Creek beginning at a hickory above the land that Bullock lived on running thence west 320 poles to a corner hickory thence north 320 poles to a corner red oak thence east 320 poles to a corner hickory thence south to the beginning . . ."[112]  The second section was situated "beginning at a hickory near a small Indian old field on Marlin's Creek running thence south 320 poles

105. Wilson, *Tinkling Spring,* p. 475.
106. *Ibid.*
107. Walter L. Lingle, *Thyatira Presbyterian Church,* Rowan County, N.C. (1753-1948) (Statesville, N.C.: Brady Publishing Co., n.d.), p. 22.
108. *Records of Augusta County,* I, 31.
109. N.C. Land Grants, XI, 10.
110. *Ibid.*
111. N.C. Land Grants, XI, 22-24. McManus was a resident of Cecil County in 1738. Cecil Judgments, S.K. No. 4 (1736-41), pp. 220, 271.
112. *Ibid.,* XI, 23.

to a corner hickory thence east 320 poles to a corner white oak thence north 320 poles to a corner hickory thence west 320 poles to the beginning . . ."[113] It was common practice on the frontier for important creeks to bear the name of the first man to settle upon them. As has already been noted, Thomas Gillespie, "the first settler west of the Yadkin River," resided on a stream known as Sill's Creek. Moreover, a certain Bullock[114] lived nearby before the summer of 1751. Yet, the creek bore the name of neither Gillespie nor Bullock, indicating the presence of a man named Sill at a very early date, probably 1748. Rowan County court records show that John Sill was living there in 1753 and 1755,[115] and it was unquestionably he for whom the creek was named. Much the same logic may reasonably be applied in the case of James Marlin.

The Sill family was in Kent County, Maryland, as early as 1711 and in Chester County, Pennsylvania, by 1723.[116] John Sill appears to have left Edgmont township, Chester County, in 1747 and to have proceeded directly to North Carolina.[117]

Marlin, like Sill, probably moved west from Chester County, where Alexander and John Marlin obtained land warrants in 1736 and 1738.[118] A James Marlin was in St. Marys County, Maryland, in 1707,[119] and the family may have originated there.

The will of Robert Wilson of Augusta County, Virginia,

113. *Ibid.,* XI, 24.

114. In 1746 David Bryan, James Houston, Israel Robinson, and James Bullock were reported as vagrants, hunting and burning the woods in the Valley of Virginia. Frederick B. Kegley, *Kegley's Virginia Frontier: The Beginning of the Southwest; The Roanoke of Colonial Days, 1740-1783* (Roanoke, Va.: Southwest Virginia Historical Society, 1938), p. 151.

115. Rowan Court Minutes, I, 8, 23.

116. Record of Births (unpaginated), St. Paul's Parish Register, Kent County, Maryland, Hall of Records, Annapolis, Md.; *Maryland Calendar of Wills,* VI, 124, VII, 176, VIII, 228; William M. Mervine, "The Scotch Settlers in Raphoe, County Donegal, Ireland," *Pennsylvania Magazine of History and Biography,* 85 volumes (Philadelphia: publication fund of the Historical Society of Philadelphia, 1904-61), XXVI, 270.

117. Chester County Tax Lists for 1722-27, 1735, 1737, 1738, 1740, 1741, 1747, and 1753 (unpaginated manuscript), Chester County Historical Society, West Chester, Pa., 1747 tax list (hereafter cited as Chester Tax Lists).

118. Chester County Land Warrants, in *Pennsylvania Archives,* Third Series, 30 vols., ed. William H. Egle (Harrisburg: State Printers, 1894-99), XXIV, 86-87.

119. Testamentary Proceedings of Maryland, 1657-1777, Maryland Hall of Records, Annapolis, Md., XIX.C, 215 (hereafter cited as Testamentary Proceedings).

written in 1745, mentions his daughter Catherine, the wife of Thomas Bell, and daughter Jennet, the wife of John Holmes.[120] The Bells originated before 1720 in Cecil or Talbot County, Maryland,[121] whence many of them removed to Philadelphia County sometime before 1739.[122] Accompanied by many of his kin, Thomas Bell removed to the Shenandoah Valley in 1741 or 1742,[123] and thence to Carolina.

The family of John Holmes, Bell's brother-in-law, was evidently in Lower Dublin township, Philadelphia County, between 1734 and 1741.[124] Holmes himself moved on to Prince Georges County in 1742[125] and proceeded from there to the Shenandoah Valley.[126] Holmes was a man of considerable prominence, for he served as constable of Augusta County in 1747 and was appointed justice of the peace for Anson County in September of the following year.[127]

Bell settled on Marlin's Creek two miles south of James Cathey.[128] Holmes' land was four miles to the northwest adjoining Thomas Gillespie on Sill's Creek.[129]

Felix and John Kennedy (or Canaday), probably from Kent County, Maryland,[130] entered the Shenandoah Valley prior to 1744.[131] Eleven years later, both were living in the Waxhaw settlement on the border between North and South Carolina,

120. Augusta County Will Books, Clerk's Office, Augusta County Courthouse, Staunton, Va., I, 1 (hereafter cited as Augusta Wills) ; Rowan Deeds, VI, 351.

121. *Records of Augusta County*, I, 311; Wilson, *Tinkling Spring*, p. 471; *Maryland Calendar of Wills*, V, 215; marriages of James Bell (1764) and of Walter Bell (1767), in Marriage Records of Rowan County (filed alphabetically on cards), Rowan County Courthouse, Salisbury, N.C.

122. Philadelphia County Court Papers, 1697-1749, 3 vols. (unpaginated), Historical Society of Pennsylvania, Philadelphia, II (1732-44) ; Philadelphia Wills, 10 vols., in Collections of the Genealogical Society of Pennsylvania, Historical Society of Pennsylvania, Philadelphia, II, 833, 879 (hereafter cited as Philadelphia Wills).

123. Wilson, *Tinkling Spring*. pp. 470-71.

124. Philadelphia Wills, II, 769; Philadelphia Landholders, 1734 (unpaginated manuscript), Historical Society of Pennsylvania, Philadelphia (hereafter cited as Philadelphia Landholders, unpaginated).

125. Prince Georges County Deeds, Hall of Records, Annapolis, Md., Liber Y, p. 503 (hereafter cited as Prince Georges Deeds).

126. *Records of Augusta County*, I, 301.

127. *Ibid.*, I, 30 ; NCCR, IV, 889.

128. N.C. Land Grants, XI, 5.

129. *Ibid.*, VI, 157.

130. Kent County Deed Books, Office of Registrar of Deeds, Kent County Courthouse, Chestertown, Md., IV, 550.

131. Wilson, *Tinkling Spring*, p. 477.

where they served in Andrew Pickens' company of militia.[132] However, Felix evidently resided for several years after 1748 in the Irish settlement, where he had a small tract on the west bank of Sill's Creek three miles above John Holmes.[133]

The presence of Alexander Dobbin in the Granville district must have afforded Governor Arthur Dobbs much pleasure, for the name is a significant one in the history of Carrickfergus, Northern Ireland. John, James, and William Dobbin were among the sheriffs of Carrickfergus during the period 1576-1681.[134] John, James, and Alexander Dobbin were in Lancaster County (probably Hanover township), Pennsylvania, at various times between 1736 and 1749.[135] Prior to 1736, however, Alexander Dobbin was probably a minor in Lower Darby township, Chester County.[136] He appeared in the Irish settlement in the fall of 1749[137] and settled on Second Creek,[138] though no land grant was issued in his name until after the colonial period.

When Richard Graham settled on the upper reaches of Second Creek on or before April 11, 1749, he unquestionably had at least one neighbor. That man, whose house was a mile upstream[139] from Graham, was John Withrow. It cannot be determined when Withrow first appeared; the records show only that he was present by September, 1749.[140] However, since the creek was named for Withrow rather than Graham, the prior arrival of the latter does not appear likely.

John Withrow was in Birmingham township, Chester County, as early as 1732.[141] He may have removed to the Marsh Creek

132. Robert N. McNeely, "Union County and the Old Waxhaw Settlement," *The North Carolina Booklet*, 26 vols. (Raleigh, N.C.: Daughters of the Revolution, 1901-26), XII (No. 1), 8-9.

133. N.C. Land Grants, VI, 235.

134. Names of mayors and sheriffs from Carrickfergus, 1568-1688, in Dobbs Papers, Southern Historical Collection, University of North Carolina, Chapel Hill, N.C.

135. Lancaster Common Pleas, vols. VIII (1735-36), XI (1738-39); Lancaster County Appearance Dockets (unpaginated manuscripts), 1747-52, Office of the County Commissioner, Lancaster, Pa., Dockets for 1747-48 and 1749 (hereafter cited as Lancaster Appearance Dockets, unpaginated).

136. Chester Tax Lists, tax list for 1737-38.

137. *NCCR*, IV, 959.

138. Rowan Deeds, X, 258. It is probable that John Dobbin, who died in Rowan County in 1761, was a brother of Alexander. James (who died in 1791) was evidently the son of John.

139. Rowan Deeds, II, 254.

140. Rowan County Civil and Criminal Cases, 1753-64, 4 folders, State Department of Archives and History, Raleigh, N.C., Folder No. 2 (1753-56).

141. Chester Tavern Petitions, II (1729-36), 78.

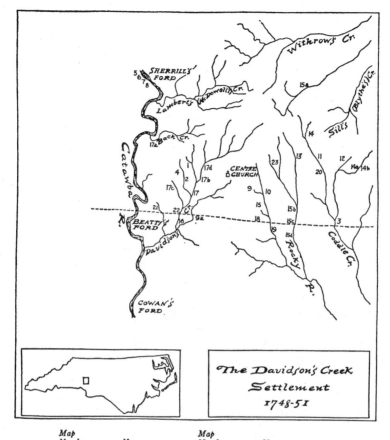

The Davidson's Creek
Settlement
1748-51

| Map Number | Name | Map Number | Name |
|---|---|---|---|
| 1 | John Davidson and George Davidson, Sr. | 15b | Alexander Osborne (sold to James Robinson, 1753) |
| 2 | George Davidson, Jr. (sold in part to William Rees, 1759) | 15c | Alexander Osborne (sold to James Dunn, 1753; sold by Dunn to James Potts, 1759) |
| 3 | David Templeton | | |
| 4 | James Templeton | 15d | Alexander Osborne (sold to James Harriss, 1753) |
| 5 | Adam Sherrill | | |
| 6 | Ute Sherrill | 16 | Edward Given (sold to John Given, 1757) |
| 7 | William Sherrill | | |
| 8 | Abenton Sherrill | 17 | John McConnell |
| 9 | John Bravard | 17a | John McConnell (sold to John McCune, 1762) |
| 9a | John Bravard (sold to Andrew Lynn, 1753) | | |
| 10 | Robert Bravard | 17b | John McConnell (sold to John, Thomas, and Robert Johnston, 1764) |
| 11 | Walter Carruth | | |
| 12 | Adam Carruth (sold to David Kerr, 1762) | 17c | John McConnell |
| | | 17d | John McConnell (sold to Moses Andrew, 1759) |
| 13 | Jane Carruth (sold to James and Robert Carruth, 1756) | | |
| | | 18 | John McWhorter |
| 14 | James Huggen | 19 | Henry Potts |
| 14a | James Huggen (sold to Hugh McQuown, 1755) | 20 | Thomas Cook (sold in part to Stephen Potts, 1762) |
| 14b | James Huggen (sold to Hugh Parks, 1753) | 21 | John Thomson (minister) |
| | | 22 | Samuel Baker |
| 15 | Alexander Osborne | Location Unknown    Joseph Reid | |
| 15a | Alexander Osborne (sold to Patrick Gracy, 1754) | 23 | Henry Hendry |

settlement in western Lancaster County after 1740[142] and from there to the Irish settlement.

Davidson's Creek is a rather lengthy stream that rises in the southern portion of present-day Iredell County and flows southwestward into the Catawba two miles south of the Granville line. The upper reaches of this creek became the center of a third accumulation of pioneers on the northwest Carolina frontier prior to the summer of 1749. Not only was the Davidson's Creek settlement the earliest to be established as far west as the Catawba River, but it also became the nucleus of the Centre Presbyterian Congregation, established sometime between 1752 and 1755.

On November 26, 1748, a grant of 650 acres was surveyed for John Davidson (or Davison) "beginning at a black oak on the north side of a creek called Davidson's Creek that runneth into Catawba River on the North side thence south 400 poles to a stake then west 260 poles to a stake then north 400 poles to a hickory then east 260 poles to the first station."[143] The chain carriers for the surveyor[144] were James Templeton and George Davidson.[145]

In 1724, a John Davidson settled on Chickaslunga Creek in the Susquehanna Valley.[146] Accompanied by William Davidson, he crossed the Susquehanna before 1734 and settled in the vicinity of Letort's Spring.[147] At the same time, Robert Davidson[148] was living in the Middle Octoraro Creek settlement (south-

142. *Pennsylvania Archives,* Second Series, 19 vols., reprinted under direction of the Secretary of the Commonwealth, ed. John B. Linn and William H. Egle (Harrisburg: Clarence M. Busch, State Printer of Pennsylvania, 1896), IX, 801; tombstones in Lower Marsh Creek Cemetery.

143. John Davidson survey, in the George F. Davidson Collection, 1748-1887 (1,660 items in 5 boxes), Duke University Library, Durham, N.C.

144. The surveyor was "C. (probably Charles) Robinson."

145. George Davidson, brother of John, was the father of William Lee Davidson, Whig general killed at Cowan's Ford in 1780.

146. "Assessment Lists and Other Manuscript Documents of Lancaster County Prior to 1729," comp. H. Frank Eshleman, *Papers and Addresses of the Lancaster County Historical Society,* 65 vols. (Lancaster, Pa., 1897-1961), XX, 183.

147. The site of present Carlisle, Pennsylvania. The Blunston Licenses, 1734-35, Land Office, Capitol Building, Harrisburg, pp. 9-11 (hereafter cited as Blunston Licenses).

148. This Robert Davidson, probably the father of Major John Davidson of Mecklenburg County, arrived in America in January, 1729, aboard the "Deligance of Glascow" in company with Walter and Adam Carruth. Chalmers G. Davidson, *Major John Davidson of Rural Hill, Mecklenburg County, N.C., Pioneer, Industrialist, Planter* (Charlotte, N.C.: Lassiter Press, Inc., 1943), pp. 2-3; *New Jersey Wills,* XXIII, 202-3.

eastern Lancaster County),[149] John Davidson was in West Caln township (Chester County),[150] and George and Samuel Davidson were in East Nottingham township (Chester County).[151] In 1739, Alexander Davidson died in Strasburg township, Lancaster County, leaving sons John and Samuel.[152] Many of these Davidsons migrated to the Shenandoah Valley,[153] whence John and George Davidson removed to the northwest Carolina frontier.

John Davidson died in 1749 on the headwaters of the creek which bears his name.[154] His 650-acre survey was granted to his brother George, who also acquired additional tracts in 1752 and 1753.[155]

James and John Templeton were neighbors of George and Samuel Davidson in East Nottingham township.[156] David Templeton was tax collector for Harmony Ridge (Lancaster County) in 1742.[157] Members of this family trekked to Carolina with the Davidsons. James Templeton's land adjoined that of John and George Davidson, while David Templeton settled on Coddle Creek, six miles to the eastward.[158]

Henry Hendry (or Henry), a schoolmaster,[159] settled near the Granville line on the waters of Rocky River.[160] He probably originated in East Nottingham township, where numerous Henrys were neighbors of the Davidsons.[161]

The most picturesque, and probably the most significant, of the early settlers on the Catawba was the Sherrill family. Not only were the Sherrills trail-blazers in the settlement of western North Carolina, but they also played a key role in opening up the Susquehanna Valley. As noted earlier, William Sherrill was among the earliest of the so-called Conestoga traders, and he was joined in 1720 by Adam, Rudil, and Samuel Sherrill as residents in Conestoga township.[162]

149. Donegal Presbytery, 1A, 9.
150. Chester Tax Lists, tax lists for 1737-38.
151. Chester Tax Lists, tax list for 1735.
152. Lancaster Wills, A-1, 39.
153. Wilson, Tinkling Spring, p. 425.
154. "Anson Abstracts," pp. 127, 129.
155. Rowan Deeds, VI, 565, IV, 83; N.C. Land Grants, VI, 140.
156. Chester Tax Lists, tax lists for 1737-38.
157. Lancaster Minute Book, p. 58.
158. N.C. Land Grants, VI, 139; X, 304.
159. Davidson, John Davidson, p. 3.
160. Rowan Deeds, V, 222.
161. Chester Tax Lists, tax list for 1737-38.
162. "Lancaster Assessment Lists," p. 162. See also p. 31n above.

Soon after 1730 the Sherrills moved into western Maryland where, in 1738, Adam Sherrill obtained a tract of land in the "back parts" of Prince Georges County on the Potomac River immediately opposite the modern village of Falling Waters, in Berkeley County, West Virginia.[163]

Several of the Sherrills were in the Shenandoah Valley in 1747,[164] whence William, Adam, Abenton, Ute, and Yont moved on to the Catawba.[165] There they established themselves on both sides of the river at a shallow, island-studded crossing to which they gave their name.[166]

John G. Herndon, author of a number of articles containing references to early settlers of Carolina, has an excellent account of the history of the Brevard family. Of Huguenot origin, the Brevards made their way to northern Ireland after the revocation of the Edict of Nantes and came to America sometime prior to 1711.[167] They settled in Maryland, where, in 1726, John Brevard was an elder from "Upper Elk" in attendance at a meeting of the New Castle Presbytery.[168]

Sometime after 1740, three of John Brevard's sons (Robert, John, and Zebulon) left Maryland (probably upon the death of their father) and set out for North Carolina.[169] There, in 1747 or 1748, John and Robert entered upon land on the headwaters of Rocky River, located between the Davidson and Templeton families.[170]

163. A. G. Tracy, Tract Map of Washington County, Md., (photostatic copy), Hall of Records, Annapolis, Md.; *The Black Books,* No. 1, pp. 60-61.

164. *Records of Augusta County,* I, 414; II, 509.

165. *Ibid.,* I, 414; *NCCR,* IV, 946, 959. This family is of French (probably Huguenot) origin. The anglicized name "Sherrill" is derived from the French "Chérel." Albert Dauzat, *Dictionnaire etymologique des noms de famille et prénoms de France* (Paris: Libraire Larousse, 1951), p. 123. For a listing of additional settlers whose names indicate a French origin, see Appendix G.

166. N.C. Land Grants, XI, 19; Rowan Deeds, IV, 77-78, 659. Descendants of these Sherrills have erected a marker two miles southwest of Sherrill's Ford which carries an inscription to the effect that Adam Sherrill and eight sons crossed the Catawba there in 1747.

167. John G. Herndon, "John McKnitt (ca. 1660-1714) and Some of His Kinfolk: Alexanders-Brevards-Dales," *Publications of the Genealogical Society of Pennsylvania,* 22 vols. (Philadelphia: Edward Stern and Co. [and subsequent publishers], 1895-1961), XVI, 92.

168. "Records of the Presbytery of New Castle Upon Delaware," *Journal of the Presbyterian Historical Society,* 39 vols. (Philadelphia: Presbyterian Historical Society, 1901-61), XV, 113.

169. Herndon, "John McKnitt," XVI, 92; *NCCR,* IV, 1046-47.

170. *NCCR,* IV, 951. N.C. Land Grants, XI, 4-5; II, 10; X, 310.

The Carruths originated in Renfrew County, Scotland.[171] After 1600, numbers of them joined the repopulation of northern Ireland, where the name may be found in a Belfast muster role of 1631.[172] In Ballymartin Parish, County Antrim, the will of James Carruth was proved in 1728. It mentioned sons Alexander, James, John, Walter, and Adam, and "overseer" John Huggen.[173]

Alexander, Walter, and Adam Carruth, accompanied probably by members of the Huggen family, migrated to Pennsylvania in 1729[174] and settled in Lancaster County.[175] Alexander died in 1739, and his estate was administered by Adam Carruth, John Houston, and James Huggen.[176] The Carruths were in the Shenandoah Valley in 1745,[177] and Walter (accompanied by Adam and Alexander's widow, Jane) removed to Carolina three years later, where he settled on the headwaters of Coddle Creek.[178]

James Huggen settled on land adjoining Carruth. His earliest grant bears the date March 25, 1752.[179] Although it cannot be proved that he and his son John were in North Carolina in 1749, the close family relationship—of at least twenty years standing and on both sides of the Atlantic—would seem to warrant the conclusion that James Huggen accompanied Walter Carruth to Carolina.

Jethro Rumple, J. H. Wheeler, and C. L. Hunter all stated in their works dealing with western North Carolina that Alexander Osborne was born in New Jersey. The author has discovered nothing to refute their contention. Osborne was in Lancaster County, Pennsylvania, in 1735 and was still residing there (in Paxtang township) ten years later.[180] He removed to North

171. Harold B. Carruth, *Carruth Family: Brief Background and Genealogical Data of Twenty Branches in America* (Ascutney, Vt., 1952), p. 7.

172. *Ibid.*, pp. 19-20.

173. *Ibid.*, p. 21.

174. *New Jersey Wills*, XXXIII, 203-4.

175. Carruth, *The Carruth Family*, p. 22; Lancaster Common Pleas, vol. XI (1738-39), vol. XII (1739-41).

176. Carruth, *The Carruth Family*, p. 22.

177. Wilson, *Tinkling Spring*, p. 472.

178. *NCCR*, IV, 951; Rowan Deeds, III, 397; N.C. Land Grants, VI, 125-127.

179. N.C. Land Grants, VI, 156; XI, 14.

180. Lancaster Common Pleas, vol. VII (1734-35); *Notes and Queries, Historical, Biographical and Genealogical, Relating Chiefly to Interior Pennsylvania*, 3 ser. (12 vols.), ed. William H. Egle (Harrisburg: Harrisburg Publishing Co. [reprinted from *Harrisburg Daily Telegraph*], 1878-1901), ser. 3, vol. II, p. 230.

Carolina before the spring of 1749[181] and settled on the head-waters of Rocky River, less than two miles from the homes of John and Robert Brevard.[182]

The Given (or Givan) family settled in Somerset County, Maryland, where the name appears as early as 1709.[183] Samuel Given, who received a Blunston license to settle in the Cumberland Valley in 1735,[184] was in the Shenandoah Valley three years later.[185] Edward, John, and James, probably his sons, were there by 1747.[186] Edward Given went to the Catawba Valley in 1748 or 1749 and settled on the west bank of the Catawba near Davidson's Creek where it crossed the Granville line.[187]

Thus, before the end of 1749, three distinctive settlements had developed in the Yadkin-Catawba basin. By far the largest was the Irish settlement, but the other two, situated at three of the four major fords[188] permitting east-west travel to and from the region, were no less important.

At least forty-three settlers[189] may be identified as residents before 1750 in Lord Granville's domain between the Yadkin and Catawba. As indicated earlier, there were almost certainly many more. The purpose of the next chapter will be to identify others among these early settlers of the northwest Carolina frontier.

181. *NCCR,* IV, 951. On April 11, 1749, Osborne was appointed one of the first justices of the peace for Anson County. The others were Charles Robinson, James Mackilwean, Joseph White, Edmund Cartledge, William Phillips, Samuel Davis, Thomas Smith, James Cathey, John Holmes, Alexander Osborne, Walter Carruth, John Brevard, and John Brandon.

182. N.C. Land Grants, XI, 18.

183. *Maryland Calendar of Wills,* III, 152; IV, 49; V, 164.

184. Blunston Licenses, p. 4. It is not clear whether Samuel Given belonged to the Somerset County family. He may have emigrated from Ulster to Pennsylvania.

185. Orange County Deeds, III, 12; IV, 88.

186. *Records of Augusta County,* II, 508, 440.

187. N.C. Land Grants, V, 390; VI, 152.

188. Shallow Ford and Trading Ford on the Yadkin and Sherrill's Ford on the Catawba. The fourth was located five miles south of the spot where Granville's line crossed the Catawba. It was known as Beatty's Ford.

189. In all likelihood, a sufficient number of these pioneers had adult married sons numerous enough to raise the total number of identifiable families to approximately sixty.

# IV

# GROWTH OF THE
# WESTERN
# SETTLEMENT, 1750-1751

During the years 1750 and 1751, thirty additional settlers appear in the colonial and county records as inhabitants of the fertile land west of the Yadkin. Of this number, two-thirds entered the Irish settlement; most of the remainder settled near Davidson's Creek.

Four Alexander families settled at New Munster, on the east side of Elk River in Cecil County, Maryland, before 1715.[1] These families contributed heavily to the westward and southward migration. A William Alexander was in Cecil County in 1738,[2] while the roster of the Cecil County militia in 1740 included Moses (ensign), James (cornet), Nathaniel, John, Joseph, and Theophilus Alexander.[3] Eleven years later David Alexander, described as "one of the first elders at Head of Christiana," died at the age of seventy-nine.[4]

James Alexander of Cecil County migrated to Lancaster County, Pennsylvania, before 1737.[5] He and his son William

1. Charles A. Hanna, *The Scotch-Irish, or the Scot in North Britain, North Ireland, and North America*, 2 vols. (New York: Knickerbocker Press, 1902), II, 60.

2. Cecil County Judgments, S.K. No. 3 (1723-30) and S.K. No. 4 (1730-32, 1736-41, 1741-43, 1746-47), Hall of Records, Annapolis, Md., S.K. No. 4 (1736-41), p. 226 (hereafter cited as Cecil Judgments).

3. "Colonial Militia, 1740, 1748," *Maryland Historical Magazine*, 56 vols. (Baltimore: published under authority of the Maryland Historical Society, 1906-61), VI, 46-47 (hereafter cited as "Colonial Militia").

4. George Johnston, *History of Cecil County, Maryland, and the Early Settlements Around the Head of Chesapeake Bay and on the Delaware River with Sketches of Some of the Old Families of Cecil County* (Elkton, Md.: published by the author, 1881), p. 141.

5. Lancaster County Common Pleas Dockets, 1729-51, Office of the County Commissioner, Lancaster, Pa., vol. VIII (1735-36) (hereafter cited as Lancaster Common Pleas; these documents are collected in twenty-three chronological listings of cases in pamphlet form [for the most part unpaginated], each one containing cases for approximately two years. In this study, reference is made by volume [pamphlet] and year).

were in the Shenandoah Valley in 1747 and moved on to Carolina within three years.[6] James Alexander acquired a 640-acre tract on the upper reaches of Cathey's Creek, while William's land was two miles away adjoining Felix Kennedy.[7] Following James's death in 1753, William Alexander seems to have moved to the site of Salisbury.[8]

In 1749, "James Allison and Mary his wife of Cecil County" sold land previously bought from one Hugh Lawson.[9] Two years later "James Allison and Mary his wife" were granted 350 acres on the Carolina frontier "lying on both sides of Crane Creek including the Trading Camps running up the path that goes to the Irish Settlement . . ."[10] and an additional 320 acres adjoining Matthew Lock and John Brandon, senior.[11]

On April 3, 1751, James Allison's brother Andrew, of Colerain township, Lancaster County, Pennsylvania,[12] recorded a land warrant for 640 acres on both sides of Fourth Creek approximately ten miles west-northwest of Richard Graham's house.[13]

The McConnells were in Nantmeal township, Chester County, in 1737.[14] The will of John McConnell, proved in Colerain town-

6. Howard M. Wilson, *The Tinkling Spring, Headwater of Freedom: A Study of the Church and Her People* (Richmond Va.: Garrett and Massie, Inc., 1954), pp. 296, 470; Anson County Deed Books, Office of Registrar of Deeds, Wadesboro, N.C., B-1, 315 (hereafter cited as Anson Deeds); *The Colonial Records of North Carolina,* 10 vols., ed. William L. Saunders (Raleigh, N.C.: Printers to the State, 1886-90), IV, 1039 (hereafter cited as *NCCR*); Frederick B. Kegley, *Kegley's Virginia Frontier: The Beginning of the Southwest; The Roanoke of Colonial Days, 1740-1783,* Roanoke, Va.: Southwest Virginia Historical Society, 1938), p. 41; Rowan County Deed Books, Office of Registrar of Deeds, Rowan County Courthouse, Salisbury, N.C., Book III, 495 (hereafter cited as Rowan Deeds).

7. Colonial Land Grant Records of North Carolina, vols. V, VI, VII, X, XI, and XV, State Library, Raleigh, N.C., XI, I (hereafter cited as N.C. Land Grants.)

8. Rowan Deeds, III, 21, 495.

9. Cecil County Deed Books, Office of the Registrar of Deeds, Cecil County Courthouse, Elkton, Md., VII, 164 (hereafter cited as Cecil Deeds).

10. N.C. Land Grants, XI, 1.

11. *Ibid.*

12. Lancaster County Land Warrants, 1733-61 (unpaginated manuscript, arranged alphabetically), Office of the County Commissioner, Lancaster County Courthouse, Lancaster, Pa., Allison entries for August 16 and 24, 1749 (hereafter cited as Lancaster Warrants); Rowan County Will Books, Clerk's Office, Rowan County Courthouse, Salisbury, N.C., A, 1 (hereafter cited as Rowan Wills).

13. *NCCR,* IV, 1239-40; N.C. Land Grants, XI, 1.

14. Chester County Tax Lists for 1722-27, 1735, 1737, 1738, 1740, 1741, 1747, and 1753 (in unpaginated manuscripts), Chester County Historical Society, West Chester, Pa., tax lists for 1737-38 (hereafter cited as Chester Tax Lists).

ship, Lancaster County, in 1754, mentioned his sons John and Alexander McConnell and his son-in-law Andrew Allison.[15] Six years later, an Alexander McConnell died in Anson County, leaving "my case of pistols and cutlash . . . to my cousin Andrew McConnell of Roan County," and "to my cousin John McConnell of Roan County my silver stock buckle."[16] Andrew McConnell had removed to Orange County, Virginia, in 1740,[17] and it is probable that his cousins John and Alexander accompanied him. John McConnell settled on the waters of Davidson's Creek before the spring of 1750.[18]

Besides the McConnells, other pioneers known to have been in the Davidson's Creek settlement prior to 1752 were John McWhorter, Henry Potts, Thomas Cook, Joseph Reid, and the Reverend John Thomson. It is probable that Samuel Baker, Thomson's son-in-law, was also among those present, for he was operating a public mill on the waters of Davidson's Creek in 1753.[19]

Alexander McWhorter was an inhabitant of New Castle County, Delaware, in 1730;[20] eighteen years later Hugh McWhorter made a will in Pencader Hundred, New Castle County.[21] John McWhorter, son of Hugh, moved to Lancaster County,

15. Lancaster County Will Books, Clerks Office, Lancaster County Courthouse, Lancaster, Pa., B-1, 81 (hereafter cited as Lancaster Wills).

16. "Anson County, North Carolina, Abstracts of Early Records," *The May Wilson McBee Collection,* ed. May Wilson McBee (Greenwood, Miss.: May Wilson McBee, 1950), p. 114 (hereafter cited as "Anson Abstracts").

17. Wilson, *Tinkling Spring,* p. 427.

18. N.C. Land Grants, XI, 17.

19. Samuel Baker originated either in the Kennett-Marlborough area of Chester County or in the Conestoga Creek district in the Susquehanna Valley, where "Robert Baker and son" were living in 1722. "Assessment Lists and other Manuscript Documents of Lancaster County Prior to 1729," comp. H. Frank Eshleman, *Papers and Addresses of the Lancaster County Historical Society,* 65 vols. (Lancaster, Pa., 1897-1961), XX, 176 (hereafter cited as "Lancaster Assessment Lists") ; Chester Tax Lists, tax lists for 1722-27; Rowan Wills, A, 20; Rowan County Court of Pleas and Quarter Sessions, 1753-1869, typed copy in 3 vols. (part of the original manuscript, torn, faded, and very difficult to read is in the State Department of Archives and History, Raleigh, N.C.), Salisbury Public Library, Salisbury, N.C., I, 1 (hereafter cited as Rowan Court Minutes).

20. New Castle County Court of Common Pleas, 1703-17, 1727-40 (the original lists are in folders undesignated save by a penciled number on the outside cover), Hall of Records, Dover, Del., Folder XVII (1731), 9 (hereafter cited as New Castle Common Pleas).

21. Will of Hugh McWhorter, New Castle County Wills (identified by means of a card index), Hall of Records, Dover, Del., (hereafter cited as New Castle Wills).

where he became associated with the Cathey family before 1737.[22] Seven years later he was among the earliest inhabitants of the Marsh Creek settlement in western Lancaster County.[23] In 1750[24] he removed to North Carolina and settled on the headwaters of Rocky River adjoining Robert Brevard.[25]

Henry Potts and Thomas Cook applied for land warrants in Anson County in the fall of 1750.[26] There is little evidence to indicate the origins of either, but what there is seems to show that Potts came from Dorchester, Queen Annes, or Kent County, Maryland.[27] Cook evidently originated in Donegal township, Lancaster County, or New London township, Chester County,[28] and removed thence to Carolina. Potts settled on the Catawba near Alexander Osborne, while Cook's land was located on a branch of Coddle Creek.[29]

One of the older settlers in the Davidson's Creek district was Joseph Reid, who died on the Catawba in 1750, the probable year of his arrival.[30] Reid evidently originated in Kent County, Maryland, whence he removed to the Shenandoah Valley as early as 1738.[31]

22. Lancaster Common Pleas, vols. IX (1736) and X (1737-38).

23. Daniel I. Rupp, *The History and Topography of Dauphin, Cumberland, Franklin, Bedford, Adams, and Perry counties; Containing a Brief History of the First Settlers, Notices of the Leading Events, Incidents and Interesting Facts, Both General and Local, in the History of these Counties, General and Statistical Descriptions of All the Principal Boroughs, Towns, Villages, etc.* (Lancaster, Pa.: Gilbert Hills, Proprietor and Publisher, 1846), p. 54.

24. Frederick County Court Judgments, 1748-59, Hall of Records, Annapolis, Md., Judgments for 1748-50, p. 84 (1749) (hereafter cited as Frederick Judgments).

25. N.C. Land Grants, XI, 17. McWhorter's sister Jane was the wife of John Brevard.

26. *NCCR*, IV, 1046-47.

27. *The Maryland Calendar of Wills*, 8 vols., comp. and ed. Jane [Baldwin] Cotton (Baltimore: Kohn and Pollock, Inc., 1904-28), V, 125, III, 117, 236 (hereafter cited as *Maryland Calendar of Wills*); Dorchester County Deed Books, Office of Registrar of Deeds, Dorchester County Courthouse, Cambridge, Md., VIII, 90; Rowan Wills, A, 197; Rowan Deeds, IV, 351.

28. Chester Tax Lists, tax lists for 1737-38, 1741, 1747; William H. Egle, *History of the Commonwealth of Pennsylvania, Civil, Political, and Military, from its Earliest Settlement to the Present Time, Including Historical Descriptions of Each County in the State, Their Towns, and Industrial Resources* (Philadelphia: E. M. Gardner, 1883), p. 180; Lancaster Common Pleas, vol. VII (1734-35); "Lancaster Assessment Lists," p. 167.

29. N.C. Land Grants, XV, 3; Rowan Deeds, IV, 584.

30. "Anson Abstracts," p. 118.

31. *Ibid.; Maryland Calendar of Wills*, III, 241; Orange County Deed Books, Office of Registrar of Deeds, Orange County Courthouse, Orange, Va., IV, 148, VI, 239; Philadelphia Wills, 10 vols., in Collections of the Genealogical Society

On March 25, 1752, a grant of 627 acres was made to John "Thompson" situated between Davidson's Creek and the Catawba River.[32] The Granville line formed the southern boundary of the tract. This was the homeplace of the celebrated Presbyterian preacher, undoubtedly the first licensed minister to make his home in the rapidly filling country west of the Yadkin. This grant, like several others issued to Thomson, contained the proviso that within three years three acres for every hundred must be cleared and in cultivation.[33] Before 1755, however, Thomson was dead.

The Reverend John Thomson was ordained at Lewes, Delaware, in 1717.[34] In 1739, he was appointed by the Donegal Presbytery to attend the needs of settlers in the valley of Virginia. In May of that year the Philadelphia Synod noted a petition from people in North Carolina requesting the appointment of a minister to correspond with them. Thomson was selected and made a number of visits to Carolina,[35] in all probability centering his activities after 1748 on the growing settlements west of the Yadkin. In 1750, Thomson left his Amelia County, Virginia, home and established residence in the Davidson's Creek settlement.[36]

While expansion of the Catawba settlement was thus taking place, the Irish settlement was growing even more rapidly. In addition to the Alexander and Allison families, at least twenty settlers entered upon the fertile fields and meandering creeks of what is today Rowan County. Before the end of 1750, George and John Cowan, Arthur Patten (or Patton), Archibald Hamilton, John Nisbet, Robert Tate, Lorentz Schnepp, and Peter Arndt had settled there. A year later appeared the names of Samuel Young, Robert McPherson, John Lynn, James Deacon (or Deason), David Fullerton, George Henry, Robert Harris, David Houston, and William, Charles, Samuel, and John Burnett.

of Pennsylvania, Philadelphia, II, 577 (hereafter cited as Philadelphia Wills) ; Rowan Court Minutes, I, 20.

32. N.C. Land Grants, XI, 19.

33. Mary Elinor Lazenby, Lewis Graveyard, With Mention of Some Early Settlers Along Fifth Creek, Iredell County, N.C. (Statesville, N.C., n.d.), p. 3.

34. E. F. Rockwell, "The Gospel Pioneer in Western North Carolina," The Historical Magazine, and Notes and Queries Concerning the Antiquities, History, and Biography of America, 23 vols., in 3 ser., (Boston: C. Benjamin Richardson and others, 1857-75), XXIII (3rd ser., vol. III), 144-45.

35. Ibid.

36. J. G. Herndon, "The Reverend John Thomson," Journal of the Presbyterian Historical Society, 36 vols. (Philadelphia: Presbyterian Historical Society, 1901-58), XXI, 34-35.

The Cowans, who were in Pennsylvania as early as 1721, resided in the West Caln-Salsbury district on the border between Chester and Lancaster counties.[37] John and George removed to North Carolina in the spring or summer of 1750 and settled next to one another within a mile of Alexander Dobbin.[38]

An order from Governor Dobbs, dated March 18, 1756, directed that a road be built "from Salisbury to Charleston by way of Cold Water at the end of Lord Granvilles line . . . to pass by Mr. Martin Phifer's (formerly Arthur Pattons)."[39] Little is known about Patton, whose house was located on, or perhaps a short distance south, of the Granville boundary. He did not remain in North Carolina but moved on southward, settling in the Long Cane district of South Carolina. Patton built a fort there in 1762 during the Cherokee Indian wars.[40]

Archibald Hamilton settled at the source of Gillespie's Back Creek in 1750.[41] He seems to have originated in Prince Georges County, Maryland, and to have entered the valley of Virginia sometime between 1740 and 1747.[42]

John Nisbet (or Nesbit) was born in 1705 in either Essex or Middlesex County, New Jersey.[43] After reaching his majority he went to Pennsylvania, probably in the company of Alexander Osborne, and settled before March, 1736, on a branch of Pequea Creek in Lancaster County.[44] The Nisbet family papers record

37. The Taylor Papers: Being a Collection of Warrants, Surveys, Letters, &C. Relating to the Early Settlement of Pennsylvania (including correspondence for the period 1723-50 and scattered miscellaneous items for the period 1672-1775 in unnumbered volumes), 10 vols., Historical Society of Pennsylvania, Philadelphia, unnumbered volume of correspondence (hereafter cited as Taylor Papers); "Lancaster Assessment Lists," p. 173; Chester County Will Books, Clerk's Office, Chester County Courthouse, West Chester, Pa., VI, 244 (hereafter cited as Chester Wills); Rowan Wills, B, 196, E, 207.

38. NCCR, IV, 1039, 1046-47; Rowan Deeds, IV, 137, VI, 533.

39. Rowan Court Minutes, p. 37.

40. R. L. Meriwether, The Expansion of South Carolina, 1729-1765 (Kingsport, Tenn.: Southern Publishers, Inc., 1940), pp. 134, 246.

41. N.C. Land Grants, VI, 154; NCCR, IV, 1046-47.

42. Maryland Calendar of Wills, IV, 9, 136, V, 23, 86; Wilson, Tinkling Spring, p. 475.

43. John Nisbet History in the Nisbet Papers, Southern Historical Collection, University of North Carolina, Chapel Hill, N.C. (hereafter cited as Nisbet Papers.); Calendar of New Jersey Wills, in Documents Relating to the Colonial History of the State of New Jersey, First Series, vols. XXX and XXXIII, ed. A. Van Doren Honeyman (vol. XXX) and William Nelson (vol. XXXIII) (Somerville, N.J.: Unionist Gazette Association, 1918 [vol. XXX], and Paterson, N.J.: Press Printing and Publishing Co., 1901 [vol. XXXIII]), XXX, 353, 356 (hereafter cited as New Jersey Wills).

44. Taylor Papers, V, 889.

his removal to North Carolina in 1750,[45] though he may have traveled southward the previous year with his friend Osborne. The closeness of their association is reflected in the marriage of Nisbet's son John to Mary Osborne, daughter of Alexander.[46]

The will of William Tait (or Tate), proved in Derry township, Lancaster County, in 1749, refers to the children of Robert Tate.[47] William H. Egle stated that Robert Tate was on the Reverend John Roan's list of those paying stipends and left Derry township after 1745.[48] In 1742, Robert Tate witnessed a deed from James Boyd to James Huey on Looney's Mill Creek in the Shenandoah Valley.[49] In 1750, the sheriff of Augusta County reported that Robert Tate had "gone to carolina."[50]

It is more difficult to determine when the earliest German settlers migrated to the Carolina frontier than it is to discover where they came from. The Germans, mostly of Rhineland origin, had in many cases not been naturalized. Furthermore, they were a minority and spoke a language totally unfamiliar to the first clerks, tax assessors, and justices of Anson or Rowan counties. Consequently, the early German immigrants rarely petitioned for warrants or surveys and were seldom issued land grants. They ventured but little into the English-speaking areas of the county and generally conducted their legal affairs among themselves.

The public records reveal but two German settlers—Lorentz Schnepp and Peter Arndt—in the area of the Irish settlement prior to 1752. It is possible—even likely—that these and other Germans were among the earliest pioneers (1747-48) on the northwest Carolina frontier; but the evidence does not show it.

Lorentz Schnepp, aged twenty-one, arrived in Philadelphia aboard the "Samuel," out of Rotterdam, in 1733.[51] Within six

45. John Nisbet History, Nisbet Papers.
46. *Ibid.*
47. Lancaster Wills, A-1, 187.
48. *Notes and Queries, Historical, Biographical and Genealogical, Relating Chiefly to Interior Pennsylvania,* 3 ser. (12 vols.), ed. William H. Egle (Harrisburg: Harrisburg Publishing Co., [reprinted from *Harrisburg Daily Telegraph,* 1878-1901], 1894-1901), ser. 3, vol. I, p. 363 (hereafter cited as Egle, *N&Q*).
49. *Chronicles of the Scotch-Irish Settlements in Virginia, Extracted from the Original Court Records of Augusta County, 1745-1800,* 3 vols., comp. and ed. Lyman Chalkley (Rosslyn, Va.: Commonwealth Printing Co., 1912), III, 289 (hereafter cited as *Records of Augusta County*).
50. *Ibid.,* II, 415.
51. *Pennsylvania German Pioneers: A Publication of the Original Lists of Arrivals in the Port of Philadelphia from 1727 to 1808,* 3 vols., comp. and ed.

years he was living in the Opequon Creek district,[52] where Jost Hite (or Heit) had settled a colony of Germans as early as 1726. He removed to North Carolina sometime prior to September, 1750, and settled in the great bend of the Yadkin, two miles east of the trading ford.[53]

The ship "Hope," from Rotterdam, brought Hermann Arndt to Philadelphia in 1733.[54] With him were his three sons, Peter, Michael, and Jacob, and a daughter, Anna Maria. Peter, the eldest son (twenty-one years of age), had evidently married in Europe, and his wife, Katrina, was six years his senior.[55] On November 1, 1751, a German language newspaper in Philadelphia carried the following advertisement:

Herman Arndt arrived in this country nineteen years ago from Hanau, with his three sons Peter, Michael, and Jacob and daughter Anna Maria. His son Heinrich, a stocking-weaver, arrived this year, and he seeks the other members of the family. He is living near the Reformed Church in Philadelphia.[56]

In order to see his brother Peter, Heinrich Arndt would have been faced with a journey of more than four hundred miles, for Peter Arndt had been living in North Carolina for at least a year.

Peter Arndt, unlike most of his countrymen, had apparently become associated with the English and Scotch-Irish. His house was located near several large springs on the site of the future town of Salisbury.[57] It probably stood within two miles of the home of William Alexander and was used as a meeting place by the county court between 1753 and 1755.[58]

Ralph Beaver Strassburger (Norristown, Pa.: Pennsylvania German Society, 1934), I, 107-12.

52. *Records of Reverend John Casper Stoever, Baptismal and Marriage, 1730-1779* (Harrisburg: Harrisburg Publishing Co., 1896), p. 13.

53. *NCCR*, IV, 1046-47.

54. Strassburger, *German Pioneers*, I, 116-18.

55. *Ibid.*

56. *Genealogical Data Relating to the German Settlers of Pennsylvania and Adjacent Territory from Advertisements in German Newspapers Published in Philadelphia and Germantown, 1743-1800*, comp. Edward W. Hocker (Germantown and Philadelphia, 1935), p. 29.

57. Jethro Rumple, *A History of Rowan County, North Carolina, Containing Sketches of Prominent Families and Distinguished Men* (Salisbury, N.C.: J. J. Bruner, 1881), pp. 61-65; N.C. Land Grants, VI, 96; Rowan Deeds, II, 42-46.

58. Rumple, *Rowan County*, p. 61.

In April, 1751, a petition was made for a land warrant in Anson County by Samuel Young.[59] The evidence concerning the origin of this man is contradictory. His tombstone, in the burying ground of the Third Creek Presbyterian Church, carries the following inscription:

> SAMUEL YOUNG
> Born in Scotland 1721
> Educated at University of Edinburgh
> Came to America 1748
> Settled in Rowan County, N.C.
> Died 1793

The public records, however, tell a different story. Young undoubtedly originated in the northern portion of Cecil County, where, between 1740 and 1750, the Youngs were associated with the Irvin, Kerr, and Armstrong families.[60] Before 1751 he married Margaret, the daughter of William McKnight of West Caln township, Chester County.[61] Young settled in North Carolina on the banks of Third Creek, four miles north of Richard Graham.[62]

The name Robert McPherson is closely associated with the origins of no less than four different frontier settlements: the Shenandoah Valley, where Robert McPherson proved his importation in 1741;[63] the Monocacy Valley in Maryland, where Robert McPherson signed a petition in 1739 requesting the creation of Frederick County;[64] the Marsh Creek settlement of western Lancaster County, where Robert McPherson was among the initial settlers in 1743;[65] and the northwest Carolina frontier, where Robert McPherson petitioned for a land warrant in 1751.[66] It would appear that the Robert McPherson with whom

59. *NCCR*, IV, 1238.

60. Rowan Wills, D, 250; "Colonial Militia," pp. 46-48; New Castle Common Pleas, XXV (1732-40), 31-33; Rowan Deeds, XI, 426; Will of Samuel Kerr, New Castle Wills; *Maryland Calendar of Wills*, VI, 223, VIII, 25; Chester Tax Lists, tax list for 1737-38.

61. John K. Fleming, *In Freedom's Cause: Samuel Young of Rowan County, N.C.* (Salisbury, N.C.: Rowan Printing Co., 1958), p. 11.

62. N.C. Land Grants, XI, 21.

63. Wilson, *Tinkling Spring*, p. 427.

64. John W. Wayland, *The German Element of the Shenandoah Valley of Virginia* (Charlottesville, Va.: published by the author, 1907), p. 58.

65. Rupp, *Dauphin . . . and Perry Counties*, p. 54.

66. *NCCR*, IV, 1242-43.

this study is concerned migrated from the Monocacy Marsh Creek region, where he was associated with Hugh McWhorter.[67]

John, Andrew, and James Lynn (Linn) were originally inhabitants of Talbot or Queen Annes County, Maryland.[68] John Lynn (probably a relative) was in the Shenandoah Valley before August, 1746, on a tract of land located between the Augusta County courthouse and Tinkling Spring Presbyterian Church.[69] James Lynn (designated as "architectus") appears on record there in August, 1747, and Andrew Lynn three years later.[70]

John Lynn went to North Carolina in 1751 and bought 312 acres from George Cathey in February of the following year.[71] This transaction was a rather significant one, because Lynn sold twelve of these acres early in 1753 to a "Congregation known by the Congregation belonging to ye Lower Meeting House between the Yadkin River and the Catawba River adherring to a Minister licensed from a Presbytery belonging to the old Synod of Philadelphia."[72] This was the origin of Thyatira Presbyterian Church. It is possible that James and Andrew accompanied John Lynn to Carolina in 1751, for both obtained land there in the spring of 1753.[73] In any event, both John and Andrew Lynn proceeded to the "Waxhaw settlement" where Andrew died before the spring of 1762.[74]

In 1731, Thomas Sharp, of Duck Creek, Kent County, Maryland, referred in his will to his "friend Elizabeth Deacon."[75] Although the available evidence is insufficient, it indicates that James and Elizabeth Deacon came from the narrow strip of territory lying within the bounds of two Kent counties, one in Delaware, the other in Maryland.[76] On June 24, 1751, the Deacons obtained a 640-acre tract of land "beginning at David Fullerton's easternmost corner at a hickory thence west 80 chains along the said

67. Rupp, *Dauphin . . . and Perry Counties*, p. 54.
68. Queen Annes County Deed Books, Office of Registrar of Deeds, Queen Annes County Courthouse, Centreville, Md., I.K. (B), 62.
69. *Records of Augusta County*, I, 20.
70. *Ibid.*, I, 280; II, 756; III, 261, 286.
71. Anson Deeds, B-1, 179.
72. Rowan Deeds, I, 46.
73. *Ibid.*, I, 29, 39.
74. Rowan Deeds, II, 7; *NCCR*, VI, 759; Robert N. McNeely, "Union County and the Old Waxhaw Settlement," *The North Carolina Booklet*, 26 vols. (Raleigh, N.C.: Daughters of the Revolution, 1901-26), XII (no. 1), 8-9.
75. Philadelphia Wills, II, 577.
76. Rowan Court Minutes, p. 20; *Maryland Calendar of Wills*, III, 241; "Anson Abstracts," p. 118; N.C. Land Grants, XI, 8.

Fullerton's line to a small hickory thence south 80 chains crossing a creek to a stake thence east 80 chains to a stake thence north 80 chains crossing the said creek to the first station . . ."[77] This land, part of the 4,480 acres acquired by James McManus of Northampton County, North Carolina, was situated on Sill's Creek less than three miles downstream from Thomas Gillespie.

As may be deduced from the above description, another resident of the Irish settlement in 1751 was David Fullerton, who originated in Salsbury township, on the border between Chester and Lancaster counties.[78] Fullerton's land, also a part of the large grant made to McManus, was not deeded him by the latter until 1761,[79] at which time Fullerton had been living on the land at least ten years. He died before November, 1772, at which time his son William sold the land to John Lock.[80]

Another of the tracts of James McManus, bearing date April 27, 1751, carried the following description: "on the North Branch of Sills Creek beginning at George Henrys corner hickory running thence west 320 poles to a corner red oak thence north 320 poles to a corner hickory thence east 320 poles to two corner pines thence south to the beginning . . ."[81] It is possible that the George Henry referred to never actually lived on this land; there is no further reference to him in the Rowan County records. His origins are also cloaked in obscurity.[82] Nevertheless, a role in the settlement process was evidently his.

Robert Harris migrated to North Carolina from Essex County, New Jersey.[83] He made application for a land warrant in Anson County in October, 1751;[84] it is conjectural whether he was

77. N.C. Land Grants, XI, 8.
78. Lancaster Warrants, entry for 1755; Lancaster County Land Warrants, in *Pennsylvania Archives, Third Series,* 30 vols., ed. William H. Egle (Harrisburg: State Printers, 1894-99), XXIV, 407 (hereafter cited as *Pennsylvania Archives,* Third Series); Lancaster Wills, D-1, 462.
79. Rowan Deeds, IV, 913.
80. *Ibid.,* VIII, 58.
81. N.C. Land Grants, XI, 23.
82. A George Henry died in Baltimore County, Maryland, in 1746. The inventory of his estate included the statement that the "appraiser knows not of any relation left by the deceased." Probate Records of Maryland, 1635-1776, Maryland Hall of Records, Annapolis, Md., liber 34, folio 332.
83. Mrs. S. J. Kiefer, "Genealogical and Biographical Sketches of the New Jersey Branch of the Harris Family in the United States," in the John Abner Harris Papers, Southern Historical Collection, University of North Carolina, Chapel Hill, N. C.
84. *NCCR,* IV, 1246. Harris' brother James Harris acquired 600 acres in 1753 "in the forks of Rocky River"; his nephew Samuel Harris 355 acres "on

at that time residing north or south of the Granville line. Harris' land in the Irish settlement, located on Second Creek, was granted him February 28, 1760.[85] Three years later he was living in Mecklenburg County, where he served as a justice of the peace.[86]

The Houstons were among the Ulster Scots who streamed into Lancaster County after its separation from Chester County in 1729. Among the numerous Houstons in Lancaster was David Houston, who obtained a Blunston land warrant in 1737 to settle in the Cumberland Valley.[87] He removed to Anson County in 1751 and settled midway between the Davidson's Creek and Irish settlements on a 640-acre tract adjoining James Huggen.[88]

Charles Burnett departed from West Caln township, Chester County, sometime between 1740 and 1747.[89] Accompanied by his kinsmen John and Samuel Burnett,[90] Charles joined the southward migration and settled on a 512-acre tract adjoining the lands of Samuel Burnett and Thomas Bell.[91] John Burnett's land grant, dated June 24, 1751, was located near the source of the south fork of Crane Creek, seven miles southeast of Charles and Samuel.[92]

The Burnetts did not remain long in the Granville district. Like John Lynn and Felix Kennedy, they moved on to the Waxhaw settlement, where Samuel Burnett served with Kennedy in Pickens' militia company.[93] Charles Burnett died in or near the Waxhaws before 1763.[94]

---

the south fork of Fourth Creek" in 1762. N.C. Land Grants, VI, 158; Anson Deeds, I, 323.

85. N.C. Land Grants, VI, 154. Harris sold this land to Henry Robinson on January 21, 1763. Rowan Deeds, V, 538.

86. Rowan Deeds, V, 538; *NCCR*, VI, 799.

87. The Blunston Licenses, 1734-35, Land Office, Capitol Building, Harrisburg, Pa., p. 18.

88. N.C. Land Grants, VI, 166.

89. Chester Tax Lists, tax lists for 1740, 1747.

90. "Anson Abstracts," p. 131.

91. N.C. Land Grants, XI, 5.

92. *Ibid.*

93. McNeely, "Old Waxhaw," pp. 8-9.

94. "Anson Abstracts," p. 131.

# V

## MARCH 25, 1752

The date March 25, 1752, is a significant one in the history of the Carolina frontier for two reasons. It marked the last new year's day in England and her colonies under the Julian system of chronology,[1] and it was the date on which land grants were issued to forty-nine persons dwelling west of the Yadkin and north of Lord Granville's boundary. This was the largest number of grants issued by Granville's agents on any one date.

It is probable that March 25 was selected as a celebration of the new year—but why 1752? Why was there not a similar mass issuance of grants in 1751 or in 1753? The proceedings of the colonial assembly would seem to furnish the answer. At a meeting of the Governor's Council at New Bern April 1, 1751, it was recorded that

The Secretary represented to his Excellency and the Councill that great numbers of people who have petitioned for land have never taken out warrants for surveying the same in pursuit of their Petitions and in Order to obtain a Title and that divers others who have taken out Warrants have nevertheless neglected to have their lands admeasured and return thereof made into the Secretary's office, and that others again who have obtained grants in consequence of warrants surveyed and returned have for many years neglected to take out Patents thereby eluding the payments not only of the fees due to the several officers thereon but also of his Majesties Quit Rents.[2]

1. Through the year 1752, March 25 marked the beginning of each new year in England. The Gregorian calendar was adopted in the sixteenth century by most Roman Catholic countries, but England adhered to the Julian system until 1752. The British government then decreed that the day following September 2, 1752, should become September 14, a loss of eleven days. *Proceedings and Debates of the British Parliaments Respecting North America,* 5 vols., edited by Leo F. Stock (Washington, D.C.: Carnegie Institute of Washington, 1924), I, xiii; *The World Almanac and Book of Facts for 1958,* edited by Harry Hansen (New York: *New York World Telegram* Corporation, 1958), p. 425.

2. *The Colonial Records of North Carolina,* 10 vols., ed. William L. Saunders

The council considered the secretary's report and ordered that a list of all approved warrants be posted "at the Council Chamber and other proper places"[3] together with a notice that the warrantees take out their patents[4] "within eight Months from this date"[5] or forfeit their right and title to the land. "It was further ordered that all persons making entry of lands shall pay down the fees of the warrant at the time of making such entry . . . and . . . that all persons applying for a patent shall pay down the fees of such patents at the time of such application."[6] It would seem apparent that many settlers, some of whom had been living on Granville's domain for four years without legal title to their land, took quick action upon the issuance of this proclamation to legalize their claims. New arrivals were entering the region almost daily, and the necessity for legal ownership become increasingly urgent.

Reference in this study has already been made to thirty[7] of the forty-eight grantees of March 25. The others were Samuel Blythe, Robert Allison, Thomas Allison, Fergus Graham, James Hill, Henry Huey, Andrew Kerr, John Kerr, James Lambert, Thomas McQuown, James Miller, William Morrison, Robert Reed, Henry White, Moses White, Benjamin Winsley, Alexander McCulloch, and John McCulloch.[8]

The two Allisons, William Morrison, and James Miller joined Andrew Allison in forming the nucleus of what was to become known as the "Fourth Creek settlement."

---

(Raleigh, N.C.: Printers to the State, 1886-90), IV, 1243 (hereafter cited as *NCCR*).

3. *Ibid.*

4. This involved payment for the land, payment of quit rents, and payment for an official survey which would then be recorded.

5. *NCCR*, IV, 1244.

6. *Ibid.*

7. They are John Dunn, John Nisbet, Matthew Lock, George Lock, John Brandon, Richard Brandon, William Brandon, Alexander Cathey, George Cathey, James Cathey, Thomas Bell, James Alexander, William Alexander, Charles Burnett, James Huggen, John Huggen, Samuel Young, Richard Graham, Andrew Allison, John McConnell, John Brevard, Robert Brevard, James Graham, Thomas Gillespie, John McWhorter, Edward Hughes, George Davidson, George Davidson, Jr., Alexander Osborne, and the Reverend John Thomson.

8. Colonel John Edwards, who was granted 1,280 acres on Fourth Creek, was not a resident of the region. Edwards, a close friend of James McManus, lived in Northampton County, North Carolina. Northampton County Will Books, Office of Clerk of the Court, Northampton County Courthouse, Jackson, N.C., I, 122; Northhampton County Deed Books, Office of Registrar of Deeds, Northampton County Courthouse, Jackson, N.C., I, 302.

There seems little doubt that Robert and Thomas Allison were close kin of Andrew, for both settled on the waters of Fourth Creek within two miles of his house.[9] Their origin cannot be positively determined, but the evidence most strongly suggests that they went to North Carolina from London Britain township, Chester County, or from the waters of Octoraro Creek, on the border between Lancaster and Chester counties.[10]

William Morrison was one of four or five brothers who migrated from northern Ireland with their father James in 1730.[11] William and Hugh Morrison settled in Nantmeal township, Chester County, before 1737.[12] William then moved to Colerain township, Lancaster County, where he grew prosperous.[13] He was tax collector for the township in 1746.[14] William Morrison's brothers Andrew and James were also living in Lancaster County (probably Drumore township) during the period 1742-47,[15] and both followed him to North Carolina.[16]

9. Rowan County Deed Books, Office of Registrar of Deeds, Rowan County Courthouse, Salisbury, N.C., I, 194 (hereafter cited as Rowan Deeds); Colonial Land Grant Records of North Carolina, vols. V, VI, VII, X, XI, and XV, State Library, Raleigh, N.C., XI, 2 (hereafter cited as N.C. Land Grants).

10. Chester County Tax Lists for 1722-27, 1735, 1737, 1738, 1740, 1741, 1747, and 1753 (unpaginated manuscripts), Chester County Historical Society, West Chester, Pa., tax lists for 1737-38 and 1740 (hereafter cited as Chester Tax Lists). Lancaster County Will Books, Clerks Office, Lancaster County Courthouse, Lancaster, Pa., A-1, 179; I-1, 2; B-1, 81 (hereafter cited as Lancaster Wills). Rowan County Will Books, Clerk's Office, Rowan County Courthouse, Salisbury, N.C., C, 178 (hereafter cited as Rowan Wills).

11. Morrison Family Data in the John Abner Harris Collection, Southern Historical Collection, University of North Carolina, Chapel Hill, N.C. (hereafter cited as Morrison Data).

12. Chester County Administration Dockets, Office of Registrar of Wills, Chester County Courthouse, West Chester, Pa., I, 171 (hereafter cited as Chester Administrations); Morrison Data.

13. Lancaster County Common Pleas Dockets, 1729-51, Office of the County Commissioner, Lancaster, Pa., vol. X (1737-38) (hereafter cited as Lancaster Common Pleas). These documents are collected in twenty-three chronological listings of cases in pamphlet form (for the most part unpaginated), each one containing cases for approximately two years. In this study, reference is made by volume (pamphlet) and year.

14. Commissioners Minute Book, 1729-70, Office of County Commissioner, Lancaster, Pa., p. 75 (hereafter cited as Lancaster Minute Book).

15. Morrison Data; Lancaster Minute Book, pp. 44, 92; Lancaster County Land Warrants, 1733-61 (unpaginated manuscripts, arranged alphabetically), Office of County Commissioner, Lancaster County Courthouse, Lancaster, Pa., Morrison entry for 1747 (hereafter cited as Lancaster Warrants); Lancaster County Land Warrants, in Pennsylvania Archives, Third Series, 30 vols., ed. William H. Egle (Harrisburg: State Printers, 1894-99), XXIV, 472, 478 (hereafter cited as Pennsylvania Archives, Third Series).

16. N.C. Land Grants, VI, 195.

The first tract obtained by William Morrison on the Carolina frontier adjoined the land of John McConnell in the Davidson's Creek settlement.[17] In November, 1753, he bought the land on Third Creek where he built his house.[18] Morrison, who was operating a mill on the frontier in 1752, claimed he was "the first Inhabiter of the country,"[19] a claim which Andrew Allison, at least, might well have disputed. William Morrison died in 1771 at the age of sixty-seven; Andrew Morrison in 1770, aged fifty-two.[20]

James Miller, originally from New Castle County, Delaware,[21] settled on the north fork of Fifth Creek.[22] His 560-acre tract adjoined one of the grants acquired by the Reverend John Thomson.[23] He seems to have been in the Shenandoah Valley in the summer of 1748[24] and could have removed to North Carolina at any time thereafter. He died (probably in the Fourth Creek settlement) prior to October 21, 1761, and his farm was sold at auction.[25]

On March 25, 1752, Samuel Blythe, Fergus Graham, James Hill, Henry Huey, Andrew Kerr, John Kerr, Robert Reed, and Henry White were granted land in the Irish settlement.

Between 1718 and 1725, four of the sons and daughters of Samuel and Margaret Blythe were baptized at the first Presbyterian Church in Philadelphia.[26] In 1733, a Lancaster County land

17. *Ibid.*, XI, 17.

18. Rowan Deeds, III, 372.

19. William S. Powell, "Notes for a Tour of Iredell County Conducted on September 12, 1948, for the North Carolina Society of County Historians" (mimeographed), North Carolina Room, University of North Carolina, Chapel Hill, N.C., pp. 4-5.

20. *Ibid.*, p. 4; Andrew Morrison tombstone in Thyatira Cemetery.

21. New Castle County Court of Common Pleas, 1703-17, 1727-40 (the original lists are in folders undesignated save by a penciled number on the outside cover), Hall of Records, Dover, Del., folder XIV (1727-30), pp. 47, 48, 50 (hereafter cited as New Castle Common Pleas); *Calendar of Delaware Wills: New Castle County, 1682-1800,* abstracted and compiled by the Historical Research Committee of the Colonial Dames of Delaware (New York: Frederick H. Hitchcock, 1911), p. 43 (hereafter cited as *Calendar of Delaware Wills*).

22. N.C. Land Grants, XI, 16.

23. *Ibid.*

24. Howard M. Wilson, *The Tinkling Spring, Headwater of Freedom: A Study of the Church and Her People* (Richmond, Va.: Garrett and Massie, Inc., 1954), p. 472.

25. Rowan Deeds, IV, 531.

26. "Register of Baptisms, 1701-1746, First Presbyterian Church of Philadelphia," *Publications of the Genealogical Society of Pennsylvania,* 22 vols. (Philadelphia: Edward Stern and Co. [and other publishers], 1895-1961), XIX (no. 3), 284, 287, 289.

warrant was issued to Samuel Blythe, probably in Salsbury Township.[27] William Blythe appeared in Lancaster County in 1739 and was described eight years later as an "unlicensed trader" of Shippensburg.[28]

Samuel, the husband of Margaret Blythe, apparently died in Cumberland County, Pennsylvania, in 1775;[29] but a son or nephew of the same name removed to the Shenandoah Valley before 1747 and thence to Carolina.[30] Samuel Blythe settled on Sill's Creek adjoining Felix Kennedy.[31]

Fergus Graham probably migrated to North Carolina from Nantmeal township, Chester County.[32] He lived in the Irish settlement next to Alexander Cathey and witnessed the latter's will in 1766.[33] Associated as he was with the Cathey family, Graham could well be among the earliest pioneers of the trans-Yadkin region.

The origins of James Hill remain obscure. He and his wife, Agnes, acquired a 640-acre tract on a branch of Second Creek adjoining the farm of Alexander Dobbin.[34] It is doubtful if Hill ever lived in the Irish settlement. He sold the land on Second Creek to Henry Schiles in 1754.[35]

James and Henry Huey settled in Nantmeal township, Chester County, in 1739 or 1740; Robert Huey in Salsbury township,

27. *Pennsylvania Archives,* Third Series, XXIV, 355; Lancaster County Deed Books, Office of Registrar of Deeds, Lancaster County Courthouse, Lancaster, Pa., B, 90 (hereafter cited as Lancaster Deeds).

28. Lancaster Common Pleas, XII (1739-44); Charles A. Hanna, *The Wilderness Trail: Or, the Ventures and Adventures of the Pennsylvania Traders on the Allegheny Path, With Some New Annals of the Old West, and the Records of Some Strong Men and Some Bad Ones,* 2 vols. (New York and London: G. P. Putnam's Sons, Knickerbocker Press, 1911), II, 327.

29. Cumberland County Wills, Office of the Clerk, Cumberland County Courthouse, Carlisle, Pa., A, 13.

30. *Chronicles of the Scotch-Irish Settlements in Virginia, Extracted from the Original Court Records of Augusta County, 1745-1800,* 3 vols., comp. and ed. Lyman Chalkley (Rosslyn, Va.: Commonwealth Printing Co., 1912), I, 26 (hereafter cited as *Records of Augusta County*).

31. Rowan Deeds, III, 296.

32. Chester Tax Lists, tax list for 1737-38; *Record of Augusta County,* II, 303.

33. N.C. Land Grants, XI, 10; Rowan Wills, A, 39.

34. N.C. Land Grants, XI, 14; Rowan Deeds, X, 258. It is probable that Hill was from Cecil County, Maryland. Cecil County Judgments, S.K. No. 3 (1723-30) and S.K. No. 4 (1730-32, 1736-41, 1741-43, 1746-47), Hall of Records, Annapolis, Md., S.K. No. 3 (1723-30), pp. 272, 281 (hereafter cited as Cecil Judgments); Testamentary Proceedings of Maryland, 1657-1777, Hall of Records, Annapolis, Md., XXXII, 256.

35. Rowan Deeds, II, 52.

Lancaster County, in 1737.[36] William and Joseph Huey were also inhabitants of Lancaster during the period 1738-44,[37] while Robert Houghey [sic] was in New Castle County, Delaware, in 1738.[38] From these families emerged Henry Huey, who proceeded to Carolina sometime before the spring of 1752 and bought 612 acres on the north bank of Fourth Creek.[39]

The records of Chester County reveal that the lands of one William McKnight, located in West Caln township, were sold in 1761 by his son-in-law John Kerr, of Rowan County, North Carolina.[40] The Kerrs migrated to Pennsylvania in extraordinary numbers between 1720 and 1750. The records for that period reveal at least fourteen adult Kerrs living in Penn's colony.

Andrew and John Kerr obtained grants in the Irish settlement within four miles of each other. John Kerr's house was on Third Creek two miles west of Samuel Young,[41] while Andrew lived on the banks of Withrow's Creek.[42] The evidence suggests that the Kerrs were cousins rather than brothers. Andrew Kerr apparently originated in the White Clay Creek district of northern New Castle County;[43] John Kerr removed to Carolina either from Paxtang township or from the Marsh Creek settlement in western Lancaster County.[44] He may have resided briefly in the Shenandoah Valley, for in 1759 he sold a 180-acre tract on Middle River of the Shenandoah at the mouth of Christian's Creek.[45]

Members of the Reed family settled between 1738 and 1743 along both banks of Octoraro Creek in Nottingham township,

36. Chester Tax Lists, tax list for 1740; *Pennsylvania Archives*, Third Series, XXIV, 425; Lancaster Wills, B-1, 585.

37. Lancaster Minute Book, p. 62; Lancaster Common Pleas, vol. X (1737-38).

38. New Castle Common Pleas, folder XXV (1732-40), p. 11.

39. N.C. Land Grants, XI, 14.

40. Chester County Deed Books, Office of Registrar of Deeds, Chester County Courthouse, West Chester, Pa., M-2, 7 (hereafter cited as Chester Deeds).

41. N.C. Land Grants, XI, 16.

42. *Ibid.*, XI, 15.

43. Rowan Wills, B, 42; Will of Samuel Kerr, New Castle County Wills (identified by means of a card index), Hall of Records, Dover, Del.; Chester Deeds, A-2, 311.

44. Lancaster Wills, A-1, 15; J-1, 116. York County Will Books, Office of Clerk of the Court, York County Courthouse, York, Pa., A, 197. Tombstones of John Kerr (1700-49) and George Kerr (1741-1815) in Lower Marsh Creek Cemetery.

45. *Records of Augusta County*, III, 357. John and James Kerr, evidently uncles of John Kerr of Carolina, were among the original Scotch-Irish settlers of the Shenandoah Valley. They settled on Christian's Creek and Middle River as early as 1730. Wilson, *Tinkling Spring,* pp. 11-12.

Chester County, and Sadsbury township, Lancaster County.[46] Robert Reed left this region sometime after 1743 and made his way to the Irish settlement, where he obtained a land grant on Marlin's Creek adjoining George and James Cathey.[47] Reed did not live on the land for more than ten years, for he was in Orange County, North Carolina, by 1761.[48]

The Lancaster County records show that "Henry White and Johanna his wife" of Rapho township, Lancaster County, sold land there adjoining the farm of Moses White on May 22, 1749.[49] It is likely that Henry White proceeded to North Carolina shortly after this sale though he does not appear on North Carolina records until his grant of 1752. White, like James Hill, may never have lived in the Irish settlement though he owned land there. In 1757, he was numbered among those who received a tract of land for use of the Waxhaw Presbyterian Congregation.[50]

The remaining grantees of March 25, 1752, settled in the Davidson's Creek area. James McCulloch, together with his sons John and Alexander,[51] obtained land between George Davidson and the Catawba River.[52] Moses White settled on a branch of Davidson's Creek[53] as did Benjamin Winsley, the latter on land adjoining John McConnell.[54] Thomas McQuown's square-mile tract was situated "three miles below Carruth's land" on the waters of Rocky River,[55] and James Lambert acquired 560 acres on the east bank of the Catawba.[56]

James McCulloch settled in Fallowfield township, Chester County, in 1739 or 1740.[57] He went to North Carolina sometime after 1747.[58] McCulloch was another of the older pioneers along

46. Lancaster Wills, J-1, 213; Chester Administrations, II, 219; Chester County Will Books, Clerk's Office, Chester County Courthouse, West Chester, Pa., I, 287; Rowan Wills, A, 243.
47. N.C. Land Grants, XI, 18.
48. Rowan Deeds, V, 202.
49. Lancaster Deeds, A, 80.
50. R. L. Meriwether, *The Expansion of South Carolina, 1729-1765* (Kingsport, Tenn.: Southern Publishers, Inc., 1940), p. 144.
51. Rowan Wills, A, 113. N.C. Land Grants, VI, 193, 183, 187, 196; XI, 17.
52. N.C. Land Grants, VI, 193, 183, 187, 196; XI, 17.
53. *Ibid.*, XI, 21.
54. *Ibid.*, XI, 20.
55. Rowan Deeds, V, 222; N.C. Land Grants, XI, 17.
56. N.C. Land Grants, XI, 16.
57. Chester Tax Lists, tax list for 1740. Alexander McCulloch (1696-1746), who lies buried in the cemetery at Meeting House Springs, Cumberland County, Pennsylvania, may have been a brother of James McCulloch.
58. *Ibid.*, tax list for 1747.

the northwest Carolina frontier. His will, probated in 1758, mentioned four sons and a grandchild.[59]

In 1722, a small group of "newcomers from Ireland" were received by certificate into the Neshaminy Presbyterian congregation of Bucks County, Pennsylvania. Included in this group were Hugh White, Moses White, Andrew Reed, William Pickens, Israel Pickens, and Matthew Gillespie.[60]

Hugh White left Neshaminy the same year and proceeded westward, settling on Little Chickaslunga Creek in the Susquehanna Valley.[61] His sons were Hugh, John, Henry, and Moses.[62] Moses White of Neshaminy removed to New Castle County, where he was a schoolmaster at the time of his death in 1735.[63] He left sons David, Joseph, James, and John.[64]

Of the eight sons of Hugh and Moses White, two made significant contributions to North Carolina and American history. Joseph White removed to North Carolina in 1745 or 1746 and settled on the Pee Dee River south of the Granville line.[65] Together with Edmund Cartledge and William Phillips he was a key figure in the development of the Pee Dee settlement (in the vicinity of modern Wadesboro) and was one of the original justices of Anson County.[66]

Henry White (as noted above) went to North Carolina after May 1, 1749, accompanied by his nephew Moses, who settled on Davidson's Creek. The grandson of this Moses White was Hugh Lawson White, Whig candidate for President in 1852.[67]

59. Rowan Wills, A, 113. The sons were Alexander, John, Samuel, and William McCulloch.

60. "Church Record of Neshaminy and Bensalem, Bucks County, 1710-1738," ed. W. J. Hinke, *Journal of the Presbyterian Historical Society,* 39 vols. (Philadelphia: Presbyterian Historical Society, 1901-61), I, 129.

61. *Lancaster County, Pennsylvania: A History,* 3 vols., ed. H. M. J. Klein (New York and Chicago: Lewis Historical Publishing Co., Inc., 1924), I, 109.

62. *Ibid.*

63. *Calendar of Delaware Wills,* p. 31.

64. *Ibid.*

65. N.C. Land Grants, V, 246-247.

66. *NCCR,* IV, 951. Phillips also originated in New Castle County (Brandywine Hundred). New Castle Assessment Lists (Brandywine Hundred, 1739) unpaginated folder, Hall of Records, Dover, Del.

67. N.C. Land Grants, XI, 21; C. L. Hunter, *Sketches of Western North Carolina, Historical and Biographical: Illustrating Principally the Revolutionary Period of Mecklenburg, Rowan, Lincoln, and Adjoining Counties, Accompanied with Miscellaneous Information, Much of It Never Before Published* (Raleigh, N.C.: Raleigh News Steam Job Print, 1877), p. 202. Hunter was incorrect in stating that Hugh Lawson White was the grandson of Moses White of New Castle.

Benjamin Winsley was living in Cecil County as early as 1731,[68] and was still there in 1740.[69] He died in the Davidson's Creek settlement in 1759.[70]

The McQuowns,[71] who may have originated in Cecil County,[72] evidently removed to Carolina from the Hanover-Derry district of Lancaster County.[73] Thomas McQuown sold a part of his land on Rocky River to Hugh McQuown in 1755.[74]

Although inconclusive, the evidence indicates that James Lambert originated in Hunterdon or Burlington County, New Jersey.[75] It was undoubtedly James or Andrew Lambert (who settled on the South Fork of the Catawba before the spring of 1750)[76] who gave his name to the small creek which empties into the Catawba six miles north of the mouth of Davidson's Creek. In 1755, James Lambert sold his land on the Catawba to John Oliphant of Evesham township, Burlington County, or Amwell township, Hunterdon County.[77] There Oliphant built a mill which served the surrounding countryside until after the Revolution.[78]

68. Marriage Records, 1730-1889, Nottingham Monthly Meeting of Friends, Friends Library, Swarthmore College, Swarthmore, Pa., p. 5.

69. "Colonial Militia, 1740-1748," *Maryland Historical Magazine,* 56 vols. (Baltimore: published under authority of Maryland Historical Society, 1906-61), VI, 48 (hereafter cited as "Colonial Militia"); Cecil Judgments, S.K. No. 4 (1736-41), p. 132.

70. Rowan Wills, A, 164.

71. This name is spelled variously McQuown, McKune, McCune, McCowen, McCowan, McQueen, McEwen.

72. "Colonial Militia," p. 48.

73. Thomas H. Robinson, *Historical Sketch of Old Hanover Church,* with *Notes Relating to the Church at Conewago, and the New Side Graveyard in Lower Paxtang Township,* by A. Boyd Hamilton ([Harrisburg]: Dauphin County Historical Society, 1878), p. 47; Hanover Township Tax Lists, unpaginated manuscripts for 1750-51, no date, and 1756, Office of County Commissioner, Lancaster County Courthouse, Lancaster, Pa., tax list for 1750.

74. Rowan Deeds, V, 223.

75. *Calendar of New Jersey Wills, in Documents Relating to the Colonial History of the State of New Jersey,* First Series, vols. XXX and XXXIII, ed. A. Van Doren Honeyman [vol. XXX] and William Nelson [vol. XXXIII] (Somerville, N.J.: Unionist Gazette Association, 1918 [vol. XXX], and Paterson, N.J.: Press Printing and Publishing Co., 1901 [vol XXXIII]), XXX, 280, 425 (hereafter cited as *New Jersey Wills*); Records of Births and Deaths, 1675-1750, Chesterfield (N. J.) Monthly Meeting of Friends, Friends Library, Swarthmore College, Swarthmore, Pa., p. 12.

76. N.C. Land Grants, X, 321.

77. *New Jersey Wills,* XXX, 360; Henry H. Bisbee, *Place Names in Burlington County, New Jersey* (Riverside, N.J.: Burlington County Publishing Co., 1955), pp. 81, 69, 39.

78. Rowan County Court of Pleas and Quarter Sessions, 1753-1869, typed copy in 3 vols. (part of the original manuscript, torn, faded, and very difficult

John McDowell acquired a square mile of land on McDowell's (later Lambert's) Creek.[79] His father Charles McDowell, a planter in Cecil County before 1731,[80] died in Anson County in 1754.[81] Less than a year after his father's death, McDowell sold the tract on Lambert's Creek[82] and departed from the region. He was a leader in the westward movement following the French and Indian War, settling in 1768 as far west as Pleasant Gardens in present-day McDowell County.[83]

to read is in the State Department of Archives and History, Raleigh, N.C.), Salisbury Public Library, Salisbury, N.C., I, 136; Rowan Wills, B, 194. Oliphant's mill was less than two miles from Sherrill's Ford.

79. N.C. Land Grants, XI, 16. McDowell's cousin Joseph McDowell lived near the Waxhaws in 1750. It is probable that John was in the Davidson Creek settlement at that time.

80. Cecil Judgments, S.K. No. 4 (1730-32), p. 65.

81. "Anson County, North Carolina, Abstracts of Early Records," *The May Wilson McBee Collection,* ed. May Wilson McBee (Greenwood, Miss.: May Wilson McBee, 1950), p. 114.

82. Rowan Deeds, II, 278.

83. *Ibid.,* VI, 595.

# VI

## *IN THE FORKS OF THE YADKIN, 1752-1762*

Investigation of the initial settlers of that part of the Carolina frontier which later became Davie and Yadkin counties discloses two interesting facts. In the first place, the Scotch-Irish are curiously absent from the region. Secondly, with the exception of the Bryan community, there is nothing to indicate settlement prior to 1752.

The reasons for belated occupation of the land in the forks of the Yadkin are primarily geographic and economic. The region is rockier, more hilly, and less fertile than the land farther south. Too, the only entrance to the area was by way of the shallow ford, and the crossing there was controlled by Hughes, Davis, Carter, Forbush, and Bryan. It was not until the choice land to the east and south had been occupied that settlers sought out homes in the forks of the Yadkin.

The immigrants to this region were largely of English stock, though there was a substantial number of Germans. Although the land grants of many are dated much later, a majority of these settlers were undoubtedly living in the area prior to 1756. In 1761, Governor Arthur Dobbs wrote that for seven years there had been very little immigration, first because of the Indian war to the north, and then because of the war with the Cherokees in North Carolina.[1]

With the exception of a few individuals, it is impossible to state with any accuracy the year in which each settler arrived. However, as it seems certain that the large majority appeared between 1752 and 1756, this chapter shall be concerned with identifying the pioneers and indicating their origins, where known.

The German settlers north of the South Yadkin were Hans

1. *The Colonial Records of North Carolina*, 10 vols., ed. William L. Saunders (Raleigh, N.C.: Printers to the State, 1886-90), V, liv (hereafter cited as *NCCR*).

Bernhardt Steigner,[2] Johanes Bösinger,[3] Michael Kuhn,[4] Peter Böhm,[5] Jacob Völker,[6] Adam Bruninger,[7] Stophel (Christopher) Buhe,[8] Paul Brack,[9] Heinrich Heller,[10] Jacob Henkel,[11] Johann Peter Vögeli,[12] Rudolf Mertz,[13] Anthony Biehler,[14] George Lagle [sic],[15] Friedrich Schor,[16] and Friedrich Fröhlich.[17] The names of most of these immigrants may be found in the pages of Strassburger's compilation of the German arrivals in Philadelphia during the eighteenth century.[18]

Brack, twenty-one years old, reached America aboard the "Winter Galley" in 1738.[19] Steigner was a young man of twenty-four when he landed at Philadelphia, also in 1738.[20] Bruninger, less than six years old at the time, was brought to America in 1731.[21] Mertz arrived in 1743 at the age of twenty,[22] while Bösinger was twenty-five at the time of his arrival in 1736.[23] Peter

2. Colonial Land Grant Records of North Carolina, State Library, Raleigh, N.C., VI, 227 (with surveyor's plat No. 588) (hereafter cited as N.C. Land Grants).

3. N.C. Land Grants, VI, 206; Rowan County Deed Books, Office of Registrar of Deeds, Rowan County Courthouse, Salisbury, N.C., V, 345 (hereafter cited as Rowan Deeds).

4. N.C. Land Grants, VI, 106; Rowan Deeds, V, 129.

5. N.C. Land Grants, VI, 100.

6. Ibid., VI, 106; Rowan Deeds, III, 76, IV, 508.

7. Rowan County Will Books, Clerk's Office, Rowan County Courthouse, Salisbury, N.C., 8 (hereafter cited as Rowan Wills).

8. Rowan Deeds, II, 187.

9. N.C. Land Grants, VI, 106, 177.

10. Ibid., VI, 162.

11. Rowan Deeds, III, 76, 184.

12. Ibid., V, 173.

13. Ibid., XI, 203, 303.

14. N.C. Land Grants, VI, 157.

15. Ibid., VI, 106, 177; Rowan Deeds, VI, 463, 465.

16. N.C. Land Grants, VI, 218; Rowan Deeds, V, 91.

17. N.C. Land Grants, VI, 106.

18. See Appendix F.

19. Pennsylvania German Pioneers: A Publication of the Original Lists of Arrivals in the Port of Philadelphia from 1727 to 1808, 3 vols., comp. and ed. Ralph Beaver Strassburger (Norristown, Pa.: Pennsylvania German Society, 1934), I, 200, 202, 204.

20. Strassburger, German Pioneers, I, 240, 242, 243.

21. Strassburger, German Pioneers, I, 47-50. Bruninger was evidently in the Shenandoah Valley in 1753. Chronicles of the Scotch-Irish Settlements in Virginia, Extracted from the Original Court Records of Augusta County, 1745-1800, 3 vols., comp. and ed. Lyman Chalkley (Rosslyn, Va.: Commonwealth Printing Co., 1912), III, 74 (hereafter cited as Records of Augusta County); Rowan Wills, A, 8.

22. Strassburger, German Pioneers, I, 331.

23. Ibid., I, 155.

Böhm landed at Philadelphia in 1738 and settled in Strasburg township, Lancaster County.[24]

Michael Kuhn, senior and junior, landed at Philadelphia in 1753,[25] but the evidence indicates that the family of Michael Kuhn of Carolina was in Berks (then Philadelphia) County, Pennsylvania, as early as 1736.[26] George Lagle was in Lancaster County in 1750 with his kinsman Michael Lagle.[27] Friedrich Schor reached Philadelphia in 1750[28] and pushed on to the Shenandoah Valley, where he acquired seventy acres on John's Creek in 1753.[29]

Heinrich and Christoph Heller arrived in America in 1751, Georg Heinrich Heller three years later.[30] However, Nicholas, Heinrich, and Peter Heller were living near the Schuylkill River in Philadelphia County in 1738.[31] It is not clear which of these Hellers migrated to the Yadkin Valley.

Eighteen-year-old Peter Vögeli landed at Philadelphia in 1736.[32] Thirteen years later, he and Jacob Völker were in Frederick County, Maryland.[33] In 1756, Völker obtained a 656-acre tract (adjoining Squire Boone) in the forks of the Yadkin from Jacob Henkel.[34] In 1761, Vögeli obtained 200 acres on Potts Creek, a short distance east of the Yadkin.[35] Stophel Buhe,

24. *Ibid.*, I, 238; Lancaster County Common Pleas Dockets, 1729-51, Office of County Commissioner, Lancaster, Pa., vol. XXIII (1747-48) (hereafter cited as Lancaster Common Pleas); Lancaster County Will Books, Clerk's Office, Lancaster County Courthouse, Lancaster, Pa., E-1, 253 (hereafter cited as Lancaster Wills).

25. Strassburger, *German Pioneers*, I, 513, 514, 516.

26. Rowan Wills, A, 36; *Notes and Queries, Historical, Biographical and Genealogical, Relating Chiefly to Interior Pennsylvania*, annual vols., ed. William H. Egle (Harrisburg: Harrisburg Publishing Co., 1896), p. 3 (hereafter cited as Egle, *N&Q*) ; Egle, *N&Q*, annual vol. for 1900, p. 82.

27. Lancaster Common Pleas, 1749 (unnumbered vol.). The only other spelling of this name which appears in the records is "Legall."

28. Strassburger, *German Pioneers*, I, 450.

29. Frederick B. Kegley, *Kegley's Virginia Frontier: The Beginning of the Southwest; The Roanoke of Colonial Days, 1740-1783* (Roanoke, Va.: Southwest Virginia Historical Society, 1938), p. 80.

30. Strassburger, *German Pioneers*, I, 459, 672-74.

31. Surveyors' Field Book (box no. 4) in Lightfoot Papers, 1733-1816, Historical Society of Pennsylvania, Philadelphia.

32. Vögeli could not write his name; the captain of the "Harle" (which brought Vögeli to America), in listing the ship's roster, spelled the name "Vögeli." Strassburger, *German Pioneers*, I, 155, 157-58, 160.

33. Frederick County Court Judgments, 1748-59, Hall of Records, Annapolis, Md., Judgments for 1748-59, pp. 317, 432 (1749) (hereafter cited as Frederick Judgments).

34. Rowan Deeds, III, 76. Henkel's origin is obscure.

35. Rowan Deeds, V, 173.

who bought 450 acres on Elisha's Creek from Johanes Bösinger, was twenty-five years of age upon arrival at Philadelphia in October, 1738.[36] Biehler reached America aboard the "Robert and Alice" in 1738.[37] Peeler Creek, which flows through present Davie County, was named for the Biehler family.

The records of Frederick County, Maryland, contain much valuable information concerning the English and Welsh pioneers who settled north of the South Yadkin. During the period 1749-54, the Frederick County court records reveal the presence of John and Silas Enyart,[38] Philip Howard (senior and junior) and John Howard,[39] William Roberts,[40] John Wilcockson,[41] Benjamin and Jacob Barton,[42] John Eaton,[43] Mark Whitaker,[44] Jonas and Solomon Sparks,[45] Thomas Burk,[46] William Bailey,[47] Margaret Riddle,[48] Samuel and William Francis,[49] David Jones, Jr.,[50] and Samuel Reed.

Silas Enyart lived before 1739 in Hunterdon County, New Jersey.[51] Isaac and John Wilcockson also originated in the Delaware Valley, migrating either from Burlington County (Mansfield township), New Jersey, or Bucks County, Pennsylvania.[52]

36. *Ibid.*, II, 187; Strassburger, *German Pioneers,* III, 309, I, 232-33. Strassburger deciphered the name as "Bouha."

37. Strassburger, *German Pioneers,* I, 213, 214, 216.

38. Frederick Judgments, 1748-50, p. 617 (1750); 1750-51, p. 170 (1750), Silas Enyart committed for indecent behavior to the court; 1752-53, p. 540 (1752), Silas and John Enyart in a case against Joseph Wood.

39. *Ibid.,* 1748-50, p. 221 (1749); 1751-52, p. 1030 (1752); 1752-53, pp. 680-81 (1752), the goods and chattels of Philip Howard to be attached "unless he answers for trespass"; 1753-59, p. 264 (1753).

40. *Ibid.,* 1748-50, p. 386 (1749), Roberts indicated for "stealing a hog with force of arms."

41. *Ibid.,* 1748-50, p. 389 (1749), Wilcockson made application "to keep an ordinary or House of Entertainment."

42. *Ibid.,* 1752-53, p. 573 (1752); 1750-51, p. 51 (1750), Benjamin Barton in a case of debt.

43. *Ibid.,* 1750-51, p. 283 (1750).

44. *Ibid.,* 1751-52, p. 349 (1752).

45. *Ibid.,* 1752-53, pp. 680-81 (1752), Jonas Sparks an appraiser of the estate of Philip Howard; 1750-51, p. 277 (1750).

46. *Ibid.,* 1748-50, p. 238 (1749).

47. *Ibid.,* 1748-50, p. 492 (1749), William Bayley [*sic*] in a case against Samuel Reed, millwright, of Prince Georges County.

48. *Ibid.,* 1748-50, p. 566 (1750).

49. *Ibid.,* 1748-50, pp. 394-95 (1749).

50. *Ibid.,* 1753-59, p. 1135 (1759), Jones from Salisbury Hundred.

51. Minutes of the Court of Common Pleas, Hunterdon County, N.J.; vols. I-VII (1713-56), Hall of Records, Flemington, N.J. (1737-50), 116 (hereafter cited as Hunterdon Court Minutes); Rowan Deeds, IV, 697.

52. Records of Middletown Monthly Meeting of Friends, Bucks County, Pa.,

John and Benjamin Barton may have removed to Frederick County from the same area—Bucks or Burlington County—or they may have originated in Somerset County, Maryland.[53] John Eaton, a Baptist, moved westward from Pennypack, Philadelphia County,[54] while Edward and William Roberts also migrated from Philadelphia County (Gwynedd, Providence, or Whitepaine township).[55] In 1761, Edward Roberts was granted 260 acres of land in the forks of the Yadkin on Bear Creek, where he was close neighbor to the Boones.[56]

The Howard, Sparks, and Winsuit families removed to Carolina from Maryland. Philip (senior and junior), Benjamin, and Cornelius Howard migrated from Anne Arundel County;[57] Solomon, Matthew, and Jonas Sparks from Kent or Queen Annes County;[58] and Abraham and Richard Winsuit from St. Marys

1700-1947, Friends Library, Swarthmore College, Swarthmore, Pa., p. 74 (hereafter cited as Middletown Meeting); *Calendar of New Jersey Wills*, in *Documents Relating to the Colonial History of the State of New Jersey*, First Series, vols. XXX and XXXIII, ed. A. Van Doren Honeyman [vol. XXX] and William Nelson [vol. XXXIII] (Somerville, N.J.: Unionist Gazette Association, 1918 [vol. XXX], and Paterson, N.J.: Press Printing and Publishing Co., 1901 [vol. XXXIII]), XXX, 374 (hereafter cited as *New Jersey Wills*); Rowan County Court of Pleas and Quarterly Sessions, 1753-1869, typed copy in 3 vols. (part of the original manuscript, torn, faded, and very difficult to read, is in the State Department of Archives and History, Raleigh, N.C.), Salisbury Public Library, Salisbury, N.C., I, 81 (hereafter cited as Rowan Court Minutes); N.C. Land Grants, VI, 233.

53. Middletown Meeting, Births and Deaths, 1680-1711, p. 201; Records of Births and Deaths, Burlington Monthly Meeting of Friends, Burlington County, N.J., 1678-1865, Friends Library, Swarthmore College, Swarthmore, Pa., p. 10 (hereafter cited as Burlington Meeting); Burlington Meeting, Removals, 1675-1750, p. 61; Hunterdon Court Minutes, IV (1733-36), 137; Testamentary Proceedings of Maryland, 1657-1777, Maryland Hall of Records, Annapolis, Md., XXI, 441 (hereafter cited as Testamentary Proceedings); Rowan Court Minutes, I, 50, 73, 5.

54. Egle, *N&Q*, annual vol. for 1899, p. 148; tombstones in cemetery of Eaton's Baptist Church, Davie County, N.C.; Rowan Deeds, V, 383.

55. "Landholders of Philadelphia County, 1734: A List of the Names of the Inhabitants of the County of Philadelphia, With the Quantity of Land They Respectively Held Therein, According to the Uncertain Returns of the Constables," *Publications of the Genealogical Society of Pennsylvania*, 22 vols. (Philadelphia: Edward Stern and Co. [and other publishers], 1895-1961), I (No. 4), 171, 180, 183 (hereafter cited as "Landholders of Philadelphia County").

56. N.C. Land Grants, VI, 212.

57. Harry W. Newman, *Anne Arundel Gentry* (n.p., n.d.), pp. 295-99; Rowan Wills, C, 114; Frederick Judgments, 1750-51, p. 282 (1750); Rowan Deeds, IV, 738, V, 326, VI, 455, 484.

58. Kent County Deed Books, Office of Registrar of Deeds, Kent County

County.[59] James and Thomas Burk may have originated in Baltimore or Kent County, Maryland, or they may have moved west from Bradford township, Chester County, Pennsylvania.[60] Both were in the Shenandoah Valley before 1750.[61]

Andrew, David, and William Bailey lived in Kennett township, Chester County, in 1737.[62] In 1761, David Bailey obtained 235 acres on the west side of the Yadkin at the mouth of Reedy Run; three years earlier, Andrew acquired 443 acres nearby.[63]

The records of the Monthly Meeting of Friends in Dublin, Ireland, reveal that in 1719 "William Whitaker, formerly of Timahoe but now of this city, desires a certificate to Pennsylvania."[64] Three years later, Katherine Whitaker of Dublin Meeting requested a certificate to America.[65]

James Whitaker was living in Bradford or Chichester township, Chester County, as early as 1716.[66] In 1738, the will of William Whitaker was proved in Queen Annes County, Maryland.[67] Joshua Whitaker, son of William, settled near Potts

Courthouse, Chestertown, Md., I, 426, 507; Maryland County Land Warrants, State Land Office, Annapolis, Md., liber Y.&S., no. 7, p. 131 (hereafter cited as Maryland Warrants); N.C. Land Grants, VI, 215-17; Rowan Deeds, V, 275, VI, 139.

59. Testamentary Proceedings; Rowan Deeds, VI, 435; Anson County Deed Books, Office of Registrar of Deeds, Anson County Courthouse, Wadesboro, N.C., book 1, pp. 319-20 (hereafter cited as Anson Deeds).

60. Probate Records of Maryland, 1635-1776, Maryland Hall of Records, Annapolis, Md., liber 18, folio 164, liber 20, folio 466, liber 28, folio 209 (hereafter cited as Probate Records); The Taylor Papers: Being a Collection of Warrants, Surveys, Letters, &C. Relating to the Early Settlement of Pennsylvania (including correspondence for the period 1723-50 and scattered miscellaneous items for the period 1672-1775 in unnumbered volumes), 10 vols. (volumes I-III: Chester County Warrants, 1682-1742), Historical Society of Pennsylvania, Philadelphia, II, 307, 542 (hereafter cited as Taylor Papers); Buffington and Marshall Papers, 1705-80, Chester County Historical Society, West Chester, Pa., item no. 55; Surry County Will Books, Clerk's Office, Surry County Courthouse, Dobson, N.C., II, 1 (hereafter cited as Surry Wills); Rowan Deeds, V, 105.

61. Records of Augusta County, I, 24.

62. Chester County Tax Lists for 1722-27, 1735, 1737, 1738, 1740, 1741, 1747, and 1753 (unpaginated manuscripts), Chester County Historical Society, West Chester, Pa., tax lists for 1737-38 (hereafter cited as Chester Tax Lists); Rowan Deeds, VI, 33.

63. N.C. Land Grants, VI, 100; Rowan Deeds, II, 261.

64. Gilbert Cope Collection, Collections of the Genealogical Society of Pennsylvania, Historical Society of Pennsylvania, Philadelphia, pp. 234-35.

65. Ibid.

66. Chester County Deed Books, Office of Registrar of Deeds, Chester County Courthouse, West Chester, Pa., L, 466.

67. Probate Records, liber 22, folio 32.

Creek on the east side of the Yadkin,[68] while his kinsmen William and Mark Whitaker established themselves in the forks of the Yadkin.[69]

In addition to those previously identified, at least three and possibly five of the early settlers removed to the forks of the Yadkin from Philadelphia County. Abraham Cresson settled at the mouth of Deep Creek next to George Forbush.[70] Charles Hunter settled on Dutchman's Creek.[71] In 1758, Jared Erwin "of Philadelphia County," purchased 422 acres on Dutchman's Creek "where Swain Rambo formerly lived."[72] Although inconclusive, there is evidence to suggest that Doctor John Parker may have originated in the same county,[73] and William Morgan removed to North Carolina either from Roxboro township, Philadelphia County, or East Caln township, Chester County.[74]

68. Tombstone of Joshua Whitaker, Jersey Church Cemetery, Linwood, N.C.; Marriage of Joshua Whitaker and Mary Reed, September 12, 1764, Rowan County Marriage Records, Clerk's Office, Rowan County Courthouse, Salisbury, N.C.

69. N.C. Land Grants, VI, 230; Rowan Deeds, III, 106, V, 329.

70. Rowan Deeds, IV, 205, 731; Philadelphia County Wills, Department of Records, City Hall, Philadelphia, I, 277, II, 915, 924, III, 1124 (hereafter cited as Philadelphia Wills). During the Regulator War, Cresson (a Regulator) was taken prisoner and confined at Salem. According to the Moravian Records, Cresson "wept like a child whenever a Brother went near him and begged that we would intercede for him." He was eventually released. *Records of the Moravians in North Carolina,* 7 vols., ed. Adelaide Fries (Raleigh, N.C.: Edwards and Broughton Printing Co., 1922-47), I, 462, 465, 469.

71. N.C. Land Grants, VI, 157, 163; Philadelphia County Land Warrants, in *Pennsylvania Archives,* Third Series, 30 vols., ed. William H. Egle (Harrisburg: State Printers, 1894-99), XXIV, 19, 21, 23 (hereafter cited as *Pennsylvania Archives,* Third Series); Rowan Court Minutes, pp. 37-38.

72. Rowan Deeds, II, 331. Swain Rambo was in Lancaster County in 1729 and in the Shenandoah Valley in 1748. Lancaster Common Pleas, vol. I (1729-30); *Records of Augusta County,* I, 37.

73. "Landholders of Philadelphia County," p. 169. There are other indications that Parker originated in Maryland (Somerset or Cecil County) or Bucks County, Pennsylvania. Rowan County Tax Lists for 1768, Clerk's Office, Rowan County Courthouse, Salisbury, N.C., pp. 367, 370 (hereafter cited as Rowan Tax List for 1768); N.C. Land Grants, VI, 204; Rowan Deeds, IV, 96, 760, V, 541; "Colonial Militia, 1740, 1748," *Maryland Historical Magazine,* 56 vols. (Baltimore: published under authority of the Maryland Historical Society, 1906-61), VI, 48; Cecil County Judgments, S.K. No. 3 (1723-30) and S.K. No. 4 (1730-32, 1736-41, 1741-43, 1746-47), Hall of Records, Annapolis, Md., S.K. No. 4 (1741-43), p. 139; *The Maryland Calendar of Wills,* 8 vols., comp. and ed. Jane [Baldwin] Cotton (Baltimore: Kohn and Pollock, Inc., 1904-28), VI, 186-87 (hereafter cited as *Maryland Calendar of Wills*); Middletown Meeting, Removals, 1682-99, p. 5; Bucks County Administration Dockets, Clerk's Office, Bucks County Courthouse, Doylestown, Pa., A, 8 (hereafter cited as Bucks Administrations).

74. Philadelphia Landholders, 1734 (unpaginated manuscript), Historical

Francis Fincher, from Worcestershire, England, landed at Philadelphia in 1683.[75] He settled in West Caln or New Garden, Chester County, whence a son or nephew of the same name removed to the forks of the Yadkin before 1753.[76] Fincher died in that year, leaving a wife, Sarah.[77] Another immigrant to the Yadkin Valley from the New Garden community was David Johnston (or Johnson), who settled on a branch of Dutchman's Creek.[78]

Evan Ellis also migrated from Chester County (East-town or Haverford township),[79] while Edward Underhill, Stephen Ruddle (Riddle), and John Francis originated in the Nottingham area of the Chester-Cecil border, five miles east of where the Susquehanna flows across the Maryland-Pennsylvania boundary line.[80]

Isaac, Daniel, and Jacob Feree settled on Pequea Creek in the Susquehanna Valley as early as 1722.[81] Eleven years later, Daniel and Isaac Feree signed a tavern petition in Kennet township,

Society of Pennsylvania, Philadelphia; Chester Tax Lists, tax lists for 1737-38; Rowan Deeds, VI, 593.

75. *Quaker Arrivals at Philadelphia, 1682-1750: Being a List of Certificates of Removal Received at Philadelphia Monthly Meeting of Friends,* ed. Albert C. Myers (Baltimore: Southern Book Co., 1957), p. 5 (hereafter cited as *Quaker Arrivals*).

76. Record of Marriages of New Garden Monthly Meeting of Friends, 1704-65, Friends Library, Swarthmore College, Swarthmore, Pa., p. 34; Rowan Court Minutes, I, 4; N.C. Land Grants, VI, 205; Rowan Deeds, III, 147; Chester Tax Lists, tax lists for 1737-38. In Rowan records, the name is consistently spelled "Pincher."

77. Rowan Court Minutes, I, 4.

78. Chester Tax Lists, tax lists for 1737-38; N.C. Land Grants, VI, 166. *See also* Charles E. Kemper, "Valley of Virginia Notes," *The Virginia Magazine of History and Biography,* 68 vols. (Richmond, Va.: Historical Society of Virginia, 1893-1960), XXXI, 252.

79. Chester County Will Books, Clerk's Office, Chester County Courthouse, West Chester, Pa., B-2, 139, 123; Chester County Tavern License Papers, 10 vols. (1700-54), Chester County Historical Society, West Chester, Pa., II (1729-36), 55 (hereafter cited as Chester Tavern Petitions); Rowan Deeds, II, 283; N.C. Land Grants, VI, 145.

80. *Records of Augusta County,* I, 24, 44, 78, III, 315; Rowan Deeds, II, 194, IV, 740; Marriage Records 1730-1889, Nottingham Monthly Meeting of Friends, Friends Library, Swarthmore College, Swarthmore, Pa., pp. 26, 36 (hereafter cited as Nottingham Meeting); Rowan Court Minutes, I, 10. On October 20, 1768, John Riddle, aged five years, presented testimony at the request of his father Stephen Riddle that part of John's right ear was lost through a "mortification" and not from a court punishment. Francis apparently never actually lived in Rowan; his name does not appear in the court minutes.

81. "Assessment Lists and Other Manuscript Documents of Lancaster County Prior to 1729," comp. H. Frank Eshleman, *Papers and Addresses of the Lancaster County Historical Society,* 65 vols. (Lancaster, Pa., 1897-1961), XX, 175.

Chester County.⁸² Isaac Feree subsequently proceeded to the Carolina Frontier and settled on the Yadkin, where he established a ferry in 1753.⁸³

Of the early settlers in the forks of the Yadkin, David Jones holds a place of particular prominence, for he became the first sheriff of Rowan County in 1753.⁸⁴ It is extremely difficult to state Jones's place of origin conclusively, for the name occurs repeatedly in many different places. The records reveal at least sixteen different adults of the name in Chester, Philadelphia, Bucks, and Lancaster counties between 1719 and 1748. Wills are recorded for only six of them. However, association with other known Yadkin Valley families indicates that the sheriff of Rowan probably removed from Haverford township, Chester County, to Oley township (where Squire Boone was then living) in 1733.⁸⁵ In North Carolina, David Jones lived on a 220-acre tract adjoining the land of Samuel, one of the sons of Morgan Bryan.⁸⁶

In 1755 James Jones, probably from New Kent County, Virginia, obtained a grant "in the forks of the Yadkin and Rocky Creek."⁸⁷ Two years later he bought 360 acres "on the south fork of Joseph's Creek" from David Jones.⁸⁸

Henry Jones, from Philadelphia County or from Kent County, Maryland, was an inhabitant of the Carolina frontier by March, 1753.⁸⁹ Six years later he witnessed a deed of land from Jonathan Boone to John Frohock on the east side of Hunting Creek.⁹⁰ Henry Jones may have been related to David or James Jones.⁹¹

82. Chester Tavern Petitions, II (1729-36), 101.

83. Rowan Court Minutes, I, 5.

84. *NCCR*, V, 1083. Jones held the post until 1757.

85. Chester Tavern Petitions, II (1729-36), 55; Rowan Wills, A, 33, "Landholders of Philadelphia County," p. 178.

86. Rowan Deeds, II, 294.

87. Rowan Court Minutes, I, 111; Rowan Deeds, III, 320; Vestry Book and Register of St. Peter's Parish, New Kent and James City Counties, Va., 1684-1786, transcribed and edited by C. G. Chamberlayne (Richmond, Va.: Division of Purchase and Printing, 1937), p. 469 (hereafter cited as New Kent Register); N.C. Land Grants, VI, 167.

88. Rowan Deeds, III, 538. In 1763 James Jones was jailed and fined five shillings for passing six counterfeit Virginia forty-shilling bills. Rowan Court Minutes, p. 111.

89. Philadelphia Wills, I, 25-26; Maryland Wills, 1635-1777, Maryland Hall of Records, Annapolis, Md., XXVIII, 41 (hereafter cited as Maryland Wills); *Records of Augusta County*, I, 58.

90. Rowan Deeds, IV, 92.

91. A John Jones (for whom no land grant or deed exists) died in Rowan County in 1769. His wife, Catherine, served as administratrix of his estate with

Caleb (and probably Ephraim) Osborne, kinsmen of Alexander Osborne, migrated to the Yadkin Valley from Elizabeth Town, Essex County, New Jersey.[92] In 1746, Jonathan Hunt was appointed constable for the newly chartered town of Trenton, New Jersey.[93] It may have been he who removed to North Carolina, for Jonathan Hunt was one of the justices of Rowan County in September, 1753.[94] Numbered among other early settlers who removed from the Delaware Valley to the forks of the Yadkin were William Frost, Thomas Parker, William Satterwaite, and probably Nicholas Harford.

William Frost died in Perth Amboy, New Jersey, in 1713.[95] Thomas Frost died there fourteen years later, leaving brothers Robert, James, and William.[96] A William Frost appeared in Hunterdon County, New Jersey, in 1733,[97] and it was probably he who migrated to Carolina. In 1761 he bought 480 acres on the waters of Dutchman's Creek from John Parker.[98]

Thomas Parker, who succeeded John Dunn as clerk of the court for Rowan County in 1755,[99] was living in Newtown, Bucks County, in 1731.[100] Following his father's death in 1742,[101] Parker left Pennsylvania and made his way to the Carolina frontier. He purchased a tract of land[102] in Granville County, North Carolina, in 1745, and, in 1759, he bought 545 acres in the

---

James and Thomas Jones sureties. The dead man also left a son John, aged fourteen. His association with the Joneses considered in this paper is not clear.

92. New Jersey Wills, XXX, 347.

93. "Abstracts of New Jersey Commissions, Civil and Military, from Liber A.A.A. of Commissions in the Secretary of State's Office at Trenton," *Publications of the Genealogical Society of Pennsylvania,* 22 vols. (Philadelphia: Edward Stern and Co. [and other publishers], 1895-1961), IX (no. 3), 228.

94. Rowan Court Minutes, I, 7. Other justices in 1753 were Alexander Osborne, John Brandon, John Brevard, Robert Simonton, Squire Boone, John Hanby, Alexander Cathey, Thomas Potts, James Carter, Edward Hughes, John Lynn, Thomas Lovelatty, George Smith, Walter Carruth, Andrew Allison, Joseph Tate, Alexander Cathey, and James Allison. Rowan Court Minutes, I, 3-7.

95. *New Jersey Wills,* XXXIII, 175.

96. *Ibid.,* XXX, 190.

97. Hunterdon Court Minutes, IV (1733-36), 54. It is possible that Frost originated in Bucks County. Middletown Meeting, Marriages, 1700-1947, p. 54.

98. Rowan Deeds, IV, 760.

99. Rowan Court Minutes, I, 21.

100. Bucks County, Pa., Miscellaneous Papers, 1682-1850, 2 vols., Historical Society of Pennsylvania, Philadelphia, I, 135.

101. Bucks Administrations A, 8.

102. Granville County Deed Books, Office of Registrar of Deeds, Granville County Courthouse, Oxford, N.C.

forks of the Yadkin "beginning at a small black oak corner of a tract of land surveyed for Robert Gamble" from David Jones.[103]

The Satterwaite family was in Burlington County, New Jersey, in 1714.[104] William Satterwaite removed from Burlington (or from Bucks County across the Delaware in Pennsylvania), made his way to the frontier, and bought a tract of land from John Parker.[105]

Among those present at a Quaker Meeting held in 1713 at Bristol, Bucks County, was a certain Charles Harford.[106] The surname "Harford" appears quite rarely during the period under consideration, and this reference to Charles Harford may indicate the origin of Nicholas. The latter was in the Shenandoah Valley as early as 1742.[107] Eleven years later he bought 331 acres at the shallow ford from Edward Hughes.[108]

In addition to the Forbush, Howard, Winsuit, and Sparks families, at least five of the initial pioneers north of the south Yadkin originated in Maryland. A Peter Parsons died in Somerset County, Maryland, in 1686, leaving sons Peter and John.[109] Peter, Joshua, John, and George Parsons were there in 1762, whence Peter Parsons removed to Carolina.[110] John Harmon evidently originated either in New Castle County or in Talbot County, Maryland.[111] Isaac Holdman, like the Howards, removed from Anne Arundel County,[112] while Samuel Tate's origin was Baltimore County.[113] Benjamin Thomson, and possibly James Coward, migrated from Charles County.[114]

103. Rowan Deeds, IV, 96.

104. *New Jersey Wills*, XXXIII, 37, 402.

105. Rowan Deeds, IV, 918.

106. Burlington Meeting, Removals, 1682-1882 (unpaginated).

107. *Records of Augusta County*, II, 509; III, 9. A William Harford obtained land in Lancaster County, Pennsylvania, in 1737. *Pennsylvania Archives,* Third Series, XXIV, 426.

108. Anson Deeds, book 1, pp. 319-20. Harford's will (dated 1762) mentions Martha, wife of Morgan Bryan, and sets aside "one acre around the meeting house as a buring [sic] place for the inhabitans [sic]." To what meeting house Harford referred is not clear, though it would seem to indicate the presence of a Quaker or Baptist edifice of which no record has survived.

109. Probate Records, liber 4, folio 246.

110. *Ibid.,* liber 31, folio 807; Rowan Deeds, VI, 194.

111. Delaware Land Records, Hall of Records, Dover, Del.: New Castle Reference H¹, no. 59; Testamentary Proceedings, liber 1, folio 105; Rowan Deeds, V, 91.

112. Newman, *Anne Arundel Gentry*, p. 437; N.C. Land Grants, VI, 162.

113. Testamentary Proceedings, liber 33, folio 49 (part one); Rowan Deeds, V, 134.

114. Testamentary Proceedings, liber 32, folio 50; Maryland Warrants, liber

Sussex County, Delaware, provided the origin for Henry and Elijah Skidmore. The Skidmores were in Sussex as early as 1693.[115] Elijah and probably Henry were in the Shenandoah Valley in 1755, whence they proceeded to the Yadkin.[116]

John Waggoner and Andrew, James, and John McMachan originated in New Castle County, Delaware.[117] Andrew and James McMachan subsequently obtained land warrants in Lancaster County, Pennsylvania, between 1744 and 1750.[118]

An Edward Turner was one of the original members of the Concord Monthly Meeting of Friends in Chester County, Pennsylvania.[119] Thomas Turner was in New Castle County, Delaware, in 1739.[120] Between 1755 and 1761, Edward, Thomas, and Roger Turner obtained more than two thousand acres of land on both sides of the Yadkin near the shallow ford.[121]

John Hunter removed to North Carolina from Little Britain township, Lancaster County.[122] Nathaniel Wiltshire was in Lancaster County, Pennsylvania, in 1743; Patrick Logan in 1751; Martin Wallock (Walck) before 1756; and John McGuire before 1753.[123] Wiltshire removed to the south fork of the Roanoke River in 1750, where he was wounded by the Indians five years

L.G., no. C, folio 256-57; N.C. Land Grants, XIII, 21, 114, 16. Thomson was in the Shenandoah Valley in 1753. *Records of Augusta County*, I, 69.

115. Index to Sussex County Deed Books, 1682-1842, Office of Registrar of Deeds, Sussex County Courthouse, Georgetown, Del., pp. 485, 486, 491, 501.

116. *Records of Augusta County*, II, 417; Rowan Deeds, IV, 205; Surry Wills, I, 32, 43.

117. New Castle County Court of Common Pleas 1703-17, 1727-40 (the original lists are in folders undesignated save by a penciled number on the outside cover), Hall of Records, Dover, Del., folder XIV (1727-30), p. 23 (hereafter cited as New Castle Common Pleas); tombstones of Andrew McMachan (1708-34) and William McMachan (1679-1738) in White Clay Creek cemetery; wills of Joseph and John Waggoner, New Castle County Wills (identified by means of a card index), Hall of Records, Dover, Del., (hereafter cited as New Castle Wills); Rowan Deeds, I, 9, II, 321, IV, 744; Rowan Wills, A, 109.

118. *Pennsylvania Archives*, Third Series, XXIV, 475, 477, 481.

119. *Quaker Arrivals*, p. 14.

120. New Castle Common Pleas, folder XIV (1727-30), 25; folder XXV, (1732-40), 17.

121. N.C. Land Grants, VI, 222-28; Rowan Deeds, V, 258-60.

122. Rowan Wills, D, 176.

123. Lancaster Common Pleas, vol. XIII (1743-44), vol. XX (1750-51); *Index to the Will Books and Intestate Records of Lancaster County, Pennsylvania, 1729-1850*, prepared by Eleanor Jane Fulton and Barbara Kendig Mylin (Lancaster, Pa.: Intelligencer Printing Co., 1936), p. 106 (hereafter cited as *Lancaster Index*); Rowan Court Minutes, I, 1; Rowan Deeds, VI, 67.

later.[124] In the spring of 1756, he bought from one John Pelham a tract of land near the shallow ford adjoining Edward Hughes.[125]

A Martin Walk [sic] died intestate in Lancaster County in 1756,[126] and it was probably his son who settled on the Yadkin in 1752 and whose will (1791) is on record in the Rowan County court house.[127] In 1754, Patrick Logan purchased from Isaac. Feree 677 acres on the north fork of Joseph's Creek.[128] His will, proved in 1790, is on file in the Surry County courthouse.[129]

In June, 1753, John McGuire was appointed by the Rowan court to be constable on the south side of the Yadkin.[130] It may have been he who (in company with Christopher Gist, Barney Curran, Henry Stewart, and William Jenkins) was hired by George Washington in October, 1753, to guide a party traveling to visit the French commander in the Ohio Valley.[131] He may, on the other hand, have been the "John McGuire of Pennsylvania" who served in Captain William Preston's company of rangers in the Shenandoah Valley in 1755.[132] It is not clear which of these was the "John McGuire of Lancaster County, Pennsylvania" who purchased 440 acres in the forks of the Yadkin from James Jones in 1762.[133] In any event, John McGuire died in Rowan County later that year.[134]

Fifteen additional individuals acquired land in the forks of the Yadkin prior to 1763.[135] One of these, Samuel Reed, belonged

124. Records of Augusta County, I, 40; Joseph A. Waddell, Annals of Augusta County, Virginia, From 1726 to 1871 (Staunton, Va.: C. Russell Caldwell, Publisher, 1902), p. 154.

125. Rowan Deeds, III, 209.

126. Lancaster Index, p. 106.

127. N.C. Land Grants, XI, 20; Rowan Wills, C, 44.

128. Rowan Deeds, I, 124.

129. Surry Wills, II, 169.

130. Rowan Court Minutes, I, 1.

131. Charles A. Hanna, The Wilderness Trail: Or, the Ventures and Adventures of the Pennsylvania Traders on the Allegheny Path, With Some New Annals of the Old West, and the Records of Some Strong Men and Some Bad Ones, 2 vols. (New York and London: G. P. Putnam's Sons, Knickerbocker Press, 1911), I, 371-72; II, 336.

132. Kegley, Virginia Frontier, p. 212.

133. Rowan Deeds, VI, 67.

134. Rowan Wills, A, 123.

135. N.C. Land Grants, VI, 208, 227, 236; Anson Deeds, book 1, pp. 319-20; Rowan Deeds, II, 7, IV, 909, 194, VI, 157, 179, 415; Rowan Wills, A, 248. It is possible that Johannes Gerhardt (the records invariably have this as John Garrett), a German, may have lived west of the Yadkin, though his home was apparently on the east bank. He was one of the earliest German settlers; he

to the Reed family of Cathey's settlement. Adam and William
Hall were associated with the Halls of Fourth Creek. The origins
of another seven remain too obscure to warrant discussion. They
were William Brookshire,[136] James and Philip Williams, Henry
Baker, William Lacewell, Elizabeth Sloan, and John Pelham. Of
the remaining four, William Giles and Marmaduke Kimbrough
(from New Kent County, Virginia)[137] are known to have resided
on the east bank of the river. William Churton and Richard
Vigers, two of Lord Granville's agents, lived in eastern North
Carolina.[138]

---

was granted land on the river in 1752 and made his will five years later. Rowan
Wills, A, 59; N.C. Land Grants, XI, 10.

136. Brookshire's home was in present-day Randolph County between Little
River and Uwharrie. Rowan Court Minutes, I, 193.

137. New Kent Register, p. 87; N.C. Land Grants, VI, 168-69; Rowan Deeds,
VI, 234.

138. N.C. Land Grants, VI, 131, 229. Vigers' home was in New Hanover
County; Churton lived in Hillsboro, Orange County. Ruth Blackwelder, *The
Age of Orange* (Charlotte, N.C.: William Loftin, Publisher, 1961), p. 27.

# VII

# *THE GERMANS OF*
# *PRESENT ROWAN*
# *COUNTY*

With the exception of Peter Arndt, Martin Pfeiffer and Lorentz Schnepp, the author has discovered nothing to indicate the settlement of German pioneers in what is now Rowan County prior to 1752. During the next ten years, however, the county court records, land grants, deeds, tax lists, and wills record the presence of forty-three Germans.[1] Two others, Martin Raiblen and Jacob Van Pool (probably a Dutchman), may not have lived in Rowan until after 1762,[2] while Alexander Clingman may or may not have been a German.[3]

It must be emphasized that some of these German pioneers may have been living on the Carolina frontier for several years prior to 1752, but proof is lacking.[4] However, of the forty-three German immigrants considered in this chapter, only four are known to have landed in Philadelphia after 1751. An additional five seem to have been sons of earlier settlers. With the exception of Anthony Salz, Michael Bonacher, Conrad Bullen, Adam and

1. This figure does not include Arndt and Schnepp, the sixteen German settlers known to have been living in the forks of the Yadkin prior to 1763, and five others to be discussed in connection with the establishment of Salisbury.

2. Rowan County Will Books, Clerk's Office, Rowan County Courthouse, Salisbury, N.C., C, 57, F, 37 (hereafter cited as Rowan Wills); Probate Records of Maryland, 1635-1776, Maryland Hall of Records, Annapolis, Md., liber 27, folio 45 (hereafter cited as Probate Records).

3. Rowan County Deed Books, Office of Registrar of Deeds, Rowan County Courthouse, Salisbury, N.C., II, 234 (hereafter cited as Rowan Deeds); Colonial Land Grant Records of North Carolina, State Library, Raleigh, N.C., LI, 124 (hereafter cited as N.C. Land Grants).

4. Bishop Spangenberg wrote that there were no Germans in the area around Salisbury in 1752. William H. Gehrke, "The German Element in Rowan and Cabarrus Counties" (unpublished master's thesis, University of North Carolina, 1934), p. 30. Governor Arthur Dobbs' statement that twenty-two families of German or Swiss origin had been living on his western lands for seven or eight years may have included a few of the Dutch Second Creek settlers. It is impossible to be certain (see p. 23 above).

Peter Büttner, and Peter Eary [*sic*] the remainder may be traced to Pennsylvania. The arrivals of at least twenty-eight of the forty-three German settlers are recorded in Strassburger's invaluable compilation of the German immigrants who landed at Philadelphia.[5]

Curiously, except for the grants issued to Peter Arndt, Georg Schmidt, and Peter Schmidt, every one of the land grants and deeds obtained by these German settlers bore the date 1760, 1761, or 1762. Lorentz Schnepp, who applied for a land warrant in September, 1750, was not issued a grant until December, 1761.[6] As most of the original Rowan County Germans were in the colonies by 1755, and as the French and Indian War broke out the previous year, it is probable that a majority of them immigrated to Carolina between 1752 and 1755. The first appearance of these settlers in the Rowan County court records occurred in 1755, when Paulus Biefel was presented with £15 *s.* for taking care of a sick man.[7]

In addition to the twenty-five immigrants known to have landed at Philadelphia, Killen and Philip Ernhardt, Lorentz Lingel, Martin Pfeiffer, Georg Henrich Birrer (or Berger), Michael Behringer, Jacob Braun, and probably Friedrich Fischer[8] removed to Carolina from Pennsylvania. The two Ernhardts migrated southward from the Delaware Valley. Killen Ernhardt obtained a land warrant in Northampton County, Pennsylvania, in 1752,[9] while Philip had acquired land four years earlier in Bucks County.[10] Lorentz Lingel does not appear in Strassburger's work, but Paulus and Johnann Jacob Lingel arrived in Philadelphia in

5. See Appendix F.

6. Rowan Deeds, IV, 877.

7. Minutes of Rowan County Court of Pleas and Quarterly Sessions, 1753-1869, typed copy in 3 vols. (part of the original manuscript, torn, faded, and very difficult to read, is in the State Department of Archives and History, Raleigh, N.C.), Salisbury Public Library, Salisbury, N.C., I, 26 (hereafter cited as Rowan Court Minutes).

8. In Rowan County records, these names were usually written differently. See Appendix F.

9. Northampton County Land Warrants, in *Pennsylvania Archives*, Third Series, 30 vols., ed. William H. Egle (Harrisburg: State Printers, 1894-99), XXVI, 70 (hereafter cited as *Pennsylvania Archives*, Third Series). Northampton was formed from Bucks County in 1752; N.C. Land Grants, VI, 96.

10. Bucks County Land Warrants, in *Pennsylvania Archives*, Third Series, XXIV, 124; Rowan Deeds, V, 101.

1737.[11] There is evidence to indicate that Lorentz may have been a son of one or the other.[12]

A Martin "Fyfer" settled in 1734 on the waters of Conestoga Creek in Lancaster County, Pennsylvania.[13] He was collector of taxes in Mannheim township in 1752 and died intestate there the same year.[14] Martin "Phyfer," probably the son of the Conestoga Creek "Fyfer," settled in North Carolina before March, 1756.[15] He may have been living in Coldwater Creek as early as 1747.[16]

It is possible that Georg Henrich Birrer (Berger) and Michael Behringer (Beriger) actually had the same surname. Birrer acquired a land grant in 1761; Behringer bought a portion of it from Birrer the following year.[17] In 1769, Michael and Katherine "Barager" leased fifty acres to Peter "Eddleman" of Northampton County, Pennsylvania. The lease was proved by "George Henry Barager, Esquire."[18]

Four different Jacob Brauns arrived at Philadelphia between 1749 and 1753.[19] The Jacob Braun who purchased 392 acres adjoining the land of Michael Braun[20] could have been one of

11. *Pennsylvania German Pioneers: A Publication of the Original Lists of Arrivals in the Port of Philadelphia from 1727 to 1808,* 3 vols., comp. and ed. Ralph Beaver Strassburger (Norristown, Pa.: Pennsylvania German Society, 1934), I, 179, 181, 183.

12. *Notes and Queries, Historical, Biographical and Genealogical, Relating Chiefly to Interior Pennsylvania,* annual vols., ed. William H. Egle (Harrisburg: Harrisburg Publishing Co., 1899), pp. 192-93, 205-6, 214; Rowan Deeds, IV, 622.

13. The Taylor Papers: Being a Collection of Warrants, Surveys, Letters, &C. Relating to the Early Settlement of Pennsylvania (including correspondence for the period 1723-50 and scattered miscellaneous items for the period 1672-1775 in unnumbered volumes), 10 vols., vol. of correspondence, item no. 3148.

14. Commissioner's Minute Book, 1729-70, Office of County Commissioner, Lancaster, Pa., p. 100; *Index to the Will Books and Intestate Records of Lancaster County, Pennsylvania,* 1729-1850, prepared by Eleanor Jane Fulton and Barbara Kendig Mylin (Lancaster, Pa.: Intelligencer Printing Co., 1936), p. 94.

15. Rowan Court Minutes, I, 37; Gehrke, "The German Element," p. 46.

16. Charles H. Phifer, *Genealogy and History of the Phifer Family* (Charlotte, N.C.: George E. Wilson, 1910), p. 8.

17. N.C. Land Grants, VI, 102; Rowan Deeds, IV, 748.

18. Rowan Court Minutes, II, 209. "George Berrier" was on Conestoga Creek, Lancaster County, in 1737. Lancaster County Land Warrants, 1733-61 (unpaginated manuscripts, arranged alphabetically), Office of County Commissioner, Lancaster County Courthouse, Lancaster, Pa.

19. Strassburger, *German Pioneers,* I, 413, 482, 498, 521.

20. N.C. Land Grants, VI, 111; Michael Braun may have been living in New Castle County, Delaware, in 1739. His massive stone house (built in 1766) still stands two miles east of Granite Quarry, North Carolina. New Castle

these. The biographers of Michael Braun of Rowan stated that he had a brother Jacob.[21]

The case of Friedrich Fischer is similar to that of the Brauns. Four Friedrich Fischers disembarked at Philadelphia between 1749 and 1753.[22] The author has no information to indicate which of these removed to Carolina.

Of those settlers known to have arrived at Philadelphia between 1730 and 1755, little is known concerning their activities before migrating to Rowan. Johannes Ägader[23] was in Bucks County, Pennsylvania, in 1734 and in 1752.[24] Elizabeth, the daughter of Herman Hartmann, was baptized in 1740 in the Monocacy Valley of Maryland.[25] Georg Brünner and Barbara Tempelmann were married at Lebanon, Lancaster County, Pennsylvania, in 1748.[26] Philip Wirbel was an inhabitant of the lower Jordan Valley, upper Bucks County, in 1750.[27]

Christian, a son of Michael Eller (or Öhler), was born in the Algau district of Bavaria in 1724.[28] A "Johann Peter Öhler" arrived in Philadelphia in 1730[29] and may have been the father of

County Court of Common Pleas, 1703-17, 1727-40 (the original lists are in folders undesignated save by a penciled number on the outside cover), Hall of Records, Dover, Del., folder XXV (1723-40), p. 19.

21. Richard L. Brown, *A History of the Michael Brown Family of Rowan County, North Carolina, Tracing Its Line of Posterity from the Original Michael Brown to the Present Generation and Giving Something of the Times One Hundred and Fifty Years Ago Together With Many Historic Facts of Local and National Interest* (n.p., published under the auspices of the Michael Brown Family Association, 1921), pp. 38, 187; Rowan Deeds, IV, 253; N.C. Land Grants, VI, 103.

22. Strassburger, *German Pioneers,* I, 394, 489, 509-11, 536. Fischer bought 112 acres along both sides of Crane Creek in 1762. Rowan Deeds, IV, 704.

23. Johannes Ägader and his son Heinrich were both in Rowan by 1761, although only the latter received a grant of land. Rowan Deeds, V, 33; Rowan Wills, A, 2.

24. Bucks County Land Warrants, in *Pennsylvania Archives,* Third Series, XXIV, 109-10; Miscellaneous Manuscripts, Northampton County, Pa., 1727-58, in Historical Society of Pennsylvania, Philadelphia, p. 77.

25. *Records of Reverend John Casper Stoever, Baptismal and Marriage, 1730-1779* (Harrisburg: Harrisburg Publishing Co., 1896), p. 14 (hereafter cited as *Stoever Record*); Rowan Deeds, IV, 833.

26. Rowan Deeds, IV, 482, VI, 48; *Stoever Record,* p. 62; N.C. Land Grants, VI, 104-5, 111.

27. David G. Williams, "The Lower Jordan Valley Pennsylvania German Settlement," *Proceedings and Papers Read Before the Lehigh County Historical Society,* 24 vols. (Allentown, Pa.: published by the Society, 1908-61), XVIII, 20; Rowan Deeds, IV, 681.

28. James W. Hook, *George Michael Eller and Descendants of His in America* (New Haven, Conn.: n.d.), pp. 433-35; Rowan Deeds, V, 347.

29. Strassburger, *German Pioneers,* I, 31-33.

Christian and Jacob Eller of Rowan County, but it seems more likely that Christian crossed the Atlantic on the "Restauration" in 1747. On the last day of 1762, Jerg Lembgen was co-purchaser with Jacob Eller of 320 acres on the Yadkin's west bank,[30] indicating a probable association antedating the movement to Carolina.

Jacob Volenweider and Barbara Frick were married at Philadelphia's German Reformed Church May 27, 1762.[31] Volenweider's Rowan County land grant was acquired August 26 of the same year.[32]

Because of the late date of their arrivals, Ströher, Rohn, Rintelmann, and Jacob Eller probably migrated at once to Carolina.[33] Heinrich Grob was a Swiss who landed at Philadelphia in 1743 and proceeded to the valley of Virginia.[34] In 1752, he attempted to build two saw and grist mills on or near Reedy Creek, a branch of the Shenandoah, but before he could complete the task "the inhabitants were drove from their plantations by the Indians and . . . [Grob] . . . left the country and never finished neither of said mills."[35]

If little is known of the settlers who entered the colonies through Philadelphia, even less information exists regarding those not found in Strassburger's three volumes. Adam (and probably Peter) Büttner was in Frederick County, Maryland, between 1743 and 1752.[36] His disappearance from Frederick County records in 1753 may mark the year of his departure for Rowan County.

Peter Eary and Anthony Salz possessed adjoining land grants on the south fork of Crane Creek in Rowan.[37] Nothing further

30. Rowan Deeds, V, 36. The Ellers probably removed to Carolina from Frederick County, Maryland. Hook, *Michael Eller*, p. 437.

31. "Record of Pennsylvania Marriages Prior to 1810," *Pennsylvania Archives*, Second Series, 19 vols., reprinted under direction of Secretary of Commonwealth, ed. John B. Linn and William H. Egle (Harrisburg: Clarence M. Busch, State Printer of Pennsylvania, 1896), VIII, 739.

32. N.C. Land Grants, VI, 150.

33. Rowan Deeds, V, 36, 328, IV, 846, 828; N.C. Land Grants, VI, 211.

34. Mrs. A. K. Spence, "Heinrich Grobb (Henry Grubb), Swiss Emigrant to Virginia," *Virginia Magazine of History and Biography*, 69 vols. (Richmond, Va.: Historical Society of Virginia, 1893-1961), L, 69-74.

35. *Ibid.*, L, 69-70. Mrs. Spence is mistaken in surmising that Grobb returned to Pennsylvania. N.C. Land Grants, VI, 152; Rowan Deeds, V, 377.

36. Frederick County, Maryland, Court Judgments, 1748-59, Hall of Records, Annapolis, Md., Judgments for 1748-50, p. 599 (1750). Büttner, "late of Frederick County, farmer," had made a promissory note in Frederick County in 1743; Judgments for 1752-53, p. 108 (1752).

37. N.C. Land Grants, VI, 144, 215.

is known of either, except that many Earys were in Loudoun County, Virginia, after 1732.[38] Similarly, all that can be said of Michael Bonacher is that his land adjoined that of Peter Veit on Crane Creek, four miles north of Salz and Eary.[39]

The other Germans who acquired grants and deeds in Rowan prior to 1763 were Stephen Braun;[40] Conrad and Jacob Arndt;[41] Georg, Peter, and Michael Schmidt;[42] and probably "Claus Thompson."[43] Braun was the son of Jacob Braun, while the two Arndts were probably sons of Peter Arndt. Nothing is known of Michael Schmidt. He may have been a son of George or Peter Schmidt. Conrad Kern, like Peter Eary, may have removed from Loudoun County, Virginia.[44]

The available data, then indicates that a majority of the German settlers migrated to Rowan from Lancaster and Bucks counties in Pennsylvania and from Frederick County, Maryland. Many, like Schnepp and Grob, tarried in the Shenandoah Valley. Jacob Braun removed to Carolina from Winchester,[45] while Philip Ernhardt lived for a short time on Smith's Creek.[46]

Of the forty-five German immigrants (including Lorentz Schnepp and Peter Arndt), all possessed legal title to their land by 1763 except Johannes Ägader, Johann Götz, and Peter Büttner.

38. "The Pennsylvania Germans in Loudoun County, Virginia," *Pennsylvania German Magazine,* 15 vols. (Lebanon, Pa.: P. C. Croll [and others], 1900-14), IX (no. 3), 127 (hereafter cited as "Loudoun County Germans"). Salz left a will in 1778. Rowan Wills, B, 109. Eary may not have lived in Rowan County. He sold all of the land granted him within three weeks to Fischer, Wirbel, and Michael Schmidt. Rowan Deeds, IV, 681, 701, 704.
39. Rowan Deeds, IV, 875; V, 37. Veit and Christian Eller proved the will of Johannes Bösinger in 1772. Rowan Court Minutes, II, 6.
40. Rowan Deeds, IV, 549.
41. *Ibid.,* IV, 727, 746.
42. N.C. Land Grants, VI, 214-15; Rowan Deeds, IV, 701.
43. A Nicklaus Thommen, aged twenty-four, reached Philadelphia in 1736 aboard the "Princess Augusta." The list of tax delinquents in the Shenandoah Valley (1753-54) contains the statement that "Luse" Thompson and "Cres" Thompson had "gone to Carolina." Strassburger *German Pioneers,* I, 164; *Chronicles of the Scotch-Irish Settlements in Virginia Extracted from the Original Court Records of Augusta County, 1745-1800,* 3 vols., comp. and ed. Lyman Chalkley (Rosslyn, Va.: Commonwealth Printing Co., 1912), II, 415 (hereafter cited as *Records of Augusta County*).
44. "Loudoun County Germans," IX (no. 3), 127. In 1762 Kern bought 308 acres from his cousin, Conrad Michael. Rowan Deeds, IV, 923; VI, 170.
45. Gehrke, "The German Element," p. 16.
46. *Records of Augusta County,* III, 345. The name of this creek may indicate the Virginia origin of the Schmidts, as Ernhardt's land in Carolina was located less than eight miles from that of Peter Schmidt.

Eight of the pioneers bought their land from previous settlers, twenty-one obtained grants from the agents of Lord Granville, and twelve purchased land from the agents of Henry McCulloh. McCulloh, a wealthy Englishman living at Turnham Green, Essex, had acquired one hundred thousand acres of land on the Yadkin River "and the branches thereof" for speculative purposes from Granville in 1745.[47] Approximately sixteen thousand acres of this vast tract lay a few miles east of Salisbury in what is now Rowan County.

The evidence indicates that there were no Germans living anywhere west of the Yadkin in 1746, and few indeed prior to 1752. Ten years later, however, they formed a significant part of the northwest Carolina frontier.

47. Rowan Deeds, IV, 866. McCulloh's son, Henry Eustace McCulloh, was sent from England in 1761 to act as land agent. An excellent account of McCulloh's speculative activities may be found in Charles G. Sellers, Jr., "Private Profits and British Colonial Policy," *William and Mary Quarterly,* 3rd ser., 18 vols. (Williamsburg, Va.: Institute of Early American History and Culture, 1944-61), VIII, 535-51. "Henry McCulloh gave the idea of an American stamp duty its first written form, which . . . was examined and endorsed by Bute, New Castle, Pelham, Halifax and Grenville and was finally accepted by the latter as the basis for his . . . revenue measure of 1765." James High, "Henry McCulloh: Progenitor of the Stamp Act," *North Carolina Historical Review,* 39 vols. (Raleigh, N.C.: State Department of Archives and History, 1924-62), XXIX (no. 1), 24.

# VIII

# THE WESTERN
# SETTLEMENTS,
# 1752-1762

By 1762, at least sixty-two pioneers had settled with their families on the fertile, undulating savannah land along the upper reaches of Third and Fourth Creek. Like most of the other settlers considered in this study, the newcomers were Scottish and Scotch-Irish Presbyterians from Maryland and Pennsylvania. Although a majority of the Fourth Creek settlers were "but lately come from Ireland," a considerable number were from families long settled in the colonies. Joining James Miller, the Allisons, and Morrisons in what is today Iredell County were immigrants bearing such established Maryland names as Watt, Lewis, Alexander, Stevenson, Ireland, Elliott, Potts, and Barry.

The Watt family was in Kent and St. Marys counties, Maryland, before 1722.[1] William and James Watt, probably brothers, made their way to Carolina by way of the Cumberland Valley.[2]

Richard Lewis resided in Cecil County, Maryland, in 1740.[3] His grandfather or great-uncle died there in 1720.[4] Roger Lawson (and probably Allen Alexander) also originated in Cecil County,

1. *The Maryland Calendar of Wills,* 8 vols., comp. and ed. Jane [Baldwin] Cotton (Baltimore: Kohn and Pollock, Inc., 1904-28), III, 189, V, 151, 155, 184 (hereafter cited as *Maryland Calendar of Wills*); Colonial Land Grant Records of North Carolina, State Library, Raleigh, N.C., VI, 232, 235 (hereafter cited as N.C. Land Grants); Family data (Watt[s]), in John Abner Harris Papers, Southern Historical Collection, University of North Carolina, Chapel Hill, N.C., (hereafter cited as Harris Papers).

2. Family data (Watt[s], Bowman, Allison), Harris Papers; Cumberland County Register's Dockets, Clerk's Office, Cumberland County Courthouse, Carlisle, Pa., A, 93.

3. Probate Records of Maryland, 1635-1776, Maryland Hall of Records, Annapolis, Md., liber 27, folio 45 (hereafter cited as Probate Records); "Colonial Militia, 1740, 1748," *Maryland Historical Magazine,* 56 vols. (Baltimore: published under authority of Maryland Historical Society, 1906-61), VI, 48 (hereafter cited as "Colonial Militia"); N.C. Land Grants, VI, 180.

4. *Maryland Calendar of Wills,* V, 21.

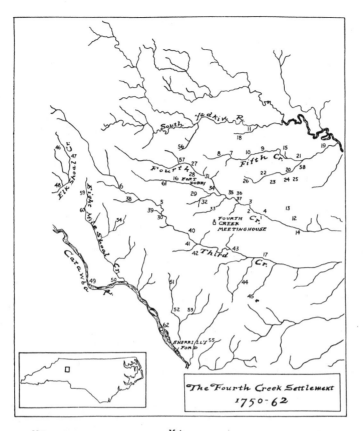

The Fourth Creek Settlement
1750-62

| Map Number | Name | | Map Number | Name |
|---|---|---|---|---|
| 1 | Andrew Allison | | 30 | James Watt |
| 2 | Thomas Allison | | 31 | James McIlwaine |
| 3 | Robert Allison (sold to Margaret McKee, "newcomer," in 1760) | | 32 | John McCulloch (never lived on this land; sold to Hugh Waddell in 1756) |
| 4 | Adam Allison | | 33 | John Oliphant (sold to Fergus Sloan in 1755) |
| 5 | William Morrison | | 34 | John Edwards |
| 6 | James Morrison | | 35 | Robert Simonton (sold to John Allison in 1757) |
| 7 | Andrew Morrison | | 36 | Theophilus Simonton |
| 8 | James Miller (Walter Lindsay acquired this land in 1761) | | 37 | William Simonton |
| 9 | James Hall | | 38 | George Erwin |
| 10 | Thomas Hall | | 39 | William Carson |
| 11 | Hugh Hall | | 40 | William Stevenson |
| 12 | George Hall (sold to David Andrew in 1762) | | 41 | George McDonald |
| 13 | Alexander Reed | | 42 | Joseph Davis |
| 14 | Samuel Reed | | 43 | Christopher Erwin |
| 15 | Andrew Reed | | 44 | John Fleming |
| 16 | George Reed | | 45 | Peter Fleming |
| 17 | Robert Reed | | 46 | William Ireland |
| 18 | John Jack | | 47 | John Ireland |
| 19 | John Archibald | | 48 | Allen Alexander |
| 20 | William Archibald | | 49 | Richard Lewis |
| 21 | James Roseborough | | 50 | Jacob Thomas |
| 22 | James Mordah | | 51 | David Black |
| 23 | John Mordah | | 52 | Samuel Cavin (sold to Robert Carson in 1762) |
| 24 | Hugh Bowman | | 53 | Robert Cavin |
| 25 | William Bowman | | 54 | John McKee |
| 26 | Samuel Thornton (sold to Patrick Duffie in 1757) | | 55 | William Erwin |
| 27 | Andrew Barry (George Davidson held legal title to this land and sold it to William Rea in 1755) | | 56 | James Potts |
| | | | 57 | John Potts |
| | | | 58 | Roger Lawson |
| 28 | Michael Robinson | | 59 | George Elliott |
| 29 | William Watt | | 60 | Richard Robinson |
| | | | 61 | Samuel Harriss |
| | | | 62 | John Leech |

while the family of William Stevenson was living on Maryland's Eastern Shore as early as 1672.[5] It is probable that few families contributed a greater number of persons to the southward movement than the Stevensons. Andrew, David, James, Thomas, John, and William Stevenson were all in the valley of Virginia between 1740 and 1755.[6] John and William Ireland originated in Calvert County, Maryland, where the family settled before 1725.[7] George Elliott's origin seems to have been Queen Annes County,[8] while James and John Potts came from Queen Annes, Kent, or Dorchester.[9] Andrew Barry was court commissioner for Cecil County in 1736.[10] He was also a lieutenant in the county militia but refused to serve.[11]

Other pioneers who migrated to the Fourth Creek settlement from Maryland were John Archibald and probably David Andrew. Archibald was a member of the Cecil County militia

5. Cecil County Deed Books, Office of Registrar of Deeds, Cecil County Courthouse, Elkton, Md., III, 284 IV, 13 (hereafter cited as Cecil Deeds). Lawson's wife was evidently a daughter of Morgan Patten of Cecil County. *Maryland Calendar of Wills*, I, 71, VI, 74, VII, 117; N.C. Land Grants, VI, 220; Iredell County Will Books, Clerk's Office, Iredell County Courthouse, Statesville, N.C., I, 37.

6. *Chronicles of the Scotch-Irish Settlements in Virginia, Extracted from the Original Court Records of Augusta County, 1745-1800*, 3 vols., comp. and ed. Lyman Chalkley (Rosslyn, Va.: Commonwealth Printing Co., 1912), III, 29, 39, 276, 7, 264 (hereafter cited as *Records of Augusta County*); Howard M. Wilson, *The Tinkling Spring, Headwater of Freedom: A Study of the Church and Her People, 1732-1752* (Richmond, Va.: Garrett and Massie, Inc., 1954), p. 428.

7. Probate Records, liber 40, folio 618; Maryland Wills, 1635-1777, Maryland Hall of Records, Annapolis, Md., XXIX, 416 (hereafter cited as Maryland Wills) ; *Maryland Calendar of Wills*, V, 122, VII, 206; N.C. Land Grants, VI, 168; Rowan County Deed Books, Office of Registrar of Deeds, Rowan County Courthouse, Salisbury, N.C., V, 11 (hereafter cited as Rowan Deeds).

8. *Maryland Calendar of Wills*, II, 109, VI, 140; Queen Annes County Deed Books, Office of Registrar of Deeds, Queen Annes County Courthouse, Centreville, Md., R.T. (A), 17-18; N.C. Land Grants, VI, 143; Rowan County Will Books, Clerk's Office, Rowan County Courthouse, Salisbury, N.C., B, 214 (hereafter cited as Rowan Wills).

9. *Maryland Calendar of Wills*, III, 117, 236, V, 125, VIII, 90; N.C. Land Grants, XV, 3, VI, 205; Rowan Deeds, IV, 351; Rowan Wills, A, 197.

10. Cecil County Judgments, S.K. no. 3 (1723-30) and S.K. no. 4 (1730-32, 1736-41, 1741-43, 1746-47), Hall of Records, Annapolis, Md., S.K. no. 3, p. 449, S.K. no. 4 (1736-41), p. 1 (hereafter cited as Cecil Judgments) ; Rowan Deeds, III, 215. Although he had land on Fourth Creek, the evidence indicates that Barry lived in Anson County south of the Granville line. "Anson County, North Carolina, Abstracts of Early Records," *The May Wilson McBee Collection*, ed. May Wilson McBee (Greenwood, Miss.: May Wilson McBee, 1950), pp. 27, 127 (hereafter cited as "Anson Abstracts").

11. "Colonial Militia," p. 46.

in 1740.[12] His brother William was living in West Nottingham township, Chester County, at the same time.[13] David and James Andrew (who bought 320 acres from Henry White in May, 1762)[14] were evidently sons of John Andrew, who died somewhere in Rowan County in 1757.[15] Although inconclusive, the evidence suggests that John Andrew originated in Anne Arundel, Dorchester, or Queen Annes County (where the name appears as early as 1724),[16] and moved to the Middle Octoraro settlement of eastern Lancaster County, where he was an elder in the Presbyterian Church in 1740.[17]

The Erwins migrated from Cecil County and from Chester County, Pennsylvania. George Erwin lived in Nantmeal or London Britain township before 1747,[18] while Christopher Erwin obtained a warrant for land in the Middle Octoraro settlement as early as 1733.[19] A William Erwin was residing in West Nottingham township, Chester County, in 1740 and departed within seven years.[20] The records of Sadsbury township of the same county reveal a William Erwin in 1747.[21]

Other pioneer settlers in the Fourth Creek settlement who

12. Cecil County Will Books, Clerk's Office, Cecil County Courthouse, Elkton, Md., XXVII, 393; "Colonial Militia," p. 47; Rowan Wills, A, 3, 251; N.C. Land Grants, VI, 94; Chester County Tax Lists for 1722-27, 1735, 1737, 1738, 1740, 1741, 1747, and 1753 (unpaginated manuscript), Chester County Historical Society, West Chester, Pa., 1740 tax list (hereafter cited as Chester Tax Lists); N.C. Land Grants, VI, 95.

13. Chester Tax Lists, tax list for 1740; N.C. Land Grants, VI, 95.

14. Rowan Deeds, IV, 725, 668. The deed to James Andrew was located ". . . on Gillespies Creek, being a part of Henry White's place where he did live. . . ." David Andrew also acquired 137 acres in the forks of the Yadkin. N.C. Land Grants, VI, 96.

15. Rowan County Court of Pleas and Quarterly Sessions, 1753-1869, typed copy in 3 vols. [part of the original manuscript, torn, faded and very difficult to read is in the State Department of Archives and History, Raleigh, N.C.], Salisbury Public Library, Salisbury, N.C., I, 41 (hereafter cited as Rowan Court Minutes).

16. *Maryland Calendar of Wills*, VII, 152, VIII, 60, 188; Maryland Wills, XXXI (Part Two), 935.

17. Records of the Donegal Presbytery (typed copy), vols., 1A and 1B (Philadelphia: Presbyterian Historical Society, 1937), 1B, 284 (hereafter cited as Donegal Presbytery).

18. Chester Tax Lists, tax lists for 1740 and 1747; N.C. Land Grants, VI, 145.

19. Donegal Presbytery, 1A, 9; N.C. Land Grants, VI, 144.

20. Chester Tax Lists, tax lists for 1740 and 1747; N.C. Land Grants, VI, 143.

21. Chester Tax Lists, tax list for 1747.

migrated from Chester County were John Jack,[22] Samuel Thornton (Bradford township),[23] Michael Robinson (Marlborough township),[24] David Black (Bradford township),[25] William and Robert Carson (Caln or Londonderry township),[26] Jacob Thomas (Vincent, Radnor, or Willistown township),[27] John and Peter Fleming (Caln or Londonderry township),[28] Patrick Duffie (Caln township),[29] and members of the large Reed family, which held lands in the adjoining townships of West Fallowfield (Chester County) and Bart (Lancaster County).[30] The Mordahs (or Murdocks) settled first in West Nottingham township, Chester County, as early as 1734.[31] They moved to Donegal or Derry township, Lancaster County, between 1740 and 1744,[32] whence James and John Mordah removed to Carolina.

The Hall family migrated to the Fourth Creek settlement from

22. John Jack removed from Sadsbury or Fallowfield township, Chester County, to Frederick County, Maryland, sometime between 1734 and 1754. Chester Tax Lists, tax lists for 1737-38; The Taylor Papers: Being a Collection of Warrants, Surveys, Letters, &C. Relating to the Early Settlement of Pennsylvania (including correspondence for the period 1723-50 and scattered miscellaneous items for the period 1672-1775 in unnumbered volumes), 10 vols., Historical Society of Pennsylvania, Philadelphia, vol. of correspondence, item no. 3141 (hereafter cited as Taylor Papers); Frederick County Will Books, Hall of Records, Annapolis, Md., A-1, 19.

23. Chester Tax Lists, tax list for 1753; N.C. Land Grants, VI, 223.

24. Chester Tax Lists, tax list for 1747; N.C. Land Grants, VI, 209.

25. Chester Tax Lists, tax lists for 1737-1738; N.C. Land Grants, VI, 109.

26. Chester Tax Lists, tax lists for 1737-38; Chester County Land Warrants, *Pennsylvania Archives,* Third Series, 30 vols., ed. William H. Egle (Harrisburg: State Printers, 1894-99), XXIV, 68 (hereafter cited as *Pennsylvania Archives,* Third Series); Records of Augusta County, III, 9, 18, 55; N.C. Land Grants, VI, 132; Rowan Deeds, V, 439. William and Robert Carson were sons of William, senior, who died in 1760 or 1761. Rowan Wills, A, 49; Rowan Court Minutes, I, 78. William Carson, Jr., was the grandfather of Christopher (Kit) Carson, the famous scout. William S. Powell, "Notes for a Tour of Iredell County Conducted on September 12, 1948, for the North Carolina Society of County Historians" (mimeographed), North Carolina Room, University of North Carolina, Chapel Hill, N.C., p. 4.

27. Chester Tax Lists, tax lists for 1740 and 1747. Thomas was probably born in Sussex County, Delaware. Index to Sussex County Deed Books, 1682-1842, Office of Registrar of Deeds, Sussex County Courthouse, Georgetown, Del., pp. 525-27; N.C. Land Grants, VI, 225.

28. Chester County Deed Books, Office of Registrar of Deeds, Chester County Courthouse, West Chester, Pa., K, 418.

29. Chester Tax Lists, tax list for 1753.

30. See above, pp. 68-69.

31. Donegal Presbytery, 1A, 34; Chester Tax Lists, tax list for 1740; Rowan Deeds, II, 64, V, 472.

32. Family data (Murdock), Harris Papers.

Donegal or Derry township, Lancaster County.[33] James Hall, patriarch of the family, was the son of Hugh Hall, who lived in Donegal township as early as 1723.[34] The sons of James Hall were Thomas, James, Hugh, Robert, and Alexander.[35] George Hall, probably a cousin of James, also migrated to Carolina from Lancaster County, where he obtained two hundred acres in 1737.[36]

At least a dozen additional pioneers removed to the Fourth Creek settlement from Lancaster County. James Roseborough was an inhabitant of the Paxtang-Derry-Donegal area after 1745.[37] The three Simontons migrated from Paxtang or Conestoga township,[38] and John Allison either from adjacent Derry or from the Octoraro Creek settlement.[39] Hugh and William Bowman were closely associated with the Watt and Allison families in the Cumberland Valley. Hugh Bowman and William Watt were married to two of the daughters of James Allison, who died in the Cumberland Valley in 1762.[40]

Robert and Samuel Cavin, too, appear to have migrated to Carolina from the fertile plain between South Mountain and the Alleghenies. They were probably sons or nephews of Samuel Cavin who signed the Westminster Confession of Faith when the Presbytery of Donegal was organized in 1732.[41] He died in 1750 and lies buried in the Silver Spring Church Cemetery eight miles west of present-day Harrisburg.

John McKee died in Derry township in 1748;[42] James McKee

33. Family data (Hall), Harris Papers; Rowan Deeds, V, 266, IV, 729; N.C. Land Grants, VI, 158, 155, 166, 161.

34. Family data (Hall), Harris Papers.

35. Family data (Hall), in James King Hall Collection, Southern Historical Collection, University of North Carolina, Chapel Hill, N.C.

36. Lancaster County Land Warrants, *Pennsylvania Archives,* Third Series, XXIV, 425.

37. *Notes and Queries, Historical, Biographical and Genealogical, Relating Chiefly to Interior Pennsylvania,* 3 ser. (12 vols.), ed. William H. Egle (Harrisburg: Harrisburg Publishing Co. [reprinted from *Harrisburg Daily Telegraph,* 1878-1901], 1894-1901), ser. 3, vol. I, p. 362 (hereafter cited as Egle, *N&Q*); Rowan Deeds, III, 492.

38. Rowan Wills, A, 157; Rowan Deeds, II, 18, 310, III, 396.

39. Rowan Deeds, II, 149; Lancaster County Will Books, Clerk's Office, Lancaster County Courthouse, Lancaster, Pa., J-1, 4 (hereafter cited as Lancaster Wills); Rowan Wills, A, 157, C, 178. See also pp. 52-53, 65 above.

40. Family data (Allison, Bowman, Watt[s]), Harris Papers; N.C. Land Grants, VI, 103; tombstone of William Bowman in Thyatira Cemetery.

41. Rowan Court Minutes, I, 85; N.C. Land Grants, VI, 131; Rowan Deeds, V, 439.

42. Lancaster Wills, I-1, 330.

in the same place fourteen years later.[43] Margaret McKee was evidently the sister of the latter.[44] John McKee, who settled on the headwaters of Eight Mile Shoal Creek, a tributary of the Catawba, was undoubtedly a near relative.[45] Another emigrant from the Derry region was William Rea, who bought 320 acres ("being also part of a tract formerly entered on said creek by Andrew Berry, esq.") from George Davidson in 1755.[46] Rea may not have lived on this land, for he was a resident of Orange County, North Carolina, in 1763.[47]

Fergus Sloan, who was a landless itinerant in Salsbury township, Lancaster County, in 1750,[48] bought a 560-acre tract in Carolina from John Oliphant[49] five years later.[50] Sloan's purchase was of unusual importance. Within a few months, portions of this tract were bought from Sloan for the construction of Fort Dobbs and for the erection of the first Fourth Creek Meeting House.[51]

George McDonald and James Mackilwean (McIlwaine) evidently originated in that part of Pennsylvania later to become Delaware. McDonald came from a family which settled on Red Clay Creek in New Castle County as early as 1705.[52] McIlwaine,

43. *Ibid.*, B-1, 621.

44. Rowan Deeds, IV, 209; Lancaster Wills, I-1, 330, B-1, 621.

45. N.C. Land Grants, VI, 197.

46. This settler should not be confused with William Reese (or Rees), a Welsh Baptist who settled on Davidson's Creek in 1759 (see p. 130). William Rees (1709-1808), who lies buried in Centre Churchyard, emigrated to Carolina from Cecil County, or New Castle County, Delaware. Rowan Deeds, IV, 83; *Maryland Calendar of Wills*, VI, 180; Taylor Papers, II, 236; Cecil Judgments, S.K. no. 3 (1723-30), p. 41; "Records of the Welsh Tract Baptist Meeting, Pencader Hundred, New Castle County, Delaware, 1701 to 1828. Copied from the Original Records in the Possession of the Meeting Officials," *Papers of the Historical Society of Delaware*, 67 vols. (Wilmington, Del.: Historical Society of Delaware), XLII, 42-43.

47. Rowan Deeds, V, 354.

48. Lancaster County Tax Lists for 1750, 1751, 1754, 1756, 1758, and 1759 (manuscripts, identified by date and township), Office of County Commissioner, Lancaster County Courthouse, Lancaster, Pa., 1750 list for Salsbury township.

49. Oliphant moved to the Catawba River. See p. 71 above.

50. Rowan Deeds, II, 34.

51. Rowan Deeds, II, 258; N.C. Land Grants, XI, 9; Northampton County Will Books, Clerk's Office, Northampton County Courthouse Jackson, N.C., I, 122 (hereafter cited as Northampton Wills).

52. *Calendar of Delaware Wills: New Castle County, 1682-1800*, abstracted and compiled by the Historical Research Committee of the Colonial Dames of Delaware (New York: Frederick H. Hitchcock, 1911), p. 13; Frederick B. Kegley, *Kegley's Virginia Frontier: The Beginning of the Southwest; the Roanoke of Colonial Days, 1740-1783* (Roanoke, Va.: Southwest Virginia

who may have been living on Fourth Creek as early as 1749,[53] evidently originated in the Cool Spring district of Sussex County, Delaware.[54]

Little is known of the origin of Walter Lindsay, John Leech, or Joseph Davis. Lindsay, who moved to Rowan from the Shenandoah Valley,[55] was made a major in the militia in 1764 and qualified as a justice of the peace for Rowan County the same year.[56] He may have originated in Prince Georges County, Maryland.[57] The origin of Richard Robinson will be considered in the next chapter.

Two of the early landowners in the Fourth Creek settlement lived elsewhere in North Carolina. Colonel John Edwards was a prominent resident of Northampton County and friend of James McManus;[58] Hugh Waddell's home was at Belfont, Bladen County.[59]

While the Fourth Creek settlement thus grew into a well-defined community, similar expansion occurred a few miles to the south. During the ten-year period following the rash of land grants on March 25, 1752, at least forty settlers are recorded as having acquired land in the Davidson's Creek settlement. Several of these pioneers, being sons, nephews, or brothers of settlers previously considered, had the same origins as their kin. These included James and Robert Carruth, Hugh McQuown, James Harriss, John Given, Hans McWhorter, Joseph Gillespie, Samuel Allison, James Dunn, and Moses White. Others have themselves

Historical Society, 1938), pp. 504-5; Delaware Land Records, Hall of Records, Dover, Del., New Castle County References M1, nos. 1 and 2.

53. *The Colonial Records of North Carolina,* 10 vols., ed. William L. Saunders (Raleigh, N.C.: Printers to the State, 1886-90), IV, 951 (hereafter cited as *NCCR*); N.C. Land Grants, VI, 188; Anson County Deed Books, Office of Registrar of Deeds, Anson County Courthouse, Wadesboro, N. C., book 1, p. 211 (hereafter cited as Anson Deeds). Mackilwean was one of the original justices of Anson County.

54. Tombstone of James McIlvaine (1693-1754) in cemetery of Cool Spring Presbyterian Church, Sussex County, Delaware.

55. Kegley, *Virginia Frontier,* p. 82; *Records of Augusta County,* III, 470; Rowan Deeds, IV, 531. Davis' land in Carolina adjoined that of George McDonald. Rowan Deeds, V, 164.

56. Rowan Court Minutes, I, 124.

57. *Maryland Calendar of Wills,* VI, 181.

58. Northampton Wills, I, 122; Northampton County Deed Books, Office of Registrar of Deeds, Northampton County Courthouse, Jackson, N.C., book 1, p. 302. Most of the land acquired for the construction of Fort Dobbs was appropriated from Edwards. Rowan Deeds, IV, 532; N.C. Land Grants, XI, 9.

59. Rowan Deeds, III, 348, VI, 398; N.C. Land Grants, VI, 237.

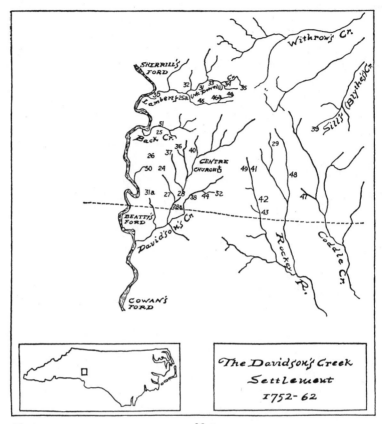

*The Davidson's Creek Settlement 1752-62*

| Map Number | Name | Map Number | Name |
|---|---|---|---|
| 24 | James McCulloch | 35 | Jeremiah Streator |
| 25 | John McCulloch (sold to Alexander Robertson, 1758) (sold by Robertson to John Thompson, 1759) | 36 | Andrew Allison |
| | | 37 | Samuel Allison |
| | | 38 | Hugh Lawson |
| | | 39 | Francis Beatty |
| 25a | John McCulloch (sold to William Neill, 1758) | 40 | William McRae (sold to Catherine Barry, 1762) |
| 26 | Alexander McCulloch | 41 | John Dickey |
| 27 | Moses White | 42 | Hanse McWhorter |
| 28 | Benjamin Winsley | 43 | Joseph Gillespie (sold to Gilbert Strayhorn, 1758) |
| 28a | Benjamin Winsley (sold in part to Patrick Hamilton, 1758) | 44 | John Gullick (sold to Abraham Jetton, 1762) |
| 29 | Thomas McQuown | 45 | William Hall |
| 30 | James Lambert (sold to John Oliphant, 1755) | 46 | John Hall |
| | | 46a | John Hall (sold to David Hall, 1762) |
| 31 | John McDowell (sold to William Neill, 1754) | 47 | John Sloan |
| 31a | John McDowell | 48 | William Denny |
| 32 | Andrew Neill | 49 | James Crawford |
| 33 | James Neill | 50 | William Morrison (sold to James Tennant, 1754) |
| 34 | Robert Adams and James Neill (Adams of Mecklenburg County) | 51 | John Parks |
| | | 52 | Robert Johnston |

been previously discussed in this study. They are John Oliphant, Andrew Allison, Andrew Lynn, and William Morrison. Of the remainder, at least ten are known to have migrated from Maryland.

The three Neills originated in Charles or Anne Arundel County, and were residents of New London township, Chester County, in 1750.[60] Hugh Lawson,[61] Moses Andrew, John Gullick, and John McCune were in Cecil County in 1740.[62] Catherine Barry removed either from Talbot or Cecil County,[63] James Tennant emigrated from Kent County,[64] and John Dickey proceeded to Carolina from Charles or St. Marys County.[65]

The father of James Robinson settled on the north branch of the Shenandoah River in 1739.[66] After the elder Robinson's death in 1751, James removed to Carolina. The evidence is inconclusive regarding the origin of James Robinson, senior.

Probably from Maryland originally,[67] but living in Chester County in 1753, were James Potts (London Britain township)[68] and James McKown (or McEwen). McKown, possibly a kinsman of John McCune of Cecil County, removed from Sadsbury township[69] to Carolina and died in Rowan in 1766 at the age of

60. *The Black Books: Calendar of Maryland State Papers* (Annapolis, Md.: Hall of Records Commission, 1943), no. 1, p. 27; *Maryland Calendar of Wills,* VI, 39, 181; Family data (Neill), Curry Collection, Southern Historical Collection, University of North Carolina, Chapel Hill, N.C.; N.C. Land Grants, VI, 200-1; Rowan Deeds, II, 278, 299; Chester County Tavern License Papers, 10 vols. (1700-54), Chester County Historical Society, West Chester, Pa., VIII (1749-50), 67 (hereafter cited as Chester Tavern Petitions).

61. See pp. 52, 94 above. Hugh Lawson was in Milford Hundred, Cecil County in 1724. Nine years later, he obtained land there from Roger Lawson, whose name appears in the Cecil County records as early as 1712. Cecil Judgments, S.K. no. 3 (1723-30), p. 145; Cecil Deeds, III, 284, IV, 13.

62. Cecil Judgments, S.K. no. 3 (1723-30), p. 145; "Colonial Militia," pp. 46-48, 50; N.C. Land Grants, VI, 177; Rowan Deeds, IV, 59, 915.

63. "Colonial Militia," p. 46; Rowan Court Minutes, I, 34; Maryland Wills, XXIV, 388, 436, XXVII, 60; Rowan Deeds, IV, 687; *Maryland Calendar of Wills,* III, 205.

64. *Maryland Calendar of Wills,* VIII, 281; Probate Records, liber 33, folio 128. Tennant removed from Rowan to Orange County, N.C., before 1765. Rowan Deeds, III, 23; VI, 71.

65. Inscription in Store Account Book (1755-86) of John Dickey, Merchant, in Duke University Library, Durham, N.C.; N.C. Land Grants, VI, 137-38.

66. *Records of Augusta County,* III, 21, 105, 544; Anson Deeds, book 1, p. 273.

67. See p. 96 above.

68. Chester Tax Lists, tax list for 1753; Rowan Deeds, IV, 351.

69. Charles E. Kemper, "Valley of Virginia Notes," *The Virginia Magazine of History and Biography,* 68 vols. (Richmond, Va.: Historical Society of Virginia, 1893-1960), XXXI, 250.

forty-nine.[70] A John McKown (McEwen), possibly the father of one or both, was an elder in the "Forks of the Brandywine" community of the Donegal Presbytery in 1740.[71]

Other immigrants to the Davidson's Creek area from Chester County were Patrick Hamilton (Edgmont or London Britain),[72] John Sloan (London Britain),[73] William Denny (Nottingham or Birmingham),[74] and Robert Johnston (or Johnson).[75]

William Hall removed to Carolina before 1753, probably from Chester County.[76] He and his sons John and David settled on Lambert's Creek,[77] where the elder Hall died prior to April, 1760.[78] Hugh and John Parks apparently originated in New Castle or Cecil County.[79] Neither William McRae (or McRee) nor Patrick Gracy appear in the records of Virginia or the middle colonies. They may have been among the few settlers who proceeded directly from Great Britain. McRae originated in county Down, Ireland, and was in the Davidson's Creek settlement

70. Tombstone of James McEwen, Fourth Creek Church Cemetery, Statesville, N.C.

71. Donegal Presbytery, 1B, 284.

72. Chester Tax Lists, tax list for 1740; Rowan Deeds, II, 368.

73. Chester Tax Lists, tax list for 1753; N.C. Land Grants, VI, 216.

74. M. C. D. Dixon and E. C. D. Vann, *Denny Genealogy,* 3 vols. (New York: National Historical Society, 1944), I, 95-96, 105 (hereafter cited as *Denny Genealogy*) ; Chester Tax Lists, tax lists for 1737-38; William Henry Foote, *Sketches of North Carolina, Historical and Biographical, Illustrative of the Principles of a Portion of Her Early Settlers* (New York: Robert Carter, 58 Canal Street, 1846), p. 168. Denny originated in Burt, County Tyrone, Ireland. *Denny Genealogy,* II, 25-26.

75. Johnston, who married Lillias Corbett in 1737 at the First Presbyterian Church in Philadelphia, removed to Carolina from Kennet or New Garden township before 1756, settling first in Orange County. At his death in 1757, a tract of 611 acres on the headwaters of Rocky River was purchased by John McConnell in trust for Johnston's three underaged sons, John, Robert and Thomas. "Record of Pennsylvania Marriages prior to 1810," *Pennsylvania Archives,* Second Series, 19 vols., reprinted under direction of Secretary of Commonwealth, ed. John B. Linn and William H. Egle (Harrisburg: Clarence M. Busch, State Printer of Pennsylvania, 1896), VIII, 147 (hereafter cited as *Pennsylvania Archives,* Second Series) ; Chester Tavern Petitions, III, 56, V, 35; Rowan Wills, A, 70; N.C. Land Grants, VI, 195; Alexander H. Torrence Letters and Papers, 1754-1915, Southern Historical Collection, University of North Carolina, Chapel Hill, N.C.; Rowan Deeds, II, 7. See also pp. 52-53 above.

76. Chester Tavern Petitions, III, 8; Rowan Court Records, I, 8; *Pennsylvania Archives,* Second Series, VIII, 119, 400.

77. Since 1747, this creek has borne at least seven names. First known as Rambo's Mill Creek, it has since been variously designated as McDowell's, Lambert's, Byers's, Falls's, Nails's (Neill's), and Cornelius'.

78. Rowan Court Minutes, I, 77; N.C. Land Grants, VI, 161, 183; Rowan Deeds, V, 266.

79. Rowan Wills, B, 123; Rowan Deeds, I, 33; N.C. Land Grants, VI, 196.

as early as May, 1752.[80] According to Patrick Gracy's great-granddaughters, he migrated to America from Ireland in 1740.[81] Gilbert Strayhorn, a tailor, evidently bought his land from Joseph Gillespie for speculative purposes. He was a resident of Orange County, North Carolina, at the time.[82] Alexander Robertson was in Drumore township, Lancaster County, Pennsylvania, in 1735,[83] while Jeremiah Streator originated either in Chester County or in Middletown township, Bucks County.[84]

Evidence is inconclusive regarding the origins of the remaining pioneers who entered land on or near Davidson's Creek, although their close association with known Marylanders who settled there gives the impression that Robert Adams, John Thompson, and Abraham Jetton migrated from that colony (Jetton from Cecil County).[85] Stephen Potts and David Kerr may have been kinsmen of the Kerrs and Pottses mentioned previously.[86] James Crawford, who may have been on Davidson's Creek as early as 1750, evidently originated in Chester County or in New Castle County, Delaware.[87]

Thus by the end of 1762, approximately 150 adult males had obtained title to land in the Fourth Creek and Davidson's Creek settlements.[88] As the great majority were heads of families, the population of these "western settlements" may be estimated at between 500 and 700.

80. N.C. Land Grants, VI, 184; Foote, *North Carolina Sketches,* pp. 434-35.

81. Hattie S. Goodman, *The Knox Family: A Genealogical and Biographical Sketch of the Descendants of John Knox of Rowan County, North Carolina, and Other Knoxes* (Richmond, Va.: Whittet and Shepperson, Printers and Publishers, 1905), pp. 35-36; Rowan Deeds, I, 134. Gracy (1700-1810) lies buried in the cemetery at Centre Church.

82. Strayhorn's deed is dated May 24, 1758. Rowan Deeds, II, 325.

83. Donegal Presbytery, 1A, 82; Rowan Deeds, IV, 180.

84. Chester County Administration Dockets, Office of Registrar of Wills, Clerk's Office, Chester County Courthouse, West Chester, Pa., I, 48 (hereafter cited as Chester Administrations.) Marriage Records of Middletown Monthly Meeting of Friends, Bucks County, Pa., 1700-1947, Friends Library, Swarthmore College, Swarthmore, Pa., p. 13; N.C. Land Grants, VI, 201. It seems probable that Streator removed to Carolina from Chester County as Bucks County is not otherwise represented in the Davidson's Creek settlement.

85. Rowan Deeds, IV, 247, 927; N.C. Land Grants, VI, 201.

86. Rowan Deeds, V, 191; IV, 917.

87. Delaware Wills, p. 52; Chester Administrations, II, 70; Chester Tax Lists, tax lists for 1737-38; Chester County Will Books, Clerk's Office, Chester County Courthouse, West Chester, Pa., I, 348; N.C. Land Grants, VI, 102. William Crawford's land was in the Cathey settlement. Rowan Deeds, IV, 53.

88. Both were within the limits of present-day Iredell County.

# IX

## THE TRADING CAMP
## SETTLEMENT,
## 1750-1762

When John Lawson reached the Yadkin's banks in 1708, he found that an old Indian path crossed the river at a shallow, island-studded spot twenty-seven miles south of the shallow ford and eighteen miles north of where Granville's boundary was pushed west of the Yadkin in 1746. Prior to the establishment of any settlement, this "trading" ford was used by whites and Indians from the east in trading with the Saponi, Catawbas, and Cherokees.

As previously noted, James Allison of Cecil County was issued a land grant in 1751 lying six miles southwest of the trading ford and near a site often used as a traders' camp.[1] Allison, of Scotch-Irish origin,[2] undoubtedly considered himself a member of the Irish settlement. However, as the majority of those who subsequently settled around his 350-acre tract were not Scotch-Irish, it seems appropriate to designate the community which sprang up the "trading camp settlement."

In general terms, this group of settlers was located north of the Rowan County Germans and east of the Irish settlement. There were at least twenty-seven of them, some of whom resided in the German settlement.

John and Peter Dill and John Thomas, all three of whom were in the Shenandoah Valley in 1746,[3] settled on the bank of the

1. *Colonial Land Grant Records of North Carolina*, State Library, Raleigh, N.C., XI, I (hereafter cited as N.C. Land Grants).

2. Charles A. Hanna, *The Scotch-Irish, or the Scot in North Britain, North Ireland, and North America*, 2 vols. (New York: Knickerbocker Press, 1902), II, 519.

3. *Chronicles of the Scotch-Irish Settlements in Virginia, Extracted from the Original Court Records of Augusta County, 1745-1800*, 3 vols., comp. and ed. Lyman Chalkley (Rosslyn, Va.: Commonwealth Printing Co., 1912), I, 24 (hereafter cited as *Records of Augusta County*).

South Yadkin River at the spot where it flows into the Yadkin.[4] The Dill family was in Maryland before 1675.[5] John Thomas seems to have originated in Sussex County, Delaware, and to have departed for the west and south from Radnor or Willistown township, Chester County, Pennsylvania.[6]

The Craig (or Cragh) family settled in Freehold, Monmouth County, New Jersey, before 1721.[7] Members of this family were in Kent County, Maryland, by 1733.[8] Archibald and Mary Craig, with their son James, left Maryland (probably accompanied by John Howard)[9] sometime prior to 1756 and proceeded to the Yadkin Valley.

A majority of the pioneers in the trading camp settlement migrated from the shores of Chesapeake Bay. Besides the Craigs, Dills, and Howards, they included William Harrison; Edward Cusick; Thomas Evans; John Gardiner; David and John Hampton; James, Abraham, and Michael Miller; and probably Richard Walton.

The Evans, Gardiner, Harrison, and Cusick (or Cusack) families settled in Maryland before 1720. William Harrison, who was in Carolina by April, 1752, originated among the Harrisons

4. N.C. Land Grants, VI, 143; Rowan County Deed Books, Office of Registrar of Deeds, Rowan County Courthouse, Salisbury, N.C., II, 30 (hereafter cited as Rowan Deeds).

5. Testamentary Proceedings of Maryland, 1659-1777, Maryland Hall of Records, Annapolis, Md., liber 6, folio 436 (hereafter cited as Testamentary Proceedings).

6. Thomas was a relative of Jacob Thomas. See p. 98 above.

7. Calendar of New Jersey Wills, in Documents Relating to the Colonial History of the State of New Jersey, 1st ser., vols. XXX and XXXIII, ed. A. Van Doren Honeyman [vol. XXX] and William Nelson [vol. XXXIII] (Somerville, N. J.: Unionist Gazette Association, 1918 [vol. XXX] and Paterson, N. J.: Press Printing and Publishing Co., 1901 [vol. XXXIII]), XXXIII, 118 (hereafter cited as New Jersey Wills).

8. Testamentary Proceedings, liber 30, folio 353; Probate Records of Maryland, 1635-1776, Maryland Hall of Records, Annapolis, Md., liber 14, folio 391 (hereafter cited as Probate Records); The Maryland Calendar of Wills, 8 vols., comp. and ed. Jane [Baldwin] Cotton (Baltimore: Kohn and Pollock, Inc., 1904-28), VII, 38, 81, 186 (hereafter cited as Maryland Calendar of Wills).

9. Rowan Deeds, II, 360, 407; map of the town of Salisbury, N.C., drawn by W. Moore, surveyor, August 7, 1823, North Carolina Room, University of North Carolina Library, Chapel Hill, N.C.; Rowan County Court of Pleas and Quarterly Sessions, 1753-1869, typed copy in 3 vols. (parts of the original manuscript, torn, faded, and very difficult to read, is in the State Department of Archives and History, Raleigh, N.C.), Salisbury Public Library, Salisbury, N.C., I, 82 (hereafter cited as Rowan Court Minutes); Harry W. Newman, Anne Arundel Gentry (n.p., n.d.), p. 248. Archibald Craig, who established a ferry on the Yadkin, died in 1758. Mary, his widow, married John Howard.

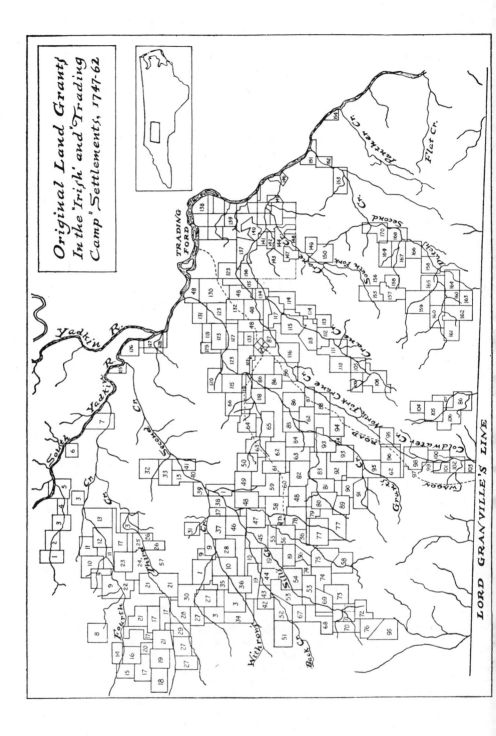

Original Land Grants
In the "Irish" and "Trading
Camp" Settlements, 1747-62

LORD GRANVILLE'S LINE

| Map No. | Name and Number of Grants (if more than one) | Map No. | Name and Number of Grants (if more than one) | Map No. | Name and Number of Grants (if more than one) | Map No. | Name and Number of Grants (if more than one) |
|---|---|---|---|---|---|---|---|
| 1 | James Dobbins (3) | 43 | Henry Barclay (Barkley) | 85 | John Lock (Locke) | 129 | Paulus Buffell (Biefel) |
| 2 | James Martin | 44 | William Niblock | 86 | John Nisbet (Nesbit) (5) | 130 | Archibald Craig |
| 3 | Robert Tate (5) | 45 | Robert Luckey (Luckie) | 87 | James Allison (2) | 131 | Conrad Michael |
| 4 | Samuel, John, and Joseph Luckey (Luckie) | Th | Thyatira Church | 88 | Mathew Lock (Locke) | 132 | Henrich Zobeli |
| 5 | Robert Johnston | 46 | James Deacon (Deason) | 89 | Charles Burnett | 133 | Elizabeth Gillespie |
| 6 | John Carson | 47 | William Sleven | 90 | David Strain | 134 | Herman Hartmann |
| 7 | Nicklaus Thommen and Johann Bernhardt Steigner | 48 | John Long (6) | 91 | Matthew Gillespie | 135 | Georg Schmidt |
| 8 | John Dobbins | 49 | James Hill | 92 | Archibald Wasson | 136 | Richard Walton |
| 9 | Henry Huey (4) | 50 | Matthew Long | 93 | Alexander Cathey (2) | 137 | Adam Büttner |
| 10 | John Withrow (3) | 51 | John Best | 94 | Richard Brandon (3) | 138 | Lorentz Schnepp |
| 11 | James Brandon (2) | 52 | Samuel Martin | 95 | James Graham (3) | 139 | "Ryal's (sic) old place" |
| 12 | Griffith Rutherford | 53 | Henry White (2) | 96 | James Patton | 140 | Johannes Bösinger |
| 13 | William Cowan (2) | 54 | John Holmes | 97 | John Russell* | 141 | Peter Veit |
| 14 | Francis Wilson | 55 | William Brandon | 98 | Samuel Woods | 142 | Michael Bonacher |
| 15 | Samuel Reed | 56 | James Cathey | 99 | George Tate* | 143 | Martin Raiblen (sic)* |
| 16 | John Wilson | 57 | James Story* | 100 | Samuel Cochrane | 144 | Peter Ströher |
| 17 | John McElwrath (5) | 58 | George Cathey (2) | 101 | Thomas Little | 145 | Christian Eller (Öhler) |
| 18 | Henry Chambers | 59 | Robert Hardin | 102 | Robert Barclay (Barkley) | 146 | Joseph Wolfskehl |
| 19 | Thomas Gillespie (4) | 60 | Andrew Cathey | 103 | Andrew and John Beard | 147 | Henrich Agader |
| 20 | Robert Steel | 61 | George Lock (Locke) | 104 | John Kilpatrick | 148 | Heinrich Fröhlich |
| 21 | John Kerr (4) | 62 | John Brandon (3) | 105 | John Brandon, Jr. (2) | 149 | Anthony Salz |
| 22 | James Hemphill | 63 | Andrew Allison (2) | 106 | Robert McPherson | 150 | Peter Eary (sic) |
| 23 | William Grant | 64 | John Todd | 107 | Robert Woods | 151 | Joseph Lobwasser |
| 24 | Michael Dickson | 65 | John Cathey | 108 | John Burnett | 152 | Killen Earnhardt (Ernhardt) |
| 25 | Mary Armstrong | 66 | John Dickey | 109 | John McConnell | 153 | Conrad Bullem |
| 26 | Samuel Young (2) | 67 | John Lawrence (Lowrance, Lorentz, Laurens) | 110 | Alexander Douglass | 154 | James McCulloch and Griffith Rutherford |
| 27 | James Stewart (4) | 68 | Mathew Woods | 111 | John Gardiner (Gardner) | 155 | John Hampton |
| 28 | Richard Graham (2) | 69 | Joshua Nichols | 112 | Thomas Evans | 156 | Jacob Van Pool* |
| 29 | Thomas Johnston | 70 | James Blyth (Blythe) | 113 | John Dunn (2) | 157 | Michael Müller (2) |
| 30 | Richard King | 71 | Samuel Blyth (Blythe) | 114 | Jacob Braun | 158 | Wendel Müller (2) |
| 31 | John and Joseph Thompson | 72 | David Woods | 115 | James Carson (3) | 159 | Christopher Rintelmann |
| 32 | Samuel Hillis | 73 | John Patterson | 116 | Hugh Waddell | 160 | Samuel Shinn (2) |
| 33 | Robert Harris | 74 | James Erwin (Irwin) (2) | 117 | Peter Schmidt | 161 | Georg Henrich Birrer |
| 34 | Humphrey Cunningham | 75 | James Alexander | 118 | Alexander McCulloch | 162 | James Carter |
| 35 | John Cowan | 76 | Walter Carruth | 119 | John Whitesides | 163 | Friedrich Litzlehr |
| 36 | Andrew Kerr (3) | 77 | Thomas Bell (2) | 120 | John Dunn and Daniel Little | 164 | Lorentz Lingel |
| 37 | David Fullerton (2) | 78 | Robert Reed | 121 | Peter Arndt | 165 | Henrich Rohn |
| 38 | Alexander Dobbins | 79 | Hugh Reed | 122 | Alexander Clingman | 166 | Richard Morebee (Morbee) |
| 39 | Malcolm Hamilton | 80 | John Huggins (Huggan) | 123 | Georg Brinner (4) | 167 | Heinrich Grob |
| 40 | William Porter | 81 | William McKnight | 124 | Salisbury Town Land | 168 | Jacob Volenweider |
| 41 | Richard Robinson (Robison) | 82 | Daniel McFeeters | 125 | James Andrew | 169 | George Magoune (sic) |
| 42 | John Kirkpatrick | 83 | Fergus Graham | 126 | John Thomas | 170 | Philip Earnhardt (Ernhardt) |
| | | 84 | Thomas Brandon | 127 | John Howard (2) | | |
| | | | | 128 | John Dill | | |

* No grant recorded prior to 1763, but referred to in descriptions of adjoining grants.

of Charles and St. Marys counties.[10] The family was in Charles
County by 1654.[11] The progenitors of Thomas Evans settled in
Calvert, St. Marys and Somerset counties between 1677 and
1714.[12] The Gardiner family was in St. Marys County in 1718,[13]
while that of Edward Cusick lived in the same county as early as
1703.[14]

The Hamptons, like the Craigs and Gardiners, have a history
which includes both Maryland and New Jersey. One branch of the
family lived in Cecil County (whence John and David Hampton
removed to Carolina) in 1722;[15] another was in Freehold,
Monmouth County, New Jersey, before 1710.[16]

Abraham, James, and Michael Miller (evidently close kin of
James Miller of Fourth Creek) migrated southward from Cecil
County, Maryland, or New Castle County, Delaware.[17] Richard

10. Anson County Deed Books, Office of Registrar of Deeds, Anson County
Courthouse, Wadesboro, N.C., book 1, pp. 202-3 (hereafter cited as Anson
Deeds) ; Rowan Deeds, V, 529; marriage of Joseph Harrison, June 30, 1762,
in Rowan County Marriage Records, Office of Registrar of Deeds, Rowan
County Courthouse, Salisbury, N.C.; *Maryland Calendar of Wills,* VI, 23, VIII,
79, 94, 80; Maryland County Land Warrants, State Land Office, Annapolis, Md.,
liber AB&H, folio 416, liber F&F no. 7, folio 79, liber CB no. 3, folio 82,
liber DD no. 5, folio 132 (hereafter cited as Maryland Land Warrants).
11. Maryland Land Warrants, liber AB&H, folio 416.
12. Testamentary Proceedings, liber 13, folios 87, 367, liber 22, folios 324,
367, 481, 488, liber 19C, folio 100; Maryland Land Warrants, liber 19, folio 392;
James S. Brawley, *The Rowan Story, 1753-1953* (Salisbury, N.C.: Rowan
Printing Co., 1954), p. 352; N.C. Land Grants, VI, 135.
13. Testamentary Proceedings, liber 23, folios 179, 180, 300, 277, 295, liber
31, folio 428, liber 29, folios 184, 316, 380; Jethro Rumple, *A History of Rowan
County, North Carolina, Containing Sketches of Prominent Families and Distinguished Men* (Salisbury, N.C.: J. J. Bruner, 1881), p. 261; Rowan Deeds,
V, 52. As in the case of the Craigs, another branch of this Gardiner family
settled in New Jersey (Burlington County) before 1694. It is possible that
Gardiner stemmed from the Jersey branch, but the fact that his 476-acre tract
adjoined those of John Dunn and Thomas Evans indicates a Maryland origin.
It is of interest that a John Gardiner served in 1723 as elder in an unspecified
congregation within the New Castle Presbytery. *New Jersey Wills,* XXXIII,
178; "Records of the Presbytery of New Castle Upon Delaware," *Journal of
the Presbyterian Historical Society,* 36 vols. (Philadelphia: Presbyterian
Historical Society, 1901-58), XV (no. 2), 88.
14. Testamentary Proceedings, liber 23, folios 130, 179, 244; *Maryland
Calendar of Wills,* III, 14; Rowan Deeds, IV, 107, VI, 541.
15. *Maryland Calendar of Wills,* VII, 167; Rowan County Will Books,
Clerk's Office, Rowan County Courthouse, Salisbury, N.C., A, 62 (hereafter
cited as Rowan Wills) ; Testamentary Proceedings, liber 25, folio 95; N.C.
Land Grants, VI, 164.
16. *New Jersey Wills,* XXXIII, 104, 204.
17. New Castle County Court of Common Pleas, 1703-17, 1727-40 (the
original lists are in folders undesignated save by a penciled number on the

Walton, a tanner, evidently originated among the Waltons of Somerset County, Maryland, who settled there before 1686.[18]

Thomas and William Carson, probably brothers, settled very near the Cecil-Chester border in 1737 or 1738.[19] William lived in Pencader Hundred, New Castle County, until his death in 1762.[20] Thomas moved from East Nottingham township, Chester County, to Lancaster borough, Lancaster County, in 1744,[21] and thence to the Shenandoah Valley.[22] In 1748, the list of tax delinquents for Augusta County recorded the fact that Thomas Carson had "gone to Carolina."[23] Carson may well have died enroute to the Yadkin, for his name does not appear in Anson or Rowan records. James and John Carson, his sons or nephews, did settle in present-day Rowan, John on the South Yadkin in the Irish settlement,[24] and James in the trading camp settlement.[25]

John Long was a prosperous planter-merchant who removed to Carolina from Earl township, Lancaster County, Pennsylvania, sometime between 1750 and 1757.[26] John Whiteside originated

outside cover), Hall of Records, Dover, Del., folder XIV (1727-30), 47, 48, 50, folder XXI (two books), book 1, p. 56, book 2, p. 32, folder XXV (1732-40), 24 (hereafter cited as New Castle Common Pleas); Rowan Wills, B, 32, 124, A, 91; Cecil County Deed Books, Office of Registrar of Deeds, Cecil County Courthouse, Elkton, Md., VIII, 198, IX, 389; Rowan Deeds, III, 369, IV, 750; N.C. Land Grants, VI, 164.

18. Maryland Testamentary Proceedings, liber 37, folio 379; *Maryland Calendar of Wills,* II, 7, IV, 105; Rowan Deeds, IV, 866. It is possible that Walton originated in Philadelphia (see Appendix D).

19. Chester County Tax Lists for 1722-27, 1735, 1737, 1738, 1740, 1741, 1747, and 1753 (unpaginated manuscripts), Chester County Historical Society, West Chester, Pa., tax lists for 1737-38 (hereafter cited as Chester Tax Lists); Chester County Land Warrants, *Pennsylvania Archives,* Third Series, 30 vols., ed. William H. Egle (Harrisburg: State Printers, 1894-99), XXIV, 67 (hereafter cited as *Pennsylvania Archives,* Third Series); *Calendar of Delaware Wills: New Castle County, 1682-1800,* abstracted and compiled by the Historical Research Committee of the Colonial Dames of Delaware (New York: Frederick H. Hitchcock, 1911), p. 60 (hereafter cited as *Calendar of Delaware Wills*).

20. *Calendar of Delaware Wills,* p. 60; New Castle Common Pleas, folder XXV (1732-40), 33.

21. Charles E. Kemper, "Historical Notes from the Records of Augusta County, Virginia, Part I," *Papers and Addresses of the Lancaster County Historical Society,* 65 vols. (Lancaster, Pa.: 1897-1961), XXV, 91.

22. In 1747, Carson was fined and put in the stocks for swearing and insulting the court. *Records of Augusta County,* I, 30.

23. *Ibid.,* II, 413.

24. Rowan Deeds, IV, 822.

25. N.C. Land Grants, VI, 126.

26. Lancaster County Tax Lists for 1750, 1751, 1754, 1756, 1758, and 1759 (manuscripts, identified by date and township), Office of County Commissioner,

in the Pequea Creek district of eastern Lancaster County, where his family resided as early as 1721.[27] He was in Rowan County by March, 1754,[28] and was operating a public mill on or near Grants Creek three years later.[29]

Benjamin Rounsavill originated in New Jersey; John Frohock, Benjamin Milner, and probably Daniel Little in Pennsylvania. Alexander McCulloh lived in Edgecombe County, North Carolina. Little has been discovered concerning the origins of George Magoune, Richard Morbee, Henry Sloan, or Charles Kirkland.

Rounsavill migrated from Hopewell township, Hunterdon County, New Jersey,[30] and established his home on the banks of the Yadkin near the trading camp ford.[31] It is evident that Edward Hughes, Isaac Feree, and Rounsavill operated the first ferry crossings north of the Granville line for, in September, 1753, each of the three petitioned the newly established Rowan County court for a license to keep a ferry over the Yadkin River.[32]

It is probable that by 1762 John Frohock was the wealthiest and most influential inhabitant of the northwest Carolina frontier. Fifteen years had passed since the arrival of the Bryans and Catheys, James Carter and John Dunn. Frohock was the dominant figure during the decade between the end of the French and Indian War and the outbreak of the Revolution.

John Frohock was one of the four sons of John Frohock, senior, who migrated from England to America sometime between

Lancaster County Courthouse, Lancaster, Pa., Earl township tax lists for 1750 and 1758; Rowan Court Minutes, I, 93. Before his death in 1760, Long acquired nearly four thousand acres of land between Salisbury and the Yadkin River. N.C. Land Grants, VI, 176, 172, 175, 174, 178; Rowan Deeds, II, 234. A kinsman, Matthew Long, was granted 652 acres on the waters of Second Creek in 1761. N.C. Land Grants, VI, 176.

27. D. F. Magee, "The Whitesides of Colerain: The Revolutionary Captain and the Congressman," *Papers and Addresses of the Lancaster County Historical Society*, 65 vols. (Lancaster, Pa.: 1897-1961), XVII (no. 8), 227-33; "Assessment Lists and Other Manuscript Documents of Lancaster County Prior to 1729," comp. H. Frank Eshleman, *Papers and Addresses of the Lancaster County Historical Society*, 65 vols. (Lancaster, Pa.: 1897-1961), XX, 173.

28. Rowan Court Minutes, I, 12.

29. *Ibid.*, I, 49.

30. *New Jersey Wills*, XXX, 71, 79, 409. The name is probably of Huguenot origin.

31. Rowan Court Minutes, I, 5.

32. *Ibid.* Hughes' petition included the request that his ferry might be at the Shallow Ford and that he might "have the ferry Road."

1720 and 1730.[33] The Frohocks evidently came to the colonies with the Parker family, with whom they settled in the vicinity of Newtown, Bucks County, Pennsylvania.[34] There, John Frohock, Jr., probably came to know Squire Boone and James Carter.

Following the death of Thomas Parker (1742)[35] and John Frohock, senior (1748),[36] many of their kinsmen left Pennsylvania for the newly opened lands to the southward. The younger John Frohock acted as an associate of his uncle Hugh Parker, a wealthy merchant of Prince Georges (later Frederick) County, Maryland,[37] and a key figure in the trading activities of the newly organized Ohio Company.[38] After Hugh Parker's death in 1751,[39] the Frohocks and several of the Parkers (including Robert and Thomas) removed to east-central North Carolina, where they acquired land in Northampton, Edgecombe, Halifax, and Granville counties.[40] There they became closely associated with Alexander and Henry Eustace McCulloh, John Edwards, and James McManus.[41]

33. Abstracts of Bucks County Wills, 1685-1795, in Collections of the Genealogical Society of Pennsylvania, Historical Society of Pennsylvania, Philadelphia (hereafter cited as Bucks Abstracts). The other three sons were Thomas, William, and Hugh Frohock.

34. Bucks County, Pa., Miscellaneous Papers, 1682-1850, 2 vols., Historical Society of Pennsylvania, Philadelphia, I, 135; Bucks Abstracts, 52, 90, 117. The sister of John Frohock, senior, married Robert Parker, probably in England. Will of John Frohock, Rowan County Wills, State Department of Archives and History, Raleigh, N.C., vol. VIII, p. 49, folio 1 (hereafter cited as Frohock Will).

35. Bucks County Will Books, Office of Register of Wills, Bucks County Courthouse, Doylestown, Pa., A, 8.

36. Bucks Abstracts, p. 128.

37. Maryland Wills, 1635-1777, Maryland Hall of Records, Annapolis, Md., XXVIII, 128-29 (hereafter cited as Maryland Wills); Alfred P. James, *The Ohio Company: Its Inner History* (Pittsburgh: University of Pittsburgh Press, 1959), pp. 201, 205, 219. Professor James incorrectly deciphered the name as "Trohock."

38. Kenneth P. Bailey, *The Ohio Company of Virginia and the Westward Movement, 1748-1792: A Chapter in the History of the Colonial Frontier* (Glendale, Calif.: Arthur H. Clark Co., 1939), pp. 70-74, 85-116; James, *Ohio Company,* pp. 13, 23-25, 31, 35-40, 43-45, 77.

39. James, *Ohio Company,* p. 39.

40. *Abstract of North Carolina Wills, compiled from Original and Recorded Wills in the Office of the Secretary of State* by J. Bryan Grimes (Raleigh, N.C.: E. M. Uzzell and Co., State Printers and Binders, 1910), p. 226; Granville County Deed Books, Office of Registrar of Deeds, Granville County Courthouse, Oxford, N.C., C, 605 (hereafter cited as Granville Deeds); Frohock Will.

41. Frohock Will. Frohock left £100 (proclamation money) "to Miss Mary McCulloh, Daughter to my worthy and good Friend the Honourable Alexander McCulloh . . . to be given her in gold and silver." James McManus was Frohock's uncle.

John Frohock moved to Rowan County in 1759 or 1760 and probably established his residence in the town of Salisbury.[42] Before the end of 1762, Frohock owned at least six thousand acres of land in North Carolina (including six grist or saw mills), a town lot in Halifax, and lots in Salisbury.[43] Before his will was written in 1768, Frohock had acquired more than two thousand additional acres and was the possessor of thirty-eight slaves.[44] In Rumple's view, Frohock grew wealthy chiefly "by entering and selling public lands."[45] This explanation is probably sound, particularly in view of the fact that Frohock was clerk of the Rowan County court from January, 1761, until February, 1772.[46] Moreover, he was associated with three of the most important land speculators on the frontier: Alexander and Henry Eustace McCulloh[47] and James McManus.

Alexander McCulloh emigrated from Great Britain to North Carolina and settled near Halifax.[48] He held the title of cacique and was councillor of the province.[49] McCulloh was a cousin of Henry Eustace McCulloh and father-in-law of Thomas Frohock.[50] In 1758, McCulloh acquired 625 acres lying on Grants Creek two miles west of Salisbury.[51] Three years later, this land was bought by John Frohock, who built saw and grist mills where the road leading northwestward from Salisbury toward the mountains crossed the creek.[52]

In 1759, Edward Hughes was succeeded as sheriff of Rowan County by Benjamin Milner.[53] There is no evidence that Milner

42. Rumple, *Rowan County*, pp. 70-71; N.C. Land Grants, VI, 147.
43. Rowan Deeds, N.C. Land Grants, Granville Deeds.
44. Frohock Will.
45. Rumple, *Rowan County*, p. 70. In April, 1761, Frohock became "Receiver of Quit rents for the County of Rowan." Rowan Court Minutes, I, 82.
46. Rowan Deeds, IV, 359; VII, 443; VIII, 5. Frohock had succeeded Thomas Parker in the office of clerk.
47. See p. 93 above.
48. Pamphlet written (1899) by W. H. Bailey, in Blanche-Baker Papers (Manuscript Book No. 1), Southern Historical Collection, University of North Carolina, Chapel Hill, N.C.
49. *Ibid.*
50. *Ibid.* Thomas Frohock, a loyalist, returned to England with the outbreak of the Revolution.
51. Rowan Deeds, IV, 207.
52. Frohock Will; Rowan Deeds, VI, 85.
53. *The State Records of North Carolina*, 16 vols. (XI through XXVI), collected and edited by Walter Clark (Winston, N.C.: M. I. and J. C. Stewart, Printers to the State, 1895-96; Goldsboro, N.C.: Nash Bros., Book and Job Printers, 1898-1905), XXII, 833.

lived west of the Yadkin, though he undoubtedly spent considerable time in Salisbury where he conducted the affairs of his office. Milner's family came to America from Yorkshire, England.[54] They settled in Burlington County, New Jersey, and on the border between Bucks and Philadelphia counties in Pennsylvania.[55]

In North Carolina, Benjamin Milner lived on Barsheby Creek near the Moravian settlement.[56] He removed to Lunenburg County, Virginia, in 1763 or 1764[57] and apparently never returned to Carolina.

The author has discovered little to indicate the origins of the remaining pioneers in the trading camp settlement. George Magoune owned land among the Germans of southeastern Rowan.[58] Richard Morbee lived in the same area adjoining Heinrich Grob.[59] Charles Kirkland's land lay next to that of Friedrich Lytzlehr,[60] but there is nothing to indicate that he ever lived on it. Little is known of Henry Sloan, although he may have originated in Somerset County, New Jersey.[61]

On September 18, 1762, Thomas Kurr of Tulpehocken township, Berks County, Pennsylvania, and Jacob Kurr of Whippen township, Philadelphia County, Pennsylvania, appointed their "trusty and well-beloved friend Daniel Little of Salisbury" legal attorney to sell for them 765 acres of land lying on the Catawba River.[62] This note in the Rowan County court minutes constitutes the sole clue to the origin of Daniel Little, who (in company with John Dunn) was granted 654 acres on the waters of Grants

54. Alfred R. Justice Collection (Massey-Musgrave), in Collections of the Genealogical Society of Pennsylvania, Historical Society of Pennsylvania, Philadelphia, p. 45; Lunenburg County Deed Books, Office of Registrar of Deeds, Lunenburg County Courthouse, Lunenburg, Va., XII, 173, X, 112; Gilbert Cope Collection (Milner), Collections of the Genealogical Society of Pennsylvania, Philadelphia, p. 23. (hereafter cited as Cope Collection).

55. Cope Collection (Milner), p. 26; Montgomery County Deed Books, Office of Registrar of Deeds, Montgomery County Courthouse, Norristown, Pa., LV, 32.

56. Rowan Deeds, IV, 399.

57. *Ibid.*, VI, 207.

58. *Ibid.*, VI, 436.

59. *Ibid.*, III, 17.

60. *Ibid.*, V, 237.

61. Rowan Deeds, II, 307; *New Jersey Wills*, XXX, 341. Sloan made his home on the east bank of the Yadkin. William H. Foote, *Sketches of North Carolina, Historical and Biographical, Illustrative of the Principles of a Portion of Her Early Settlers* (New York: Robert Carter, 58 Canal Street, 1946), p. 171.

62. Rowan Court Minutes, I, 104.

Creek four miles northwest of Salisbury.[63] Little died in 1775 and lies buried in the "English" graveyard in Salisbury.

These twenty-seven settlers, the majority of whom were neither Scotch-Irish nor German, thus occupied the best land between the Irish settlement and the Yadkin, and provided an unbroken chain of settlement extending from Davidson's Creek to the trading ford.

63. N.C. Land Grants, VI, 141.

# X

## GROWTH OF THE IRISH SETTLEMENT, 1752-1762

By far the largest of the frontier settlements was that centered at Thyatira Church and known as the Irish settlement. During the decade after March, 1752, more than one hundred families, nearly all of Scotch-Irish origin, obtained title to lands there. Few of these immigrants were men of means, and few were elected or appointed to public office. Nevertheless, they comprised the bulk of the Presbyterian population, the largest single group on the northwest frontier.

As in the case of settlers discussed elsewhere in this study, it is not possible to determine the exact date when each of these immigrants settled in Carolina, but the majority were undoubtedly on the land by 1757. Like the initial pioneers in the Irish settlement, most of the newcomers originated in Maryland or Pennsylvania.

The will of Robert Luckie, written in 1754 in Martic township, Lancaster County, Pennsylvania, referred to sons Hugh, John, Andrew, James, Robert, and Samuel, and to daughters Isabel, the wife of William Sleven, and Ann, the wife of Samuel Hillis.[1] Also mentioned was Agnes Luckie, the wife of Robert Pendry. By 1762, John Luckie, John Luckie, Jr., Joseph Luckie, Robert Luckie, Samuel Luckie, William Luckie, William Sleven, Samuel Hillis, and Alexander Pendry were all residents of the Irish settlement.[2]

The will of James Armstrong, written in 1759 in Paxtang township, Lancaster County, mentioned brothers Abel, William,

1. Lancaster County Will Books, Clerk's Office, Lancaster County Courthouse, Lancaster, Pa., B-1, 188 (hereafter cited as Lancaster Wills).
2. Tombstone of John Luckie (1688-1773) in Thyatira Cemetery; Rowan County Deed Books, Office of Registrar of Deeds, Rowan County Courthouse, Salisbury, N.C., I, 108; II, 376, 380; III, 399, 417; IV, 367, 639; V, 78 (hereafter cited as Rowan Deeds).

and John.[3] The will also contained the statement that James Armstrong (nephew of the author of the will) had been in North Carolina in February and March, 1759, but had returned to become an executor of the estate. Within three years, James, Mary, and William Armstrong were living on Fourth Creek adjoining the land of Samuel Young.[4]

In addition to the Luckies and Armstrongs, other pioneers from Lancaster County who acquired grants or deeds in the Irish settlement were Henry Schiles (Leacock township),[5] David Strain (Hanover township),[6] Thomas Douglas (Derry or Colerain township),[7] William Cowan (Salsbury township),[8] Francis Lock (Derry or Paxtang township),[9] Patrick Campbell (Derry or Donegal township),[10] Samuel Galbraith (Derry town-

3. Lancaster Wills, B-1, 278.

4. Rowan Deeds, VI, 97, 357; tombstone of William Armstrong (1739-80) in Thyatira Cemetery. William Armstrong was killed in the Revolution.

5. Lancaster Wills, J-1, 238; Rowan Deeds, II, 52. Schiles was in Cecil County in 1726. Cecil County Judgments, S.K. no. 3 (1723-30) and S.K. no. 4 (1730-32, 1736-41, 1741-43, 1746-47), Hall of Records, Annapolis, Md., S.K. no. 3 (1723-30), pp. 272, 281 (hereafter cited as Cecil Judgments).

6. Lancaster Wills, H, 24, J-1, 239; Colonial Land Grant Records of North Carolina, State Library, Raleigh, N.C., VI, 214 (hereafter cited as N.C. Land Grants); Hanover Township Tax Lists, Office of County Commissioner, Lancaster County Courthouse, Lancaster, Pa., lists consist of unpaginated manuscripts, one undated, one dated 1750, and a third dated 1756 (hereafter cited as Hanover Tax Lists).

7. Lancaster County Land Warrants, 1733-61 (unpaginated manuscripts, arranged alphabetically), Office of County Commissioner, Lancaster County Courthouse, Lancaster, Pa. (hereafter cited as Lancaster Warrants); *Notes and Queries, Historical, Biographical and Genealogical, Relating Chiefly to Interior Pennsylvania,* 3 ser. (12 vols.), ed. William H. Egle (Harrisburg: Harrisburg Publishing Co. [reprinted from *Harrisburg Daily Telegraph,* 1878-1901, 1894-1901]), ser. 3, vol. I, p. 340 (hereafter cited as Egle, *N&Q*); Rowan Deeds, IV, 21, 213.

8. Lancaster Wills, A-1, 217, I-1, 82; Rowan Deeds, IV, 139; Rowan County Will Books, Clerk's Office, Rowan County Courthouse, Salisbury, N.C., B, 196, E, 207 (hereafter cited as Rowan Wills).

9. Lock was in Lancaster County in 1738. Lancaster Wills, A-1, 33; Derry and Paxtang Tax Lists for 1750-51 and 1756 (unpaginated manuscripts), Office of County Commissioner, Lancaster County Courthouse, Lancaster, Pa. (hereafter cited as Derry-Paxtang Tax Lists). Lock, a carpenter, became sheriff of Rowan County by 1766. Rowan Deeds, I, 103; Minutes of Rowan County Court of Common Pleas and Quarter Sessions, 1753-1869, typed copy in 3 vols. (part of the original manuscript, torn, faded and very difficult to read, is in the State Department of Archives and History, Raleigh, N.C.), Salisbury Public Library, Salisbury, N.C., I, 12 (hereafter cited as Rowan Court Minutes).

10. Lancaster Wills, B-1, 656; Charles H. Browning, "Francis Campbell," *Pennsylvania Magazine of History and Biography,* 85 vols. (Philadelphia: publication fund of the Historical Society of Pennsylvania, 1877-1961), XXVIII, 64-65 (hereafter cited as *Pennsylvania Magazine*); Rowan Deeds, III, 370.

ship),[11] Humphrey and John Cunningham (Hanover township),[12] James and John Patterson,[13] Mary Murray (Paxtang or Donegal township),[14] Dennis Lafferty,[15] Michael Dickson,[16] James and David Stewart (Hanover township),[17] Alexander Douglass,[18]

Campbell may never have lived in Carolina. He sold his land to James Armstrong and James Brandon in 1762, at which time he was referred to as "Patrick Campbell of Pennsylvania." Rowan Deeds, VI, 357.

11. Lancaster County Land Warrants, *Pennsylvania Archives,* Third Series, 30 vols., ed. William H. Egle (Harrisburg: State Printers, 1894-99), XXIV, 414 (hereafter cited as *Pennsylvania Archives,* Third Series) ; Egle, *N&Q,* ser. 3, vol. I, p. 4; Rowan Deeds, IV, 478.

12. Lancaster County Deed Books, Office of Registrar of Deeds, Lancaster County Courthouse, Lancaster, Pa., FF, 594 (hereafter cited as Lancaster Deeds) ; N.C. Land Grants, VI, 133, 178.

13. James, John, and Arthur Patterson were among the first settlers in the Susquehanna Valley. James and John were there in 1718, Arthur by 1728. Charles A. Hanna, *The Wilderness Trail: Or the Ventures and Adventures of the Pennsylvania Traders on the Allegheny Path, With Some New Annals of the Old West, and the Records of Some Strong Men and Some Bad Ones,* 2 vols. (New York and London: G. P. Putnam's Sons, Knickerbocker Press, 1911), I, 163; "Assessment Lists and Other Manuscript Documents of Lancaster County Prior to 1729," comp. H. Frank Eshleman, *Papers and Addresses of the Lancaster County Historical Society,* 65 vols. (Lancaster, Pa.: 1897-1961), XX, 180 (hereafter cited as "Lancaster Assessment Lists") ; "Register of Baptisms, 1701-1746, First Presbyterian Church of Philadelphia," *Publications of the Genealogical Society of Pennsylvania,* 22 vols. (Philadelphia: Edward Stern and Co. [and other publishers], 1895-1961), XIX (no. 3), 284, 289, 293, 297, 299; N.C. Land Grants, VI, 207; Rowan Deeds, IV, 174.

14. Robert Murray was in Cecil County in 1724, whence he evidently removed to the Conestoga settlement on the Susquehanna in 1724 or 1725. His kinsmen James and John Murray died in the Paxtang-Donegal area, James in 1747, John in 1745. Mary Murray was the widow of one of these three. Cecil Judgments, S.K. no. 3 (1723-30), p. 133; "Lancaster Assessment Lists," p. 181; Lancaster Wills, A-1, 100, I-1, 328; Rowan Wills, A, 118.

15. Lafferty appeared in the Lancaster Courts in 1743; there is nothing to indicate his place of residence in the county. Rowan Deeds, IV, 53; Lancaster County Common Pleas Dockets, 1729-51, Office of County Commissioner, Lancaster, Pa., vol. for 1743-44 (hereafter cited as Lancaster Common Pleas). These documents are collected in twenty-three chronological listings of cases in pamphlet form (for the most part unpaginated), each one containing cases for approximately two years. In this study, reference is made by volume (pamphlet) and year.

16. Lancaster Common Pleas, vol. XII (1739-43) ; N.C. Land Grants, XI, 8.

17. Hanover Tax Lists, undated and 1750; Egle, *N&Q,* ser. 1, vol. I, p. 31; Rowan Deeds, IV, 216, V, 197; N.C. Land Grants, VI, 217; *Chronicles of the Scotch-Irish Settlements in Virginia, Extracted from the Original Court Records of Augusta County, 1745-1800,* 3 vols., comp. and ed. Lyman Chalkley (Rosslyn, Va.: Commonwealth Printing Co., 1912), III, 119, 124 (hereafter cited as *Records of Augusta County*) ; Howard McKnight Wilson, *The Tinkling Spring, Headwater of Freedom: A Study of the Church and Her People* (Richmond, Va.: Garrett and Massie, Inc., 1954), p. 482.

18. Douglass was in Lancaster County in 1742 and in the Shenandoah Valley (where he was described as a stonemason) later the same year. It is conjectural

Alexander McCorkle (Paxtang or Derry township),[19] Humphrey Montgomery,[20] William and James Porter (Sadsbury or Drumore township),[21] Robert Barclay (Paxtang township),[22] and probably John and Francis Wilson (Manheim township).[23]

Before 1740, members of the Woods, Cochran, Little (or Lytle), and Patton families settled variously in Cecil County, Maryland; in Pikeland, Chichester, Nottingham, and Sadsbury townships in Chester County; and in the Paxtang-Hanover district of Lancaster County.[24] The four families were closely

whether Douglass actually lived in Carolina. Although he sold his land on Crane Creek two months after acquiring it in 1756, he was allowed twenty shillings for ten bushels of corn for the Indians in 1758. Lancaster Common Pleas, vol. XII (1739-43); Wilson, *Tinkling Spring,* p. 474; Records of Augusta County, I, 300; N.C. Land Grants, VI, 141; Rowan Deeds, III, 429. Douglass was the stonemason who constructed the foundations of the Tinkling Spring Church in 1742. Wilson, *Tinkling Spring,* p. 89.

19. McCorkle removed from Pennsylvania in 1750 and settled on the upper James River in the Shenandoah Valley. He proceeded to Carolina in 1755 or 1756. Egle, *N&Q,* ser. 3, vol. I, p. 349; *Records of Augusta County,* I, 415; Frederick B. Kegley, *Kegley's Virginia Frontier: The Beginning of the Southwest; the Roanoke of Colonial Days, 1740-1783* (Roanoke, Va.: Southwest Virginia Historical Society, 1938), pp. 80, 145 (hereafter cited as Kegley, *Virginia Frontier*); Rowan Deeds, II, 285.

20. Montgomery, who was in Lancaster County in 1751, proceeded directly to the Carolina frontier. Lancaster County Appearance Dockets (unpaginated manuscripts), 1747-52, Office of County Commissioner, Lancaster, Pa., Docket for 1751 (hereafter cited as Lancaster Appearance Dockets); Rowan Deeds, I, 69, IV, 383.

21. Members of this Porter family were in Cecil County as early as 1716. Lancaster Wills, A-1, 116; Lancaster Warrants; Cecil County Deed Books, Office of Registrar of Deeds, Cecil County Courthouse, Elkton, Md., III, 141, VI, 23 (hereafter cited as Cecil Deeds); Rowan Wills, C, 55, A, 136; Rowan Deeds, VI, 164.

22. Derry-Paxtang Tax Lists for 1756; N.C. Land Grants, VI, 110.

23. This Wilson family originated in Strabane, County Tyrone, Ireland. Thomas A. Glenn, "Genealogical Gleanings of the Wilson, or Willsons, of Ulster," *Pennsylvania Magazine,* XXXVIII, 346-47; Lancaster Wills, A-1, 50; N.C. Land Grants, VI, 230, 237.

24. Lancaster Wills, B-1, 116, 136, E-1, 178, I-1, 75, A-1, 166; Lancaster Deeds, G, 1; Cecil Deeds, III, 190, IV, 186; Maryland Wills, 1635-77, Maryland Hall of Records, Annapolis, Md., XXVII, 391 (hereafter cited as Maryland Wills); *The Maryland Calendar of Wills,* 8 vols., comp. and ed. Jane [Baldwin] Cotton (Baltimore: Kohn and Pollock, Inc., 1904-28), IV, 77, VIII, 251 (hereafter cited as *Maryland Calendar of Wills*); "Anson County, North Carolina, Abstracts of Early Records," *The May Wilson McBee Collection,* ed. May Wilson McBee (Greenwood, Miss.: May Wilson McBee, 1950), p. 119 (hereafter cited as "Anson Abstracts"); Derry-Paxtang Tax Lists of 1751; Chester County Will Books, Clerk's Office, Chester County Courthouse, West Chester, Pa., I, 278, 325, 444; Chester County Deed Books, Office of Registrar of Deeds, Chester County Courthouse, West Chester, Pa., L, 80 (hereafter cited as

related in both Maryland and Pennsylvania, and members of all four probably migrated to Carolina together.

The will of Andrew Woods, written in Hanover township, Lancaster County, in 1753, mentioned daughters Sarah Cochran and Margaret Patton.[25] In 1761, Samuel Cochran, husband of Sarah, obtained 446 acres of land on Coldwater Creek adjoining a tract belonging to Samuel Woods. [26] Sometime between 1752 and 1757, Matthew Woods, a cousin or nephew of Samuel, acquired Charles Burnett's tract on the headwaters of Grant's Greek.[27] He then sold it in 1757 to Robert Woods, whose will (dated 1766) contained reference to "Uncle Samuel" and "Aunt Sarah" Woods.[28]

John Little's will, proved in Anson County in 1755, referred to sons John and Thomas in Rowan County.[29] In that year the younger John Little bought half of Robert Reed's 645-acre tract adjoining James Cathey one mile south of Thyatira Church.[30] Thomas Little settled on Coldwater Creek next to Samuel Cochran.[31] In 1760, James Patton was granted 645 acres "lying on the ridge between Grant's Creek and Cold Waters."[32] Robert and John Patton, probably sons of James, obtained part of this land in 1761 and 1762.[33]

At least thirty of the pioneers who made their homes in the Irish settlement after 1752 emigrated from Chester County. William Bailey, from Kennet township, bought 120 acres from Robert Tate in 1757.[34] John Biggs, originally from county Antrim, Ireland,[35] evidently removed to Carolina from Chester County, as his son-in-law, James Carson, originally lived there.[36]

One branch of the McElwrath family settled in Nantmeal

---

Chester Deeds) ; Records of the Donegal Presbytery (typed copy), vols. 1A and 1B (Philadelphia: Presbyterian Historical Society, 1937), 1A, 35; Egle, *N&Q*, ser. 3, vol. 1, p. 364; Rowan Wills, A, 226, 84, 162, 163, 190, 265, C, 26.

25. Lancaster Wills, B-1, 136.
26. Rowan Deeds, V, 123; Rowan Wills, A, 226.
27. Rowan Deeds, IV, 712.
28. Rowan Wills, A, 163; Rowan Deeds, IV, 712.
29. "Anson Abstracts," p. 119.
30. Rowan Deeds, II, 106.
31. N.C. Land Grants, VI, 178.
32. *Ibid.*, VI, 205.
33. Rowan Deeds, IV, 480; V, 196.
34. *Ibid.*, II, 189. See also p. 78 above.
35. Tombstone of John Biggs (1699-1763) in Thyatira Cemetery.
36. See p. 111 above.

township, Chester County; another in Somerset County, New Jersey.[37] John McElwrath removed to the Irish settlement from one of the two and settled on Third Creek.[38]

William McKnight, the father-in-law of John Kerr, owned nearly 3,000 acres of land in Rowan County scattered throughout the Irish settlement. In 1734 McKnight lived on a 300-acre tract in Caln township "about two miles beyond the West Branch of Brandywine."[39] In Carolina he settled in the southwest corner of the Irish settlement on a 641-acre tract which he bought in 1753 from James Graham.[40]

A number of those who entered the Irish settlement from Chester County followed in the footsteps of kinsmen who had previously removed to Carolina. James and John Dobbin, brothers or cousins of Alexander Dobbin, originated in Caln or Lower Darby township.[41] John Gillespie, a cooper, removed from New

37. Chester County Tax Lists for 1722, 1727, 1735, 1737, 1738, 1740, 1741, 1747, and 1753 (unpaginated manuscripts), Chester County Historical Society, West Chester, Pa., 1740 tax list (hereafter cited as Chester Tax Lists); *Calendar of New Jersey Wills*, in *Documents Relating to the Colonial History of the State of New Jersey*, 1st ser., vols. XXX and XXXIII, ed. A. Van Doren Honeyman [vol. XXX] and William Nelson [vol. XXXIII] (Somerville, N.J.: Unionist Gazette Association, 1918 [vol. XXX], and Paterson, N.J.: Press Printing and Publishing Co., 1901 [vol. XXXIII]), XXX, 34 (hereafter cited as *New Jersey Wills*); *Records of Augusta County*, I, 151, III, 463; Wilson, *Tinkling Spring*, p. 478; Rowan Wills, A, 82; Lawyers Account Book, (1759-74), in the Macay-McNeely Papers, Southern Historical Collection, University of North Carolina, Chapel Hill, N.C.

38. Chester Tax Lists, tax list for 1740. McElwrath was evidently a man of means, for he acquired nearly three thousand acres on Third Creek between 1753 and 1759. N.C. Land Grants, VI, 187, 188, 190, 198. Thomas McElrath, the son of John McElwrath's grand nephew, was one of the original proprietors of the *New York Tribune*. In 1841 he entered into partnership with Horace Greeley in the conduct of the newspaper. Egle, *N&Q*, ser. 3, vol. III, pp. 174-75.

39. The Taylor Papers: Being a Collection of Warrants, Surveys, Letters, &C. Relating to the Early Settlement of Pennsylvania (including correspondence for the period 1723-50 and scattered miscellaneous items for the period 1672-1775 in unnumbered volumes), 10 vols. (vols. I, II, and III: Chester County Warrants, 1682-1742), Historical Society of Pennsylvania, Philadelphia, II, 236 (hereafter cited as Taylor Papers).

40. Rowan Deeds, I, 12.

41. Chester Tax Lists, tax lists for 1737-38 and 1747; N.C. Land Grants, VI, 137-39; Rowan Deeds, IV, 800. According to Alexander, John Dobbin, one of the first elders of Thyatira, was afflicted with sores. S. C. Alexander, *An Historical Address, Delivered at the Centennial Celebration of Thyatira Church, Rowan County, N.C., October 19, 1855* (Salisbury, N.C., J. J. Bruner, Printer, 1855), pp. 15-16. A list of the mayors and sheriffs of Carrickfergus, County Antrim, Ireland, for the period 1568-1688 includes the names of John, James, and William Dobbins. Arthur Dobbs Papers, Southern Historical Collection, University of North Carolina, Chapel Hill, N.C.

London township sometime after 1738.[42] He bought one hundred acres on Sill's Creek from Samuel Blyth in 1759.[43] Hugh Reed, probably from the vicinity of Octoraro Creek on the border between Chester and Lancaster counties,[44] settled three miles south of Thyatira Church on land adjoining Robert Reed.[45]

The other settlers from Chester County were William Boggan (Concord township),[46] Francis Johnston (New London or East Nottingham township),[47] John Bunting (Fallowfield township),[48] John Kirkpatrick (Nottingham township),[49] James Hemphill (Edgmont township),[50] James Docharty (Nottingham township),[51] John Poston (Fallowfield township),[52] Samuel and Robert Rankin (Sadsbury township on the Lancaster County border),[53] James Storey (West Nantmeal township),[54] Archibald Wasson (Fallowfield township),[55] Henry McHenry (Caln township),[56] and Robert Steel (New London township).[57] Joshua

42. Chester Tax Lists, tax lists for 1737-38; Rowan Deeds, IV, 349, XII, 188; Wilson, *Tinkling Spring*, pp. 475, 426.

43. Rowan Deeds, IV, 349.

44. See p. 68 above; Lancaster Appearance Dockets, docket for 1749.

45. Rowan Deeds, V, 550.

46. Chester Tax Lists, tax list for 1740; Rowan Deeds, III, 519.

47. Chester Tax Lists, tax lists for 1740 and 1747; Rowan Deeds, III, 480.

48. Chester County Orphan's Court Dockets, Minors Estates, Office of Registrar of Wills and Clerk of Orphans' Court, Chester County Courthouse, West Chester, Pa., II, 31; marriage of James Bunting, June 23, 1763, Rowan County Marriage Records, Office of Registrar of Deeds, Rowan County Courthouse, Salisbury, N.C. (hereafter cited as Rowan Marriages); Chester Tax Lists, tax lists for 1737-38, 1740, and 1747; Rowan Deeds, IV, 644.

49. Chester Tax Lists, tax lists for 1740 and 1747; Rowan Deeds, II, 139. Kirkpatrick may actually have lived just over the line in Cecil County, Maryland. Cecil Deeds, IV, 489.

50. Chester Tax Lists, tax list for 1747; N.C. Land Grants, VI, 162. Hemphill moved to Rowan County from the Shenandoah Valley in 1756. *Records of Augusta County*, II, 399.

51. Chester Tax Lists, tax lists for 1740 and 1747; Rowan Deeds, IV, 349.

52. Taylor Papers, vol. of miscellaneous items, item 3411; John Dickey Store Account Book (1755-86), Duke University Library, Durham, N.C., p. 11. Poston was living in the Davidson Creek area in 1769. Rowan Court Minutes, II, 27.

53. Chester Tax Lists, tax list for 1753; Cecil Deeds, VIII, 480; Rowan Deeds, V, 272.

54. Chester Tax Lists, tax list for 1747; Augusta County Will Books, Clerk's Office, Augusta County Courthouse, Staunton, Va., V, 530; Charles E. Kemper, "Valley of Virginia Notes," *Virginia Magazine of History and Biography*, 69 vols. (Richmond, Va.: Historical Society of Virginia, 1893-1961), XXXIV, 139; Rowan Wills, A, 148.

55. Chester Tax Lists, tax list for 1747; N.C. Land Grants, VI, 236.

56. Chester Tax Lists, tax list for 1747; Rowan Deeds, IV, 493.

57. Chester Wills, II, 193; Chester Tax Lists, tax lists for 1737-38; Rowan Deeds, VI, 81; N.C. Land Grants, VI, 215.

Nichols obtained a warrant for land in Chester County in 1737,[58] and Malcolm Hamilton did the same in 1750.[59] Robert Johnston, with his sons John, William, Thomas, and Robert, was in Lancaster County in 1745.[60] He seems to have been a cousin of Robert Johnston of Rocky River[61] and may have originated in Chester County. Johnston settled on the South Fork of the Yadkin adjoining Samuel, John, and Joseph Luckie.[62]

Approximately twenty of the newcomers to the Irish settlement originated among Maryland families, several of which had been in America for nearly one hundred years. The Thompson family was in Dorchester County before 1717 and in Baltimore County before 1738,[63] while the progenitor of the Todds settled on the Severn River near Annapolis in 1651.[64] Henry, George, John, William, and Richard Robinson (or Robison) were in Calvert, Charles, and St. Marys counties before 1680.[65] Branches of the numerous Scott family resided in every Maryland County prior to 1725,[66] appearing first in Baltimore (1670), Talbot (1681), and Calvert (1685).[67] These four families were represented in the Irish settlement prior to 1763 by John Thompson (died 1760 or 1761),[68] Joseph Thompson,[69] John Todd,[70] George

58. Chester County Land Warrants, *Pennsylvania Archives,* Third Series, XXIV, 91; Rowan Deeds, VI, 225. A Joshua Nichols appeared in the New Castle County Courts as early as 1710. New Castle County Court of Common Pleas, 1703-17, 1727-40 (the original lists are in folders undesignated save by a penciled number on the outside cover), Hall of Records, Dover, Del., folder V (1708-11), unpaginated.

59. Chester County Land Warrants, *Pennsylvania Archives,* Third Series; XXIV, 79; N.C. Land Grants, VI, 162.

60. Lancaster County Land Warrants, *Pennsylvania Archives,* Third Series, XXIV, 443-45; Rowan Wills, B, 22; marriages of John and Thomas Johnston, June 9, 1766, and November 20, 1767, Rowan Marriages.

61. Rowan Wills, B, 22; A, 70.

62. N.C. Land Grants, VI, 180.

63. *Maryland Calendar of Wills,* IV, 106; VIII, 67; VII, 121.

64. Christopher Johnson, "The Todd Family of Anne Arundel County," *The Maryland Historical Magazine,* 56 vols. (Baltimore: 1906-61), IX, 298-305; *Maryland Calendar of Wills,* VIII, 19, 139; Rowan Wills, A, 259.

65. *Maryland Calendar of Wills,* I, 45, 116, 77, 146, 177. The family was in Talbot County by 1706 and in Kent County before 1741. *Maryland Calendar of Wills,* VI, 107; VIII, 177.

66. *Maryland Calendar of Wills,* vols. I-V.

67. *Ibid.,* I, 62, 138, 156, II, 233, IV, 72, V, 174, 183, 207, VII, 114, 182; marriages of Andrew (August 11, 1769) and Thomas Scott (February 27, 1772), Rowan Marriages.

68. Rowan Wills, A, 159; Rowan Deeds, IV, 247.

69. Rowan Wills, A, 159.

70. N.C. Land Grants, VI, 226.

Robinson and his brother Richard,[71] John Robinson,[72] William Robinson,[73] John Scott, [74] John Scott, Jr.,[75] and James Scott.[76]

Other Marylanders who acquired land in the Irish settlement were James Hynds of Queen Annes County,[77] William Mackey from Cecil County,[78] Andrew and John Beard of Anne Arundel County (where both names appear as early as 1708),[79] and Hugh Mathews of Cecil County.[80] Although inconclusive, the evidence suggests that Robert Hardin originated in Talbot County, where the name appears in 1706,[81] and that the family of James and John Best was also in Talbot County as early as 1684.[82]

Members of the Chambers family settled before 1726 in the Cumberland Valley and in Derry township, Lancaster County.[83]

71. Rowan Deeds, VI, 248; N.C. Land Grants, VI, 209; Rowan Wills, C, 198, D, 91.

72. There is no will, deed, or land grant for John Robinson, but he was appointed constable "on the south side of Grants Creek to the Forks of Said Creek" in 1753. He evidently died very soon thereafter.

73. Rowan Wills, A, 143. William Robinson, who died in 1757, was probably the brother of John Robinson and uncle of George and Richard Robinson.

74. Rowan Wills, A, 147. Scott probably was in Cecil County in 1719. Cecil Deeds, IV, 128.

75. Rowan Deeds, IV, 484.

76. N.C. Land Grants, VI, 217.

77. Maryland Calendar of Wills, V, 20; Rowan Deeds, IV, 373.

78. Cecil Deeds, VI, 218; Probate Records of Maryland, 1635-1776, Maryland Hall of Records, Annapolis, Md., liber 38, folio 809 (hereafter cited as Probate Records) ; Rowan Deeds, III, 19; Anson County Deed Books, Office of Registrar of Deeds, Anson County Courthouse, Wadesboro, N.C., book 1, p. 312 (hereafter cited as Anson Deeds).

79. Rowan Court Minutes, I, 77; Maryland Calendar of Wills, III, 114, VIII, 74, 94, 152, 231; N.C. Land Grants, VI, 108. John Beard removed to South Carolina following the death of Andrew in 1761. Rowan Deeds, VII, 247.

80. Mathews was a surgeon in Cecil County in 1733. Although he subsequently removed to Philadelphia, his son continued to practice in Cecil County. The elder Mathews was among those Catholics arrested for "disaffection" during the French and Indian War. There is nothing to indicate that either ever lived in Carolina. Rowan Deeds, II, 92; Cecil Deeds, IV, 294, 363, VIII, 456; J. Thomas Scharf and Thompson Westcott, History of Philadelphia, 1609-1884, 3 vols. (Philadelphia: L. H. Everts and Co., 1884), I, 253.

81. Maryland Calendar of Wills, III, 86, VIII, 83; Records of Augusta County, I, 312; N.C. Land Grants, VI, 165.

82. Talbot County Will Books, Clerk's Office, Talbot County Courthouse, Easton, Md., book 1, p. 71; Maryland Calendar of Wills, IV, 60; N.C. Land Grants, VI, 111, 106.

83. Henry Chambers Genealogy, in Chambers Papers, Southern Historical Collection, University of North Carolina, Chapel Hill, N.C.; Alfred Nevin, Churches of the Valley: Or, An Historical Sketch of the Old Presbyterian Congregations of Cumberland and Franklin Counties, in Pennsylvania (Philadelphia: Joseph M. Wilson, 1852), pp. 138-39; Egle, N&Q, ser. 3, vol. I, pp. 76-77.

Henry Chambers left one of these groups and proceeded to Prince Georges County, Maryland, before 1739.[84] He was in Carolina by April, 1752, where he bought 640 acres on Third Creek from Thomas Gillespie.[85]

The King and Lawrence families originated in New Jersey. Richard King, a clothier, was born in Ireland, near Dublin.[86] He migrated to America in 1728, settling first in Philadelphia.[87] In 1735, following the death of his first wife, King married Margaret Barclay in Middlesex or Somerset County, New Jersey.[88] Described as "a short, thick man, quick in manner and temper,"[89] King removed to Carolina in 1755 or 1756 and settled with his sons James and Robert on the waters of Withrow's Creek.[90]

John Lawrence (or Laurents), of Huguenot origin, migrated to New York in 1710 and died in Somerset County, New Jersey, in 1745.[91] Twelve years later, his eldest son Alexander bought 524 acres from Richard King on Beaverdam branch of Withrow's Creek.[92] John, Alexander's brother, purchased 632 acres on Sill's Creek from Henry White at the same time.[93]

Griffith Rutherford has been described as "somewhat undersized, about 5 feet 8 inches, but heavily and compactly formed."[94] The Moravians noted that he had red hair and that he seemed to be an "affable, honest, friendly man."[95] The evidence regarding Rutherford's origin is contradictory. According to Long, he

84. Prince Georges County Judgments (1731, 1732, 1738-40, 1747), Hall of Records, Annapolis, Md., vol. of 1739 judgments, p. 512.

85. Anson Deeds, book 1, p. 169.

86. Family data (King), in vol. 14 of the James King Hall Collection, Southern Historical Collection, University of North Carolina, Chapel Hill, N.C. (hereafter cited as James King Hall Collection).

87. *Ibid.*

88. *Ibid.*

89. *Ibid.*

90. N.C. Land Grants, VI, 170-71; Rowan Deeds, II, 288, IV, 534; Family data (King), in vol. 14 of James King Hall Collection. Robert King, probably a brother of Richard, was collector of taxes in Little Britain township, Lancaster County, in 1742. Commissioner's Minute Book, 1729-70, Office of County Commissioner, Lancaster, Pa., p. 58.

91. T. F. Chambers, *The Early Germans of New Jersey: Their History, Churches and Genealogies* (Dover, N.J.: Dover Printing Co., 1895), pp. 439-40. The name is consistently spelled "Lowrance" in Rowan records.

92. Chambers, *Early Germans,* pp. 439-40; Rowan Deeds, III, 315.

93. Chambers, *Early Germans,* pp. 439-40; Rowan Deeds, II, 199.

94. Minnie R. H. Long, *General Griffith Rutherford and Allied Families: Harsh, Graham, Cathey, Locke, Holeman, Johnson, Chambers* (Milwaukee, Wis.: Wisconsin Cuneo Press, 1942), p. 66.

95. *Ibid.*

moved southward from New Jersey,[96] but it is possible that he originated among the numerous Rutherfords of Chester and Lancaster counties.[97]

In 1757 John Braly (or Brawley) bought 596 acres on Reedy Fork Creek, a branch of Haw River.[98] He married Sarah, the daughter of Walter Carruth, in 1758 and settled with his cousin or brother Thomas Braly in the Irish settlement.[99] In 1762, John Braly was appointed registrar of deeds for Rowan County.[100] The Bralys probably migrated directly from Ireland to Carolina.[101]

On the tombstone of William Niblock in the Third Creek cemetery is inscribed the statement that he was a native of Scotland, migrated to Rowan County in 1750, and died in 1761. In 1754, Niblock bought 350 acres of land on Withrow's Creek from Humphrey Montgomery.[102] The name Niblock does not appear in the records of Maryland and the middle colonies; it is possible that this pioneer proceeded directly from Scotland to North Carolina.

John Knox may have migrated north and west from Somerset County, Maryland, or he may have removed from Colerain, Ireland, to Pennsylvania.[103] The name appears but seldom in the records. In either event, he settled on Third Creek (where his descendants still reside) in 1757 or 1758.[104] Henry Barkley (or

96. *Ibid.*, pp. 64-65.

97. Lancaster Common Pleas, vol. XII (1739-44); Lancaster Appearance Dockets, docket for 1747-48; tombstones in cemetery of Fagg's Manor Presbyterian Church.

98. Rowan Deeds, V, 183; III, 542.

99. Harold B. Carruth, *Carruth Family: Brief Background and Genealogical Data of Twenty Branches in America* (Ascutney, Vt.: 1952), p. 164; Rowan Deeds, IV, 533; Rowan Court Minutes, I, 135.

100. Rowan Court Minutes, I, 104.

101. *Ibid.,* I, 135.

102. Rowan Deeds, II, 79.

103. *Maryland Calendar of Wills,* V, 142; "Colonial Militia, 1740-1748," *Maryland Historical Magazine*, 56 vols. (Baltimore: published under authority of the Maryland Historical Society, 1906-61), VI, 48 (hereafter cited as "Colonial Militia"); *Records of Augusta County*, III, 123; Hattie S. Goodman, *The Knox Family, A Genealogical and Biographical Sketch of the Descendants of John Knox of Rowan County, North Carolina, and other Knoxes* (Richmond, Va.: Whittet and Shepperson, Printers and Publishers, 1905), pp. 30-31; Chester Tax Lists, tax list for 1753; tombstones of John Knox (1770-77) and Samuel Knox (1726-1808) in Lower Marsh Creek cemetery; Rowan Wills, A, 72. See also Worth S. Ray, *The Lost Tribes of Carolina* (Austin, Tex.: published by the author, 1947), p. 510.

104. Rowan Deeds, II, 328.

Bartley),[105] William Grant,[106] and Jacob Crawford[107] evidently originated in Philadelphia County, while Matthew Gillespie removed from Ireland to Neshaminy, Bucks County, in 1722.[108] The origin of William Crawford, who lived in the forks of Second Creek,[109] is not clear. It seems likely, however, that he was kin to either James[110] or Jacob.

John Witherspoon, from New Castle County, Delaware, bought a tract of land on Sill's Creek from James Andrews in 1762.[111] John Kilpatrick originated in Cecil County, Maryland.[112] David McDowell, probably a kinsman of the McDowells of Cecil County, purchased one hundred acres from Samuel Blyth (also on Sill's Creek) in 1760.[113] John Hickey, a wealthy merchant of Lunenburg County, Virginia, bought 434 acres from David Strain in 1754.[114] There is no evidence that Hickey actually lived in the Irish settlement.

John Smith may have emigrated from Nottingham township, Chester County. He died before 1763, and Francis Johnston and

105. Philadelphia County Court Papers, 1697-1749, 3 vols. (unpaginated), Historical Society of Pennsylvania, Philadelphia, II (1738) ; Rowan Deeds, I, 79.

106. Philadelphia Wills, 10 vols., in Collections of the Genealogical Society of Pennsylvania, Historical Society of Pennsylvania, Philadelphia, III, 1212 (hereafter cited as Philadelphia Wills) ; N.C. Land Grants VI, 151. Grant may have been in Carolina before 1750; his 640-acre grant was surveyed for him in November of that year. Rowan Deeds, III, 370. Grant's wife was Elizabeth, a daughter of Squire Boone. Hazel A. Spraker, *The Boone Family: A Genealogical History of the Descendants of George and Mary Boone, who came to America in 1717, Containing Many Unpublished Bits of Early Kentucky History, Also a Biographical Sketch of Daniel Boone, the Pioneer, By One of His Descendants* (Rutland, Vt.: Tuttle Co., 1922), p. 61.

107. Philadelphia Wills, III, 1235; "Records of Pennsylvania Marriages Prior to 1810," *Pennsylvania Archives*, Second Series, 19 vols., reprinted under direction of Secretary of Commonwealth, ed. John B. Linn and William H. Egle (Harrisburg: Clarence M. Busch, State Printer of Pennsylvania, 1896), VIII, 352; *Genealogical Data Relating to the German Settlers of Pennsylvania and Adjacent Territory from Advertisements in German Newspapers Published in Philadelphia and Germantown, 1743-1800,* comp. Edward W. Hocker (Germantown and Philadelphia, 1935), p. 35; Rowan Deeds, V, 231.

108. See p. 70 above.

109. Rowan Deeds, IV, 53.

110. See p. 105 above.

111. Kent County Deed Books, Office of Registrar of Deeds, Kent County Courthouse, Chestertown, Md., VII, 326; Delaware Land Records, Hall of Records, Dover, Del.: New Castle Reference W³ no. 73; will of John Witherspoon, New Castle County Wills (identified by means of a card index), Hall of Records, Dover, Del.; Rowan Deeds, IV, 762.

112. "Colonial Militia," p. 49; Cecil Deeds, X, 302; Rowan Deeds, IV, 802.

113. Rowan Deeds, IV, 381.

114. *Ibid.,* I, 117.

James Carson (both of whom originated in East Nottingham) acted as securities in the administration of his estate.[115] Smith's home was on a tract of land bought from Peter Arndt in 1757.[116]

Little is known of the origins of five additional pioneers in the Irish settlement. They include John Russell,[117] Robert Gray,[118] Alpheus Paine,[119] and James and Samuel Martin.[120]

115. Rowan Court Minutes, I, 104.

116. Rowan Deeds, II, 177.

117. Russell lived on Cold Water Creek next to Samuel Woods. N.C. Land Grants, VI, 232.

118. Gray bought 320 acres from Archibald Hamilton in 1758. Rowan Deeds, II, 296.

119. Paine acquired 320 acres from Henry White in 1758. Rowan Deeds, IV, 534.

120. It is not known whether these Martins (probably of Huguenot origin) were related. James settled on the Beaver Dam branch of the South Yadkin; Samuel on Withrow's Creek. N.C. Land Grants, VI, 189; Rowan Deeds, V, 158.

# XI

## *QUAKERS AND BAPTISTS ON THE NORTHWEST FRONTIER*

Although a majority of the settlers on the northwest Carolina frontier were Scotch-Irish Presbyterians or German Lutherans, a significant number were of English or Welsh origin and of Quaker or Baptist persuasion. The importance of this group on the frontier was considerable, for most of the sheriffs, clerks of the court, lawyers, and justices of the peace were of Quaker or Baptist origin.[1]

Among those of Quaker antecedents were Edward Hughes, William Linville, and the Whitaker, Bryan, and Boone families.[2] Though not conclusive, the evidence consulted in the pursuance of this study strongly suggests that John Frohock, Thomas Parker, Samuel Shinn, Abraham Cresson, Hugh Forster, Francis Fincher, Benjamin Winsley, Moses Andrew, James Lambert, Jonathan Potts, James Carter, John Parker, Nicholas Harford, George Forbush, Charles and Jacob Hunter, Robert Gamble, Edward Underhill, John and Benjamin Barton, Elias Brock, Jonathan Hunt, William and Edward Roberts, and the three Turners were also of Quaker derivation.[3]

John Eaton, William Reese, and David Jones were Baptists.[4] Either of Baptist or Quaker origin were James, Joseph, and Henry Jones; Evan Ellis; William Morgan; Patrick Logan; Caleb and Ephraim Osborne; Stephen Riddle; John and Silas Enyart; Jared Erwin; Henry Sloan; and members of the Feree, Davis, and Wilcockson families.[5]

1. See Appendices A through E.
2. See above, pp. 30-36, 78-79.
3. See Appendices B, C, and D.
4. Rowan County Will Books, Clerk's Office, Rowan County Courthouse, Salisbury, N.C., A, 33; tombstones in cemetery of Eaton's Baptist Church. See above, pp. 77, 81, 83, 100*n*.
5. Tombstones in Boone Burying Ground, in cemetery of Eaton's Baptist Church, and in churchyard at present-day "Tanglewood," near Clemmons, N.C. See also Appendix B.

A number of other settlers of English, Irish, and Welsh derivation represented a mixture of Quaker, Baptist, Anglican, and Catholic antecedents. They were John Dunn, Thomas Evans, John and Peter Dill, John and Jacob Thomas, John Gardiner, Hugh and William Montgomery, Richard Morbee, Daniel Little, John Ryle, John and David Hampton, Benjamin Rounsavill, Henry ₋and Elijah Skidmore, Peter Parsons, John McGuire, Martin Wallock, Richard Walton, Matthew Sparks, Solomon Sparks, Jonas Sparks, David and William Bailey, James Burk, Thomas Bashford, John Francis, James Williams, William Williams, Phillip Williams, John Harmon, Samuel Tate, Isaac Holdman, Hugh Matthews, Benjamin Thompson, James Coward, Archibald and James Craig, George Cusick, William Harrison, and the Howard family.[6]

There was no Anglican or Catholic church on the northwestern frontier prior to 1768,[7] indicating that the number of settlers of those beliefs was small. Indeed, in 1765 there were only six ministers of the Church of England settled in the entire colony.[8] There may have been a Quaker meetinghouse near shallow ford and another at the site of the "Boone graveyard," but no record has been found of either.[9]

Through the activities of Benjamin Miller, pastor of the General Baptist Church at Scotch Plains, New Jersey, and of John Gano, a pastor sent by the Charleston Association, a Baptist meetinghouse was established in 1754 or 1755 on Potts Creek three miles east of the trading ford.[10] Five or six years later, a

6. These names are not represented in the burying grounds of any of the Scotch-Irish Presbyterian Churches in Carolina; moreover (with the exception of Bailey, Craig, Gardiner, Little, Tate, and Thompson), none are characteristically Scottish names. Charles A. Hanna, *The Scotch-Irish, or the Scot in North Britain, North Ireland, and North America,* 2 vols. (New York: Knickerbocker Press, 1902), pp. 519-27.

7. Jethro Rumple, *A History of Rowan County, North Carolina, Containing Sketches of Prominent Families and Distinguished Men* (Salisbury, N.C.: Published by J. J. Bruner, 1881), p. 298. Rumple felt that the number of Anglicans in Rowan County in 1768 "amounted to at least one-fourth or one-third of the whole population." This is an overstatement, even though many persons of Quaker and Catholic origin adhered to the established church after reaching the Carolina frontier.

8. Hugh T. Lefler and Albert R. Newsome, *North Carolina: The History of a Southern State* (Chapel Hill: University of North Carolina Press, 1954), p. 123.

9. Although see p. 83 above.

10. George W. Paschal, *History of North Carolina Baptists* (Raleigh, N.C.: General Board, North Carolina Baptist State Convention, 1930), I (1663-1805), 265-68.

missionary church was organized by the Separate Baptists at the shallow ford.[11] It seems probable that many of the Quaker settlers, cut off from New Garden and Cane Creek by the Moravian settlement[12] and hundreds of miles from their Quaker origins, were absorbed into these Baptist congregations.

There seems little doubt that a majority of the earliest English and Welsh immigrants were of Quaker background. Why did these people move to the Carolina frontier? What were the factors influencing Quaker migration?

Members of the Society of Friends entered the middle colonies in two great migratory waves beginning in 1676.[13] The first, which lasted approximately thirty-five years, was caused chiefly by persecution following the restoration of Charles II.[14] A veritable flood for the first decade, it slackened after the Act of Toleration in 1683, and slowed to a mere trickle after the outbreak of the War of the League of Augsburg. The religious basis for this migration was to be found in the Acts of Uniformity, passed at the time of the Restoration.[15] Moreover, the Friends refused to pay tithes, and their refusal to take oaths in court often resulted in their being the victims of fraud and deprivation.[16]

The second Quaker migration, heaviest between 1714 and 1740,[17] occurred evidently for reasons that were chiefly economic. As early as 1660, George Fox suggested that land be purchased in America for use as a Quaker colony,[18] and the low rates at which land was offered in Pennsylvania after 1700 caused many Friends to act on Fox's suggestion. The Free Society of Traders, including many Quakers, bought twenty thousand acres of land in Pennsylvania to be developed. Robert Turner, an Irish Quaker

11. *Ibid.*, p. 299.

12. Lefler and Newsome, *North Carolina*, pp. 126, 130.

13. Albert C. Myers, *Immigration of the Irish Quakers into Pennsylvania, 1682-1750, With Their Early History in Ireland* (Swarthmore, Pa.: published by the author, 1902), p. 83.

14. Myers, *Irish Quakers*, p. 83. Rufus Jones, on the other hand, felt that the causes of Quaker emigration came from within the sect itself; from the desire "to show Quakerism at work, freed from hampering conditions." Rufus M. Jones, *Quakers in the American Colonies* (New York: Russell and Russell, Inc., 1962), pp. 357, 421.

15. Myers, *Irish Quakers*, pp. 42-44.

16. *Ibid.*

17. Myers, *Irish Quakers*, p. 83. Again, Jones held that "it was not commercialism which established them so firmly in the new country." Jones, *Quakers*, p. 371.

18. Myers, *Irish Quakers*, p. 50.

and one of a committee of twelve directing the Society's activities, went to Philadelphia with seventeen indentured servants as early as 1683.[19] Settlement of the interior, which began after 1714, accelerated these early activities, leading to the establishment of land companies and the organized planting of interior settlements. Among the prominent Quaker merchants and traders who financed and advertised these speculative enterprises were Hugh Parker of Pennsylvania and Maryland;[20] Edmund Cartledge, Alexander Ross, Edward Shippen, George Croghan, and Morgan Bryan, of Pennsylvania; and Benjamin Borden of New Jersey.

It must be noted that these men and their associates

were, after all, Quakers, members of a religious sect which preached a pure spiritual religion, aloofness from the world, human equality in the sight of God, and above all, simplicity. The demands of such a religion imposed severe strains on a prosperous and rising aristocracy; it created intolerable tensions which some of them escaped by leaving the Society of Friends and joining the more fashionable, less demanding Church of England. For those who remained under the discipline of the meeting there was always the necessity of working out a practical compromise between the absolute spiritual and ethical demands of their faith and the strong pull of the world in which—socially, economically, politically—they were inextricably involved.[21]

In 1739 Benjamin Borden, born near Freehold, Monmouth County, New Jersey, obtained 92,000 acres of land in that part of the Shenandoah Valley now embraced by Rockbridge County.[22]

19. *Ibid.,* pp. 51-53.

20. Though not conclusive, the evidence indicates that Parker was a Quaker. His nephews, Thomas Parker and John Frohock, originated in southeastern Bucks County before 1725. John Frohock signed as "Nearest of Friend" in the inventory of Parker's estate (1753). Maryland Inventories, Hall of Records, Annapolis, Md., LIV, 91-92. Morgan Bryan, a known Quaker, sold his tract on Opequon Creek to Hugh Parker. *Chronicles of the Scotch-Irish Settlements in Virginia, Extracted from the Original Court Records of Augusta County, 1745-1800,* 3 vols. (Rosslyn, Va.: Commonwealth Printing Co., 1912), II, 109 (hereafter cited as *Records of Augusta County*).

21. Frederick B. Tolles, *Quakers and the Atlantic Culture* (New York: MacMillan Co., 1960), p. 84.

22. Howard M. Wilson, *The Tinkling Spring, Headwater of Freedom: A Study of the Church and Her People* (Richmond, Va.: Garrett and Massie, Inc., 1954), p. 20; *Hopewell Friends History, 1734-1934, Frederick County, Virginia; Records of Hopewell Monthly Meetings and Meetings Reporting to Hopewell,* compiled from official records and published by a joint committee of Hopewell Friends assisted by John W. Wayland (Strasburg, Va.: Shenandoah Publishing House, Inc., 1936), p. 26.

Borden was undoubtedly a Quaker,[23] though he encouraged persons of all faiths to take up land on his great tract. His history provides a good example of the dilemma in which many Friends found themselves, for he was convicted by the Augusta County courts in 1747 of using false receipts for quit rents.[24] Such action was in direct violation of Quaker doctrine, for the Philadelphia Yearly Meeting had announced in 1724 that

... whereas, in this time of general ease and liberty, too many under our profession have launched forth into the things of this world, beyond their substance and capacity to discharge a good conscience in the performance of their promises and contracts . . . it is . . . our earnest desire that all Friends, everywhere, be very careful to avoid all inordinate pursuit after the things of this world, by such ways and means as depend too much upon . . . hazardous enterprises.[25]

Squire Boone and his sons departed from Pennsylvania upon being ejected from the Exeter Monthly Meeting for refusing to apologize publicly over the marriage of Israel Boone to a young woman of contrary faith.[26] Quaker doctrine was clear on the matter. The Philadelphia Yearly Meeting of 1694 advised Friends to

Take heed of giving your sons and daughters who are believers and profess and confess the truth, in marriage with unbelievers; for that was forbidden in *all* ages. . . . It is unbecoming those who profess the Truth to go from one woman to another, and keep company and sit together, especially in the night season, spending their time in idle discourse, and drawing the affections one of another many times when there is no reality in it.[27]

The internal discipline of the Society of Friends developed during the half-century prior to 1740, the so-called "Golden Age" of the Quakers in the colonies. Members such as the Boones were disowned for "marrying out," a procedure which is believed to have

23. See Appendix B.
24. *Records of Augusta County*, I, 34.
25. Ezra Michener, *A Retrospect of Early Quakerism: Being Extracts from the Records of Philadelphia Yearly Meeting and the Meetings Composing It To Which Is Prefixed an Account of Their First Establishment* (Philadelphia: T. Ellwood Zell, 1860), p. 265.
26. John J. Stoudt, "Daniel and Squire Boone," *The Historical Review of Berks County*, 27 vols. (Reading, Pa.: published quarterly by the Society, 1935-61), I (no. 4), 108.
27. Michener, *Early Quakerism*, p. 225.

caused immense losses in numbers and in the quality of members after 1740.[28]

By the middle of the eighteenth century, the number of Quaker Meetings had "increased from about forty-three to one-hundred, comprehending, it is believed, about thirty-thousand members."[29] This significant increase was caused by immigration from Europe, the natural increase of population among Friends in the colonies, and "the numerous convincements which took place."[30]

In Maryland, numerous Quaker Meetings existed by 1750. In April, 1739, a new meetinghouse was established on Swan Creek, near the head of the Sassafras River.[31] This was in addition to those already established in Cecil and Queen Annes counties.[32] The influence of Quaker migration into this region from England, Pennsylvania, and southern Maryland undoubtedly helped produce the religious unheaval which characterized the settlements at the "head of Chesapeake" by 1739.

Quakers and German Lutherans settled in the Monocacy Valley by 1729.[33] These Friends, mostly from Salem County, New Jersey, and the Nottingham region along the Chester-Cecil border, represented the first Quaker migration in America away from navigable waters.[34] The settlement organized by Morgan Bryan and Ross in the Opequon Creek region of the Shenandoah Valley followed in 1730. The Hopewell meetinghouse (1734) in this settlement is believed to represent the first organized congregation in the valley.[35]

In addition to the Quakers who settled in the Yadkin Valley after 1746, many migrated from Pennsylvania and New Jersey to the central part of North Carolina and settled after 1750 in the

28. Henry Van Etten, *George Fox and the Quakers,* trans. and rev. E. Kelvin Osborn (London: Longmans, Green and Co., 1959), p. 119.

29. James Bowden, *History of the Society of Friends in America,* 2 vols. (London: Charles Gilpin and W. & F. G. Cash, 1850-54), II, 245.

30. *Ibid.*

31. Minutes of the Cecil Monthly Meeting of Friends, 1698-1779, Friends Library, Swarthmore College, Swarthmore, Pa., p. 112.

32. *Ibid.*

33. A. B. Faust, *The German Element in the United States, With Special Reference to Its Political, Moral, Social, and Educational Influence,* 2 vols. (New York: Steuben Society of America, 1927), I, 167-68; Jones, *Quakers,* p. 296.

34. Jones, *Quakers,* p. 296.

35. Frederick B. Kegley, *Kegley's Virginia Frontier: The Beginning of the Southwest; The Roanoke of Colonial Days, 1740-1783* (Roanoke, Va.: Southwest Virginia Historical Society, 1938), pp. 33-34.

present counties of Guilford, Randolph, Alamance, and Chatham.[36] Cane Creek Monthly Meeting was organized in present-day Alamance County in 1751, and the New Garden Meeting three years later in what is now Guilford County.[37]

It is quite extraordinary that while two permanent Quaker Meetings were established east of the Yadkin by 1762, an equally large number of Friends living west of the river[38] failed to organize a single enduring congregation. The reasons are not clear, but it is known that many of the settlers west of the Yadkin, originally of Quaker persuasion, had ceased to be Friends in good standing. In addition to the Boones, James Carter apparently abandoned his Quaker heritage, for he informed the Moravians in 1754 that he was a member of the Church of England.[39] Abraham Cresson, originally from an old Philadelphia Quaker family, seems to have left the pale, for he became a Regulator in 1769.[40] It is evident that many, if not all, of the Bryans lost their Quaker identity; Samuel, one of the sons of Morgan Bryan, became an important Loyalist officer during the Revolution.[41]

Political expediency unquestionably played an important part in the abandonment of Quakerism by many frontier settlers. With the outbreak of the colonial wars in 1739, those sects advocating nonviolence and a lenient Indian policy became highly unpopular. Moreover, the Anglican Church was the established denomination in Virginia and Carolina, quite a different situation from that prevailing in the colonies from which the immigrants came. Consequently, the more prominent of the Quaker settlers, men such as Carter, Boone, Bryan, Frohock, Parker, Milner, Hughes, and possibly Forster may well have found it politically expedient to abandon Quakerism in order to qualify more readily for sheriff, clerk, justice of the peace, constable, tax collector, coroner, or some other lucrative public trust.

36. Lefler and Newsome, *North Carolina*, p. 126.
37. *Ibid.*
38. It is evident that between fifty and one hundred families of Quaker origin lived west of the Yadkin and north of the Granville Line by 1762. According to Jones, eighty-six Friends joined the New Garden Meeting (east of the river) during the period 1754-70. Assuming that one-half of these became members prior to 1763, and that an equal number joined the Cane Creek Meeting, the disparity in numbers east and west of the river cannot have been great. Jones, *Quakers,* p. 297.
39. *Records of the Moravians in North Carolina*, 7 vols., ed. Adelaide Fries (Raleigh, N.C.: Edwards and Broughton Printing Co., 1922-47), I, 126.
40. See p. 79*n* above.
41. Rumple, *Rowan County,* p. 136.

Whether for reasons of severe church discipline, distance from the heart of Quakerism, frontier conditions, the outbreak of war, political expediency, Baptist missionary activity, or unprecedented opportunities for pecuniary gain, it seems clear that the large majority of these settlers abandoned the Quaker faith either before they reached Carolina or very shortly thereafter. The local records are silent on the matter—but this very silence is in itself the strongest evidence that such was the case.

# XII

# THE SCOTCH-IRISH
# MIGRATION

The first distinctively Scotch-Irish settlement in America was established on the Eastern Shore of Maryland between 1649 and 1669.[1] In 1681 and 1682, five Presbyterian meeting houses were organized by Francis Makemie in Somerset and Calvert counties. They were Rehoboth, Manokin, Snow Hill, Wicomico, and Patuxent.[2] The significance of these congregations may be seen in the fact that only twelve Presbyterian Churches are known to have existed throughout the thirteen colonies prior to 1700.[3]

By 1695 the Scots were quite numerous in Dorchester and Somerset counties.[4] Ford's view was that these settlements were unimportant "as a stage in the Scotch-Irish occupation of America,"[5] but it has already been seen that the movement of people from this region was of enormous significance in the settlement of northwestern Carolina. George Scot, Laird of Pitlochie, wrote in 1685 that a friend living in Maryland had sent such an encouraging account of the country that many of his acquaintances were preparing to make the voyage to Baltimore's colony.[6]

Following these early developments, and continuing throughout the first half of the eighteenth century, thousands of Scots from northern Ireland engaged in a wholesale emigration to America, settling before 1730 chiefly in Cecil County, Maryland; New Castle County, Delaware; and Chester County, Pennsylvania. Smaller numbers made their homes in Sussex County,

1. Henry J. Ford, *The Scotch-Irish in America* (Princeton, N.J.: Princeton University Press, 1915), pp. 170-71.
2. Charles A. Hanna, *The Scotch-Irish, Or, the Scot in North Britain, North Ireland, and North America*, 2 vols. (New York: Knickerbocker Press, 1902), II, 14.
3. *Ibid.*
4. Ford, *Scotch-Irish*, pp. 180-81.
5. *Ibid.*, p. 181.
6. *Ibid.*, p. 177.

Detail of Pennsylvania

Presbyterian Congregations 1698-1730

* Early German Churchs

## PRESBYTERIAN CONGREGATIONS IN PENNSYLVANIA, 1698-1730

| Meeting House | Date Established |
|---|---|
| 1. New Castle | 1698 |
| 2. Philadelphia | 1698 |
| 3. Head of Christiana | before 1708 |
| 4. Norriton | 1714 |
| 5. Abington | 1714 |
| 6. Great Valley | 1714 |
| 7. Rock | 1720 |
| 8. Lower Brandywine | 1720 |
| 9. Lower Octoraro | 1720 |
| 10. Upper Octoraro | 1720 |
| 11. Donegal | 1721 |
| 12. White Clay Creek | 1721 |
| 13. Red Clay Creek | 1723 |
| 14. Pequea | 1724 |
| 15. Nottingham | 1725 |
| 16. Neshaminy | before 1726 |
| 17. Deep Run | 1726 |
| 18. Middle Octoraro | 1727 |
| 19. New London | 1728 |
| 20. Derry | 1729 |
| 21. Paxtang | 1729 |
| 22. Faggs Manor | 1730 |
| 23. Little Britain | 1730 |
| 24. Chesnut Level | 1730 |
| 25. Plumstead | 1730 |

## LUTHERAN AND GERMAN REFORMED CHURCHES IN PENNSYLVANIA, 1748

Lutheran (four earliest)

26—New Hanover
27—Philadelphia
28—Trappe
29—Skippack

Reformed

30—Philadelphia
31—New Goshenhoppen
32—Falckner Swamp
33—Bern
34—Cacusi
35—Dunkel
36—Tulpehocken
37—Muddy Creek
38—New Providence
39—Seltenreich
40—Lancaster
41—Quittopahilla
42—Millbach
43—Egypt
44—Great Swamp
45—Tohickon

Delaware, and Kent County, Maryland. A few may have settled
in the New Jersey counties of Hunterdon, Somerset, Union,
Middlesex, and Monmouth.[7]

The fundamental causes of this movement were economic.
Repressive trade laws, rack-renting landlordism, famine, and the
decline of the linen industry were major factors in stimulating the
overseas movement of these Ulster Scots.[8] The manufacture of
woolens, northern Ireland's staple industry, was restricted in 1699
by the passage of an act forbidding the exportation of Irish
woolen goods to any part of the world except England. This act
deprived the Ulsterites of their foreign markets.

Between 1720 and 1728 thirteen Scotch-Irish churches were
established in Pennsylvania and in New Castle County, Delaware.
The first of these was the so-called Rock Church, organized in
1720 one mile from present-day Lewisville, Maryland, on the
Pennsylvania border.[9] James Logan, Secretary of the Province
of Pennsylvania, stated in 1727 that the Scotch-Irish immigrants
settled generally near the Maryland border.[10] According to Proud,
such was the volume of immigration that an estimated six thousand Scotch-Irish landed in New Castle or Philadelphia in 1729
alone.[11]

Gradually the Pennsylvania-Maryland frontier was pushed
westward toward the foothills of the Alleghenies. By 1729 a
sufficient number of pioneers had settled in the Susquehanna
Valley to warrant the creation of Lancaster County. Six ad-

7. Both Ford and Leyburn doubt the presence of large numbers of Scotch-
Irish in New Jersey before 1740. Ford, *Scotch-Irish*, pp. 250-51; James G.
Leyburn, *The Scotch-Irish, A Social History* (Chapel Hill: University of
North Carolina Press, 1962), p. 245. As has been seen, however, John Nisbet,
Alexander Osborne, John Oliphant, and possibly Henry Sloan originated in
Jersey. Other Jersey families of significance to this study included those of
Andrew and John Craig, John Gardiner, David Hampton, Thomas and William
McElwrath, William Davidson, Robert and James Harris, Margaret (Kerr)
Barclay (wife of Richard King), and James Chambers. These families may
have been Scottish—or they may have been Scotch-Irish.

8. Ford, *Scotch-Irish*, pp. 163-64, 167-68, 182-83; Hugh T. Lefler and Albert
R. Newsome, *North Carolina: The History of a Southern State* (Chapel Hill:
University of North Carolina Press, 1954), p. 75.

9. Ford, *Scotch-Irish*, pp. 262-63; Hanna, *Scotch-Irish*, II, 60-62.

10. Ford, *Scotch-Irish*, p. 264.

11. J. Smith Futhey, "The Scotch-Irish," *Papers and Addresses of the Lancaster County Historical Society*, 65 vols. (Lancaster, Pa., 1897-1961), XI,
227. This estimate is undoubtedly too high. No records of the debarkation of
Scotch-Irish immigrants exist, but the size of the Centre and Thyatira congregations in Carolina indicates that each of the twenty-five Pennsylvania churches
had two or three hundred adult members.

ditional Presbyterian meetinghouses were then established in Lancaster, Chester, and Bucks counties; they included Faggs Manor, Little Britain, Chesnut Level, Plumstead, Derry, and Paxtang.

Scotch-Irish settlers began moving west of the Susquehanna as early as 1721,[12] but were ordered to leave by the proprietary government because the Indian title had not been extinguished.[13] One of the first permanent settlers west of the Susquehanna was James Silver, whose home was located on Conodoguinet Creek in the Cumberland Valley eight miles west of Harris' Ferry. Silver built a house and grist mill in 1724 and received a Blunston license ten years later.[14] The existence of the grist mill indicates the presence of other settlers in the Cumberland Valley by 1724.

Of the 250 persons who obtained licenses from Samuel Blunston in 1734 and 1735, at least 50 are of significance to this study.[15] They include John Beard, whose land was on Conococheague Creek adjoining John Harris; James Barry; William Blythe (north side, "the waggon road"); Francis Beatty (north side, Yellow Breeches Creek); Samuel, Randle, George, Rowland, Robert, and Benjamin Chambers; James Cathey (south side, Conodoguinet Creek); William Cathey (land "now owned by George Cathey" on north side, Conodoguinet); Alexander Cathey (north side, Conodoguinet); Archibald Cathey (north side, Conodoguinet, near John Cathey and adjoining James Woods); James Clark (adjoining Samuel Given); James Crawford (north side, Yellow Breeches); Isaac Davenport (on Conodoguinet, two miles west of John Lawrence); John Davidson ("where he is already settled on Letort's Spring"); William Davison; William Docharty (adjoining Alexander Cathey and James Forster); Patrick Docharty (one mile southeast of John Potts); Robert Edmiston (adjoining Thomas Wilson); William Fullerton (next above William Hall); Francis Graham; John Hunter (head of

---

12. George P. Donehoo, *A History of the Cumberland Valley in Pennsylvania,* 2 vols. (Harrisburg: Susquehanna History Association, 1930), I, 39.

13. *Ibid.*

14. A. Boyd Hamilton, "When was the Kittatinny or Cumberland Valley Settled?" *Notes and Queries, Historical, Biographical, and Genealogical, Relating Chiefly to Interior Pennsylvania,* 3 ser. (12 vol.), ed. William H. Egle (Harrisburg: Harrisburg Publishing Co. [reprinted from *Harrisburg Daily Telegraph,* 1878-1901]), ser. 1-2, vol. III, p. 157; The Blunston Licenses, 1734-35, Land Office, Capitol Building, Harrisburg, Pa., p. 16 (hereafter cited as Blunston Licenses).

15. Blunston Licenses, 30 pages.

Conodoguinet); David Houston (adjoining John Black); John
Jones (northwest side Conodoguinet); Hans Kaighe *(sic)*
(Codorus Creek, where Thomas Linvie [Linville?] formerly
lived); Francis, William, and John Lawson; William Little; John
McKown; John and Morgan Morgan (Yellow Breeches); James
Martin; Archibald McAlister (adjoining Patrick Campbell);
William McDowell (northwest branch, Conococheague); John
McWhorter (north side, Yellow Breeches, first granted to John
Rankin); John Parker; James, John, Thomas and William Pat-
ton; James Patterson and son James; John, James, and Robert
Rutherford; James Rankin; William Ralston (south side, Conodo-
guinet, adjoining the widow Jack); William Robinson (north side,
Yellow Breeches); James Todd; John Wilson; and the Reverend
John Thompson (Conodoguinet).

Between 1734 and 1740, six Presbyterian churches were
established in the Cumberland Valley.[16] The date and location of
each clearly reflects the advance of the Scotch-Irish southward
toward the Potomac and the "back parts" of Prince Georges
County, Maryland. Silver's Spring was organized in 1734, followed by Meeting House Spring in 1734 or 1735, Big Spring in
1735 or 1737, East Conococheague (or Rocky Spring) in 1739,
Falling Spring in 1739, Mercersburg in 1738 or 1739, and Upper
and Lower Marsh Creek in 1740.

It should be noted that the records of the Presbyterian settlements in the Cumberland Valley are exceeding meagre. In at-
tempting an explanation of this unfortunate situation, one authority has concluded that the Scotch-Irish were somehow conscious
of not having found there an enduring home.[17] It was his feeling
that this attitude accounts for the indifference of the pioneers in
Pennsylvania toward the preservation of records. In 1751, the
Cumberland Valley contained a predominately Scotch-Irish population; by 1820 only one-third of the taxables were of that stock.[18]

Between 1730 and 1734 the Scotch-Irish, led by the Kerr and
Lewis families, began moving southward from the Cumberland

16. Hanna, *Scotch-Irish,* II, 103-4; Alfred Nevin, *Churches of the Valley:
Or, an Historical Sketch of the Old Presbyterian Congregations of Cumberland
and Franklin Counties, in Pennsylvania* (Philadelphia: Joseph M. Wilson,
1852), p. 25.
17. John Stewart, "Scotch-Irish Occupancy and Exodus," *Papers Read
Before the Kittochtinny Historical Society,* 10 vols. (Chambersburg, Pa.:
various publishers, 1900-22), II, 17-23.
18. *Ibid.*

and upper Potomac valleys into the Shenandoah region.[19] The fertile valleys of western Virginia extended generally from northeast to southwest, thereby lending geographical encouragement to an extension of the southward movement. Moreover, land costs in Virginia were considerably less than in Pennsylvania.[20]

William Beverley, a wealthy planter-merchant of Essex County, Virginia, saw an opportunity to profit from the influx of new settlers. Accordingly, he entered into an agreement with John and Ralph Randolph and John Robinson, and acquired 118,000 acres of land "on the River Sherando called the Manor of Beverley," upon an order of Council dated August 12, 1736.[21] Robinson and the two Randolphs subsequently released their interest to Beverley, who proceeded to sell the "manor" to new settlers in small tracts of varying size.[22] In 1739, Benjamin Borden acquired his tract of nearly 100,000 acres, thereby creating a combined speculative venture of 200,000 acres, extending southward from Augusta Church to a point near modern Lexington. The Beverley and Borden patents acted as a spur to the southward migration of the Scotch-Irish. The valley of Virginia filled rapidly after 1736, leading in turn to settlement of the northwest Carolina frontier.

Why did the Scotch-Irish leave Pennsylvania? What caused the establishment of a steady succession of Presbyterian Churches from New Castle westward and southward into Virginia? Most of the reasons were considered in the discussion of general causes for migration, but one additional cause peculiarly applicable to the Scotch-Irish deserves mention.

Pennsylvania was established by English Quakers in 1681. In 1715, the Friends represented the largest single element in the population and controlled the political and economic life of the colony.[23] By 1740 this was no longer true. The Quakers continued to dominate the colony—but were outnumbered by both

19. Howard M. Wilson, *The Tinkling Spring, Headwater of Freedom: A Study of the Church and Her People* (Richmond, Va.: Garrett and Massie, Inc., 1954), pp. 7-14.

20. Wayland F. Dunaway, *The Scotch-Irish of Colonial Pennsylvania* (Chapel Hill: University of North Carolina Press, 1944), pp. 28-29, 51.

21. Wilson, *Tinkling Spring*, p. 16.

22. *Ibid.*, pp. 16-17, 417-19.

23. Jones estimated that the Quakers comprised approximately one-half the population of Pennsylvania in 1702. Rufus M. Jones, *Quakers in the American Colonies* (New York: Russell and Russell, Inc., 1962), p. 522.

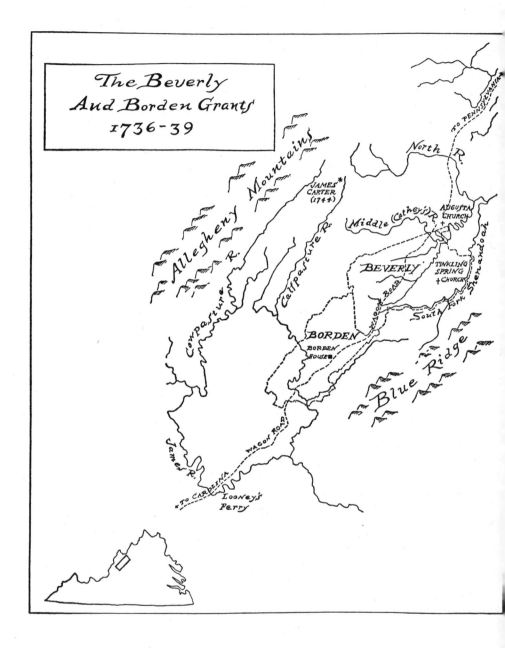

The Beverly
And Borden Grants
1736-39

Allegheny Mountains

Cowpasture R.

Calfpasture R.

JAMES
CARTER
(1744)

Middle (Cathey's) R.

North R.

TO PENNSYLVANIA

AUGUSTA
CHURCH

BEVERLY

WAGON ROAD

TINKLING
SPRING
+ CHURCH

South Fork

Shenandoah

Blue Ridge

BORDEN

BORDEN
HOUSE

James R.

WAGON ROAD

TO CAROLINA

LOONEY'S
Ferry

the Germans and Scotch-Irish.[24] Political difficulties inevitably ensued.

In 1732, in Lancaster County, Andrew Galbraith (the Scotch-Irish candidate) opposed John Wright (Quaker) in a contest for a seat in the Assembly.[25] Wright won, and there were no repercussions. In 1743, however, the Scotch-Irish forced the county sheriff to approve only those tickets acceptable to them and to make a return accordingly. The Assembly warned the sheriff, who thereupon altered the returns and permitted Samuel Blunston to take the vacant seat.[26]

Also in 1743 Richard Peters, Secretary of the Province, proceeded to the Marsh Creek settlement in an attempt to conduct surveys and dispossess the squattors. "About seventy" of the inhabitants assembled and forbade them to proceed. These persons were subsequently indicted, subdued, and forced to obtain leases.[27]

The Quaker government encouraged the Scotch-Irish to move to the frontier in order to provide a buffer against possible French and Indian hostility. Also, such a policy placed the newcomers as far as possible from the centers of political authority. The Quakers were determined to maintain control, and there can be little doubt that their efforts to do so were an important cause of Scotch-Irish emigration from Pennsylvania.

24. Benjamin Franklin estimated the population of Pennsylvania in 1766 at 160,000, of which one-third were Quakers. Jones felt this was too high a figure, fixing the probable number of Quakers in 1775 at 25,000. Jones, *Quakers*, p. 524. Schlatter estimated the number of communicants in the sixteen Reformed churches in 1746 at 15,000. Addition of the four Lutheran congregations and communicants of miscellaneous sects produces the conclusion that the Germans outnumbered the Quakers. A. B. Faust, *The German Element in the United States, with Special Reference to Its Political, Moral, Social, and Educational Influence*, 2 vols. (New York: Steuben Society of America, 1927), I, 122-23. It has already been noted that there were twenty-five Presbyterian churches in 1730, each ministering to perhaps 300 adults or 1,000 persons.

25. Daniel I. Rupp, *The History and Topography of Dauphin, Cumberland, Franklin, Bedford, Adams, and Perry Counties: Containing a Brief History of the First Settlers, Notices of the Leading Events, Incidents and Interesting Facts, Both General and Local, in the History of these Counties, General and Statistical Descriptions of All the Principal Boroughs, Towns, Villages, etc.* (Lancaster, Pa.: Gilbert Hills, Proprietor and Publisher, 1846), p. 55.

26. *Ibid.*

27. *Ibid.*, p. 54.

# XIII

# *THE GERMAN MIGRATION*

Beginning in 1690 and continuing throughout the first half of the eighteenth century large numbers of Germans emigrated from the Rhenish Palatine and other areas of the Rhine Valley. Destructive wars, religious persecutions, and extravagant accounts of the promised land of America (widely circulated by agents of ship companies and firms speculating in colonization schemes) encouraged thousands of Rhinelanders to cross the Atlantic.[1]

The War of the League of Augsburg (1689-97) and the War of the Spanish Succession (1702-14) provided the principal reason for this migration. The winter of 1688-89 was exceedingly severe in Europe, and it was during that winter that the Rhenish cities of Mannheim, Heidelberg, Worms, and Speyer were destroyed or damaged by the contending armies. Nearly five hundred thousand Germans were driven from their homes into the snow.[2]

In 1707, the struggle over succession to the Spanish throne brought new destruction to the left bank of the Rhine. Once again countless numbers were rendered homeless, providing impetus for mass emigration involving thousands of Rhinelanders.[3]

Chiefly through the efforts of William Penn and the Quakers, the migration of these people was directed toward Pennsylvania. Penn himself was half Dutch, his mother having been a native of Holland, and he made a number of preaching expeditions to that country and to Germany.[4] George Fox, the founder of the

1. Carl Hammer, *Rhinelanders on the Yadkin: The Story of the Pennsylvania Germans in Rowan and Cabarrus* (Salisbury, N.C.: Rowan Printing Co., 1947), p. 22.

2. *Ibid.*, pp. 14-15.

3. *Ibid.*

4. Sydney George Fisher, *The Making of Pennsylvania: An Analysis of the Elements of the Population and the Formative Influences that Created One of the Greatest of the American States* (Philadelphia: J. B. Lippincott Co., 1909), p. 91.

Society of Friends, had also been to Germany, and large numbers of the early emigrants from western Germany were not only encouraged by the Quakers but also partially financed by them.

Benjamin Furly, an Englishman by birth, became Penn's chief continental agent for the sale of his lands. To encourage settlement of Pennsylvania, Furly caused to be printed a German and Dutch translation of an English pamphlet entitled "Some Account of the Province of Pennsylvania in America" (London, 1681).[5] This was followed by "A Description of the New Found Province of Pennsylvania in America" (Hamburg, 1694). As a result of this advertising campaign, thirteen German families from Krefeld sailed for Philadelphia in 1683.[6]

During the next twenty years, German immigration was slight. It has been estimated that only two hundred settlers and their families arrived during this period, most of whom located at Germantown.[7] After 1702, however, the flow of immigration greatly increased. The new arrivals pushed into the country west of Philadelphia, leaving the Quakers in undisturbed possession of that city.[8]

Adding to the rapid accumulation of Germans in Pennsylvania was a substantial group from the Hudson Valley of New York. These Palatines, brought into New York in 1708 to provide labor for an ill-fated naval stores industry, traveled down the Susquehanna at the invitation of Pennsylvania's Governor Keith and settled in northern Philadelphia County between 1723 and 1728.[9]

By the middle of the eighteenth century, as a result of the simultaneous growth of the English, Scotch-Irish, and German population, desirable land had become quite scarce in Pennsylvania, and the cost of farm land rose prohibitively. By 1750, according to Gehrke, the number of Germans in Penn's colony reached seventy or eighty thousand, nearly one-half of the total population.[10] In 1752, Michael Schlatter, a leader in the Reformed

5. Julius F. Sachse, "Benjamin Furly," *The Pennsylvania Magazine of History and Biography*, 85 vols. (Philadelphia: publication fund of the Historical Society of Pennsylvania, 1877-1961), XIX, 286-87.

6. *Ibid.*

7. Fisher, *Making of Pennsylvania*, p. 91.

8. *Ibid.* Rufus Jones, however, was of the opinion that two-thirds of Philadelphia's population in 1702 was *not* Quaker. Rufus M. Jones, *Quakers in the American Colonies* (New York: Russell and Russell, Inc., 1962), p. 522.

9. Hammer, *Rhinelanders*, p. 19.

10. William H. Gehrke, "The German Element in Rowan and Cabarrus Counties" (unpublished master's thesis, University of North Carolina, 1934),

Church, estimated the German population of Pennsylvania at ninety thousand.[11]

The three chief denominations among the Pennsylvania Germans were the Lutherans, led by Henrich Melchior Mühlenberg; the German Reformed, led by Michael Schlatter; and the United Brethren (or Moravians), under the leadership of Nicholas, Count Zinzendorff.[12]

As the Lutherans had a great leader in Mühlenberg, so the German Reformed congregations found an organizer in Michael Schlatter. Most of the Palatines probably belonged to the German Reformed Church, which was akin to the Lutheran, but followed reforms instituted by Calvin and Zwingli. They were very close in their religious doctrines to the Presbyterians.[13]

When Schlatter arrived in September, 1746, he found only four preachers of the Reformed Church in Pennsylvania, while the number of communicants was approximately fifteen thousand.[14]

Between 1725 and 1734, Reformed Churches were established in Philadelphia, Lancaster, and upper Bucks counties.[15] By 1748, the congregations in Philadelphia and Berks counties included Philadelphia, New Goshenhoppen, Falckner Swamp (New Hanover), Bern, Cacusi, Dunkel's, and Tulpehocken.[16] In Lancaster County were Muddy Creek (East Cocalico Township), New Providence (Strasburg Township), Seltenreich, Lancaster, Quittopahilla, and Millbach (the last two in present-day Lebanon County).[17] In northern Bucks County were Egypt, Great Swamp, and Tohickon.[18]

---

p. 8. Gehrke's estimate is probably too high, particularly in view of the fact that in 1740 there was a larger number of Scotch-Irish congregations than German.

11. Hammer, *Rhinelanders*, p. 23. This estimate is excessive. See above, p. 145n.

12. Hammer, *Rhinelanders*, p. 22.

13. A. B. Faust, *The German Element in the United States, With Special Reference to Its Political, Moral, Social and Educational Influence*, 2 vols. (New York: Steuben Society of America, 1927), I, 122-23.

14. See above, p. 145n.

15. William J. Hinke, "Reformed Church Records of Eastern Pennsylvania Arranged Chronologically and According to Counties," *Publications of the Genealogical Society of Pennsylvania*, 22 vols. (Philadelphia: Edward Stern and Co. [and other publishers], 1895-1961), XIII, (nos. 1-2), 90-92.

16. *Ibid.*

17. *Ibid.*

18. *Ibid.*

The earliest Lutheran settlements were established before 1730 at New Hanover (near Germantown), Philadelphia, and Trappe (New Providence).[19] The Moravians under Zinzendorf reached Pennsylvania in 1738 and 1739, settling chiefly in the Lehigh Valley of northern Bucks County.[20] There were an estimated one thousand Moravians in Pennsylvania by 1762.[21]

In New Jersey, the earliest German settlements occurred in 1714, principally located in present-day Hunterdon, Somerset, Morris, Bergen, and Essex counties.[22] Approximately three hundred different German names existed in Jersey by 1762.[23]

There were few Germans in Maryland before 1725.[24] The most important settlement in that colony was established in the Monocacy Valley, where an estimated one hundred fifty taxables made up the settlement in 1747.[25] The southwestern corner of Pennsylvania's York County was included in this colony. Many of these Monocacy Valley settlers landed at Baltimore between 1725 and 1735, while others reached the area by traveling along an Indian trail extending from Wright's Ferry on the Susquehanna to the Monocacy near the point where it crosses the Maryland-Pennsylvania border.[26] This trail followed the Monocacy River for a time, then went westward through South Mountain at Crampton's Gap and continued on to the Potomac. The first group of these German pioneers settled near present-day Creagerstown.

Fifty-two licenses were issued between 1733 and 1736 to settlers desiring to take up land west of the Susquehanna along Codorus Creek. Most of these pioneers were Germans.[27]

As early as 1732, Jost Hite (Heit) of Monocacy entered the Shenandoah Valley and realized that the way was open for German expansion southward.[28] By 1735, he had established a prosperous German settlement on Opequon Creek near the Bryan

19. Faust, *German Element*, I, 116.
20. *Ibid.*, I, 125-26. Spangenberg replaced Zinzendorf in 1743.
21. *Ibid.*
22. *Ibid.*, I, 152.
23. *Ibid.*
24. *Ibid.*, I, 163.
25. Dieter Cunz, *The Maryland Germans, A History* (Princeton, N.J.: Princeton University Press, 1948), p. 67.
26. Faust, *German Element*, I, 167-68.
27. Cunz, *Maryland Germans*, p. 49.
28. Faust, *German Element*, I, 188-91.

Quaker colony.[29] At the same time, more than fifty German families were settled on nine plantations in the southeastern part of present-day Rockingham County, Virginia.[30] Winchester had German inhabitants as early as 1738; Woodstock by 1740.[31]

By 1750, favorable reports reached the Germans regarding the fertility and cheapness of land in the Granville district of North Carolina (already being populated by Scotch-Irish from the Shenandoah Valley). The successful Moravian settlement at Wachovia in 1753 greatly encouraged the southward movement of other Germans living in Maryland, Virginia, and Pennsylvania. Many Germans moved to Carolina after 1750, and the southward movement "came into full swing" by the time Spangenberg's United Brethren unloaded their wagons at Bethabara.[32]

Most of the German settlers in the forks of the Yadkin and along Second Creek in Rowan County originated, as has been described, in Pennsylvania. They were members of the Lutheran and Reformed churches, but their number was insufficient to erect a meetinghouse for the sole use of either denomination.[33] Although evidence is lacking, they are believed to have built a temporary church on Jacob Volenweider's land for the use of both groups. It was known as the "hickory church" and subsequently crumbled into ruin.[34]

There seems little doubt that the fundamental cause of German migration to the Carolina frontier was the increasing scarcity of desirable land in Pennsylvania.[35] One has but to travel across the central part of Lancaster County to realize that the German settlers, who entered Pennsylvania in large numbers a decade before the Scotch-Irish immigration, acquired most of the fertile land in the county. The land in Donegal and Drumore is far less desirable.

These facts assume great importance in the light of the physical characteristics of Rowan County, for the evidence in this

29. *Ibid.*, I, 190-91.
30. *Ibid.*, I, 188-89.
31. *Ibid.*, I, 192.
32. Hammer, *Rhinelanders*, p. 26.
33. G. D. Bernheim, *History of the German Settlements and of the Lutheran Church in North and South Carolina, From the Earliest Period of the Colonization of the Dutch, German and Swiss Settlers to the Close of the First Half of the Present Century* (Philadelphia: Lutheran Book Store, 1872), p. 244.
34. *Ibid.*
35. Hammer, *Rhinelanders*, p. 25.

respect provides a further indication that the Scotch-Irish were living in the region in considerable numbers prior to the arrival of the Germans. A type of soil known as Cecil clay, which is heavily concentrated in the well-watered region settled by the early Scots, is one of the strongest soils of the county. It is especially well-suited to the production of corn, wheat, oats, rye, clover, and grasses—the chief crops of the first settlers. It is highly productive and has a higher average value per acre than any other soil in the county.[36] On the other hand, the land in southeastern Rowan consists largely of Iredell, Alamance, or Appling loam. Though suitable for the raising of grain, this soil is considerably less productive than Cecil clay.[37] Gehrke, Fisher, and Hammer have written convincingly regarding the agricultural efficiency of the German pioneers. It is inconceivable that the Germans would have settled in the southeast had the clay soil been available. It is noteworthy, too, that virtually all of the creeks in the county have English rather than German names. This evidence added to that revealed by the court records warrants the conclusion that the Scotch-Irish were the first settlers in what is today Rowan County. Although a few Germans were among the first settlers, it seems clear that general Teutonic immigration did not begin until after 1752.

36. R. B. Hardison and R. C. Jurney, *Soil Survey of Rowan County, North Carolina* (Washington, D.C.: Government Printing Office, 1915), pp. 23-25, 47.
37. *Ibid.*, pp. 27-33.

# XIV

## *ESTABLISHMENT OF SALISBURY*

I n 1753, because of the influx of settlers, the northern portion of Anson was formed into Rowan County (named for Matthew Rowan, who became acting governor in 1753).[1] The eastern boundary of Rowan extended from where the Anson County line bisected Granville's line north to the Virginia border. There was no limit to its westward extent.

It is not known where the first court in Rowan County was held, but it probably met in a private home or in some convenient ordinary. During the spring term of the court in 1753, the county justices adjourned to the house of James Alexander.[2] On other occasions in 1753 the court convened at the house of Peter Arndt,[3] at the home of George Cathey,[4] and probably at that of Edward Cusick. The court minutes for September, 1753, stated that "Peter Aaron petitioned this court for a license to keep public house at his plantation where he now lives" and that "Edward Cusick petitioned this court for a license to keep public house at the court house."[5] Both requests were granted. Cusick's petition is curious because no courthouse, as such, had yet been built.

In the spring of 1753, the court set in motion the machinery

1. David Leroy Corbitt, *The Formation of the North Carolina Counties, 1663-1943* (Raleigh, N.C.: State Department of Archives and History, 1950), pp. 8-9.

2. Jethro Rumple, *A History of Rowan County, North Carolina, Containing Sketches of Prominent Families and Distinguished Men* (Salisbury, N.C.: J. J. Bruner, 1881), p. 61.

3. *Ibid.*

4. On September 21, 1753, it was ordered that "next court be held at Mr. George Catheys." Minutes of Rowan County Court of Pleas and Quarterly Sessions, 1753-1869, typed copy in 3 vols. (part of the original manuscript, torn, faded and very difficult to read is in the State Department of Archives and History, Raleigh, N.C.), Salisbury Public Library, Salisbury, N.C., I, 7 (hereafter cited as Rowan Court Minutes).

5. *Ibid.*, I, 6.

for administering the county. A courthouse was authorized, and was described as follows:

. . . the dimension of the court be 30 feet long and [torn] and a story and a half ["half" is scratched out] high with two floors framed . . . shingles of pine . . . with one good window [torn] of five lights of 8"/10" and one do. in each side [torn] ten foot from the end of the court house with a door in the end opposite to the bench on oval bar with banisters and bench three feet above the floor a table and proper bars for the attorneys the said house to be enclosed with proper doors and window shutters and a seat for the clerk under the bench.[6]

Construction of a sturdy prison was also ordered, its dimensions to be

18 feet long/14 foot wide and seven foot between floor and floor with a partition of logs, all the logs 10 inches thick for the whole work: roof of three foot shingles of feather edge and each corner to be lined 2 foot within and without with plank of 2 inch thick well pined and also two foot from the doors of 2 inch thick with sufficient number of spikes and substantial hinges and lock and iron grates of inch square in the windows and cross bars and staples for the doors. . . . ordered that a pair of good stocks be erected.[7]

The court also ordered that a tax of four shillings and one penny half-penny proclamation money[8] be levied on each taxable[9] in the county "for the defraying the public charges of the province and also debts due from this county and public buildings, etc."[10]

6. *Ibid.*, I, 3.

7. *Ibid.*

8. Proclamation money was "coin valued according to a proclamation of Queen Anne (1704) by which the various colonial evaluations of the Spanish pieces of eight were fixed at six shillings sterling." This attempt to unify the silver currency in the colonies failed. In March, 1754, every four-shillings proclamation bill was valued at three shillings sterling. *The Dictionary of American History*, 5 vols., 2nd ed., rev., ed. James Truslow Adams (New York: Charles Scribner's Sons, 1940), IV, 353; *The Colonial Records of North Carolina*, 10 vols., ed. William H. Saunders (Raleigh, N.C.: Printers to the State, 1886-90), V, xliv (hereafter cited as *NCCR*).

9. By an Act of Assembly in 1749, taxables were described as all white males over sixteen, all Negroes and mulattoes over twelve, and all white persons over twelve who intermarried with Negroes. *The State Records of North Carolina* (XI through XXVI), collected and edited by Walter Clark (Winston, N.C.: M. I. and J. C. Stewart, Printers to the State, 1895-96; Goldsboro, N.C.: Nash Brothers, Book and Job Printers, 1898-1905), XXIII, 345 (hereafter cited as *NCSR*).

10. Rowan Court Minutes, I, 8.

The first clerk of the court was John Dunn, who was appointed in 1753 and held the office for two years.[11] On March 20, 1754, Dunn was designated "keeper of the standard" of weights and measures, and was appointed commissioner to procure "the stamps and marks of the weights and measures."[12]

In the fall of 1753, the court authorized the purchase of a large number of books at county expense. These included William Nelson's *The Office and Authority of a Justice of the Peace* (third edition, 1745); John Godolphin's *The Orphan's Legacy, Or a Testamentary Abridgment* (including sections of wills, executors, and legacies, fourth edition, 1701); Giles Jacob's *New Law Dictionary* (1729); and Cary's *Abridgment of the Statues.*[13] James Carter was appointed commissioner to make the purchase. On March 21, 1754, the first step in the establishment of a town was taken when the court made the announcement that "James Carter, Esquire, his lordship's deputy-surveyor, produced a warrant for six hundred and forty acres of land for the use of the inhabitants of this county & c. and for the use of the prison courthouse and stocks & c. of said county by which warrant it appears he paid the sum of £1:6:8."[14] Six acres of ground were to be set aside as the "prison bounds" of the county and were to include the spot selected for building the courthouse.[15]

On February 11, 1755, the town of Salisbury was formally created when William Churton and Richard Vigers, agents for Lord Granville, made the following grant to James Carter and Hugh Forster,[16] trustees:

11. Rowan County Deed Books, Office of Registrar of Deeds, Rowan County Courthouse, Salisbury, N.C., I, 74; II, 303 (hereafter cited as Rowan Deeds).

12. By an Act of Assembly of 1741, the following standards were established for weights and measures: weights—hundreds, half-hundreds, quarter-hundreds, eighth-hundreds, seven pounds, four pounds, two pounds, one pound, one-half pound; measures—ell (cloth measure of forty-five inches), yard, one-half bushel, peck, gallon, quart, pint. A metal stamp, marked "N.C.," was authorized for use on weights of brass, tin, iron, lead, or pewter. A branding iron, with the letters "N.C.," was required for use on wood measures. *NCSR,* XXIII, 178; Rowan Court Minutes, I, 10.

13. Rowan Court Minutes, I, 8; *The Dictionary of National Biography,* 30 vols., ed. Sir Leslie Stephen and Sir Sidney Lee (London: Oxford University Press, 1937-38), VIII, 41, X, 553, XIV, 215.

14. Rowan Court Minutes, I, 11.

15. *Ibid.*

16. Hugh Forster was mentioned in the will of James Forster, innholder, of Cecil County, Maryland, who died in 1736. Fourteen months before becoming trustee for the town land of Salisbury, Forster purchased 615 acres on Horse-pen Creek of Haw River (on the Guilford Battlefield site). A saddler by trade

. . . six hundred and thirty-five acres of land for a township . . . by the name of Salisbury . . . that they might and should grant and convey in fee simple the several lots already taken up and entered . . . reserving the annual rent of one shilling for each lot . . . and likewise grant and convey . . . such lots . . . as are not already entered to such persons as shall respectively apply for the same on the payment of twenty shillings. . . . beginning at a hickory by the trading road a corner of James Carter, Esquire, then east by his land 112 poles to a spring branch then the same course 264 poles to a hickory in the said line then north 64 poles to first branch 150 poles to a hickory the same course then west 114 poles to second branch then the same course 202 poles to third branch then the same course 326 poles to fourth branch then the same course 414 poles to a post in the center of a hickory . . . then south 26 poles to fifth branch then the same course 190 poles to a path that leads to George Catheys then the same course 240 poles to the aforesaid trading road then the same course 384 poles to sixth branch then the same course 414 poles to a post then east 22 poles to said sixth branch then the same course 50 poles to Crane Creek then 68 poles crossing Crane Creek 120 poles crossing Crain Creek thence 150 poles to a post then north 50 poles to Crane Creek then 264 poles to the beginning.[17]

The lots which Carter and Forster had the responsibility of selling were marked off in a squared area cut out of the town land. Two main streets traversed the square at right angles to each other and intersected in the center. Corbin Street was laid out from northeast to southwest, along the route of the Indian trading path. Innes Street extended from northwest to southeast across the square.[18] Thus, the area set aside for the sale of lots was sub-

Forster, like Carter, removed from Cecil County to Carolina by way of the Shenandoah Valley. Rowan Deeds, III, 114, VI, 507, VIII, 470; *The Maryland Calendar of Wills*, 8 vols., comp. and ed. Jane [Baldwin] Cotton (Baltimore: Kohn and Pollock, Inc., Publishers, 1904-28), VII, 211 (hereafter cited as *Maryland Calendar of Wills*); *Chronicles of the Scotch-Irish Settlements in Virginia, Extracted from the Original Court Records of Augusta County, 1745-1800*, 3 vols., comp. and ed. Lyman Chalkley (Rosslyn, Va.: Commonwealth Printing Co., 1912), I, 112, 347, 444 (hereafter cited as *Records of Augusta County*).

17. Colonial Land Grant Records of North Carolina, State Library, Raleigh, N.C., VI, 114 (hereafter cited as N.C. Land Grants). John Whiteside was appointed treasurer for the township, a position which he held until June, 1758. He was also given responsibility for construction of the prison, a task which he apparently had difficulty in completing. Rowan Deeds, II, 13, 407; Rowan Court Minutes, I, 12.

18. Francis Corbin and James Innes were agents of Lord Granville. Corbin lived in Edenton, Innes in Wilmington.

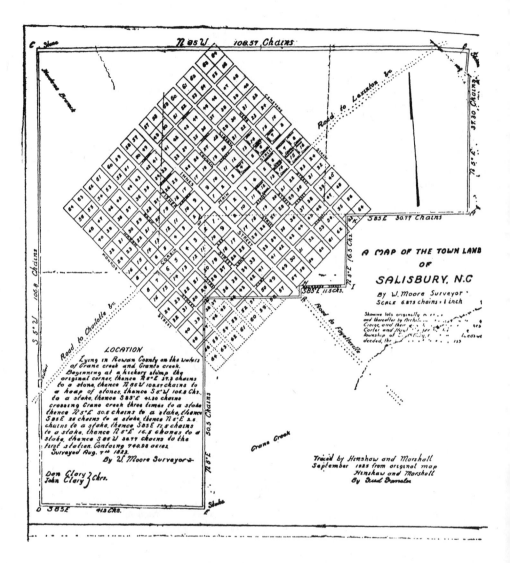

A MAP OF THE TOWN LAND
OF
SALISBURY. N.C
By W. Moore Surveyor
SCALE 6.875 chains = 1 inch

Showing lots originally ...
and thereafter by Archil...
Craige and their ... ...
Corter and Houl ... ... ...
Township of ... ... ...
deded, the ... ... ... ...

N 85 W    108.57 Chains
N 5° E    37.30 Chains
S 85 E    30.77 Chains
S 5° U    106.8 Chains
S 85 E    16.5 Chs
S 85 E    11.5 Chs
S 85 E    11.5 CHS.
N 8 E    50.5 CHAINS
D   S 85 E    413 CHS.    E

Road to Lexington Cr.
Road to Charlotte Cr.
Road to Fayetteville
Montoros Branch
Crane Creek

LOCATION
Lying in Rowan County on the waters
of Crane creek and Grants creek.
Beginning at a hickory stump the
original corner, thence N 5° E 37.3 chains
to a stone, thence N 85 W 108.57 chains to
a heap of stones, thence S 5° U 106.8 Chs.
to a stake, thence S 85° E 4.30 chains
crossing Crane creek three times to a stake
thence N 5° E 50.5 chains to a stake, thence
S 85 E 26 chains to a stake, thence N 5° E 2.5
chains to a stake, thence S 85 E 11.5 chains
to a stake, thence N 5° E 16.5 chains to a
stake, thence S 85 U 30.77 chains to the
first station. Containing 740.98 acres.
Surveyed Aug. 7th 1823.
        By W. Moore Surveyor

Dan Clary 3 chrs.
John Clary 3 chrs.

Traced by Hinshaw and Marshall
September 1823 from original map
Hinshaw and Marshall
By Sued Bameln

divided into four smaller areas, designated respectively the north, west, south, and east squares.

On April 15, 1755, Carter and Forster issued their first deed as trustees:

> . . . for and in consideration of twenty shillings . . . do hereby grant, bargain, and sell . . . unto . . . the Justices of the Peace . . . and to their successors in office forever, for the use of the public, part of that lot of land in the township of Salisbury whereon the prison is erected containing forty-eight perches (poles) . . . adjoining on Corbin Street and thence by said street northeast four perches to the corner of said street and Water Street, and thence by Water Street northwest twelve perches known and disinguished in the plan of the said town by No. 4, together with the diamond whereon the courthouse, office and stocks are erected in the center of Corbin and Inness Streets.[19]

The enterprising John Dunn resigned as clerk of the court in 1755 in order to devote full time to the practice of law.[20] He was replaced by Thomas Parker, who held the position until 1760.[21]

On June 17, 1755, Governor Dobbs undertook a trip to the western parts of his province. While discussing his trip in a letter to the Board of Trade, he made the following remark: ". . . the Yadkin . . . is a large, beautiful river where is a ferry. It is near 300 yards over, it was at this time fordable scarce coming to the horses bellies. At six miles distance I arrived at Salisbury, the county town of Rowan. The town is but just laid out, the courthouse built and seven or eight log houses erected."[22] Who were the first inhabitants of Salisbury? Who were the people dwelling in the "seven or eight log houses?"

It has already been observed that James Alexander, Peter Arndt,[23] and probably Edward Cusick[24] were living on the town lands before the formal survey of February, 1755. Alexander had died in 1753, but it is probable that his son or brother, William, succeeded to the home site. A William Alexander received title

19. Rowan Deeds, II, 81.
20. Rowan Court Minutes, I, 21; Rumple, *Rowan County*, p. 68.
21. Rowan Deeds, IV, 357, 359.
22. *NCCR*, V, 353-55.
23. Arndt purchased lots two, ten, and twenty in the east square on May 30, 1755. Rowan Deeds, II, 43, 42, 46. Each of the lots in the town consisted of 144 square poles.
24. Cusick, in conjunction with William Harrison, obtained title to lot number five in the north square on April 18, 1755. Rowan Deeds, VI, 541.

to lot number five in the south square on May 2, 1755.[25] James Carter undoubtedly lived near or inside the town line on the tract acquired by him in 1753,[26] and John Dunn may have had a legal establishment in the town by the time of Dobbs's visit.[27]

In addition to the five persons mentioned above, John Ryle, Johannes Adam, and William Montgomery were the possessors of dwellings or inns in Salisbury before the end of 1755. In April, 1755, Ryle petitioned for a license to keep an inn in Salisbury, and the following month acquired by deed lot number two in the north square fronting Corbin Street.[28] Adam was a Pennsylvania German and a potter by trade.[29] He obtained a lot in Salisbury in May, 1755.[30] Montgomery, from Philadelphia,[31] was an innkeeper in Salisbury in August, 1756,[32] and, since he received no land grant prior to 1759, probably lived on lot number two in the west square, which he bought April 15, 1755.[33]

During the spring of 1755, nine additional settlers obtained

25. Rowan Deeds, III, 21; *NCCR, IV,* 12; Howard M. Wilson, *The Tinkling Spring, Headwater of Freedom: A Study of the Church and Her People, 1732-1952* (Richmond, Va: Garrett and Massie, Inc., 1954), p. 470.

26. Rowan Court Minutes, I, 15.

27. Dunn acquired lot number five in the east square on April 17, 1755. Rowan Deeds, II, 5.

28. Rowan Court Minutes, I, 18; Rowan Deeds, VI, 514. Although it is possible that Ryle was a German (Johannes Rühl arrived in Philadelphia in 1742), the stronger evidence indicates his origin to have been Salem County, New Jersey. In 1738, a John Ryle was fined in Prince Georges County, Maryland, for not burning tobacco. A pioneer of the same name was in the Shenandoah Valley before 1743. Ryle died in Rowan County in 1769. *Pennsylvania German Pioneers, A Publication of the Original Lists of Arrivals in the Port of Philadelphia from 1727 to 1808,* 3 vols., comp. and ed. Ralph Beaver Strassburger (Norristown, Pa.: Pennsylvania German Society, 1934), I, 325; *Calendar of New Jersey Wills,* in *Documents Relating to the Colonial History of the State of New Jersey,* 1st ser., vols. XXX and XXXIII, ed. A. Van Doren Honeyman [vol. XXX] and William Nelson [vol. XXXIII] (Somerville, N.J.: Unionist Gazette Association, 1918 [vol. XXX], and Paterson, N.J.: Press Printing and Publishing Co., 1901 [vol. XXXIII]), XXX, 411 (hereafter cited as *New Jersey Wills*); Prince Georges County Court Judgments (1731-32, 1735-40, 1747), Hall of Records, Annapolis, Md., col. of 1738 judgments, p. 224; "Anson County, North Carolina, Abstracts of Early Records," *The May Wilson McBee Collection,* ed. May Wilson McBee (Greenwood, Miss.: May Wilson McBee, 1950), pp. 130, 228 (hereafter cited as "Anson Abstracts); *Records of Augusta County,* II, 509.

29. Rowan Deeds, VI, 542; Strassburger, *German Pioneers,* I, 283-85, 366-68, 403, 496.

30. Rowan Deeds, VI, 542.

31. *Ibid.,* II, 385.

32. *Ibid.*

33. *Ibid.,* II, 13.

deeds to lots in Salisbury, but there is no evidence to indicate that any of them actually lived in the town. Dobbs's reference in June to seven or eight log houses may again be cited as evidence that these nine persons did not possess dwellings in Salisbury. The purchasers were Joseph Woods, William Cadogan, George Cathey, Sr., John Newman Oglethorpe, Theodore Feltmatt, Nathaniel and Moses Alexander, Alexander Dobbin, and James Carson. Cadogan, who originated in Nantmeal township, Chester County, or in the Appoquinimink Creek district of New Castle County, Delaware, bought lot number two in the south square in April, 1755.[34] Feltmatt, possibly a German, acquired the same property a month later, indicating a fraudulent sale by the trustees.[35]

Joseph Woods, about whom the author has little information, bought lot number one in the west square.[36] John Newman Oglethorpe, a "chirurgeon" (surgeon),[37] was an Englishman who owned land along Abbotts Creek in that portion of Rowan County lying east of the Yadkin River.[38] He purchased two lots in the north square, evidently for speculative purposes.[39]

Nathaniel and Moses Alexander moved to North Carolina from Cecil County, Maryland, before 1752 and settled in Anson

34. Lancaster County Deed Books, Office of Registrar of Deeds, Lancaster County Courthouse, Lancaster, Pa., A, 40; *Calendar of Delaware Wills: New Castle County, 1682-1800,* abstracted and compiled by Historical Research Committee of Colonial Dames of Delaware (New York: Frederick H. Hitchcock, 1911), p. 33; Rowan Deeds, II, 76.

35. Rowan Deeds, III, 516. Part of this lot was located on James Carter's tract of 350 acres.

36. *Ibid.,* II, 24. There is no other record of a land grant or deed to Woods.

37. *Ibid.,* IV, 16.

38. *Ibid.,* II, 22.

39. *Ibid.,* IV, 16-17. Oglethorpe was living in Camden, South Carolina, in 1766. The itinerant Anglican minister Charles Woodmason, writing from Camden in 1768, made the following observation regarding Oglethorpe, who was a justice of the peace at the time: "And yet there is a magistrate here—but he is a Presbyterian—so are these Wretches. Instead of this Magistrate punishing these worthless sinners he protects them . . . This dirty fellow I must report to to the Governor and Council: How can Ministers suppress Vice thus openly countenanc'd and protected?" In the same year, however, during a sermon at Camden, a Presbyterian minister exclaimed:

. . . there's Mr. Oglethorpe, there he sits, God bless him, I say it in his face, He's a Jewel of a Man, and strives to compose People's Janglings all he can . . . and yet very often instead of being prais'd and Esteem'd for admonishing and reproving offenders against the Laws He is often hiss'd or hooted at when by St. Patrick would he exert his Authorityship properly.

Richard J. Hooker, *The Carolina Backcountry on the Eve of the Revolution* (Chapel Hill: University of North Carolina Press, 1953), pp. 54, 156.

(now Mecklenburg) County.[40] Nathaniel purchased lot number
nineteen in the west square, while Moses, a blacksmith, obtained
lot number eleven in the same section.[41] Both men played prominent roles in the colonial and early national history of North
Carolina. Nathaniel Alexander lived on Rocky River (in modern
Cabarrus County) and operated a mill at the spot where the
trading road from Salisbury to the Catawba Nation crossed the
river.[42] Moses Alexander became the first sheriff of Mecklenburg
County (created in 1762) and held the rank of colonel in the
county militia.[43] He had five sons, one of whom, Nathaniel,
became governor of North Carolina in 1805.[44]

Among other early purchasers of lots in Salisbury were Alexander Dobbin and James Carson. In May, 1755, Dobbin bought
lot number five in the west square, across Corbin Street from
William Alexander.[45] Carson, a tanner by trade,[46] purchased a
640-acre tract in November, 1753, adjoining the land of John
Dunn.[47] He bought a lot in Salisbury in May, 1755, and obtained
two more the following year.[48] As stated above, the majority of
these acquisitions probably represented efforts at speculation, yet
it is noteworthy that Nathaniel Alexander's lot was not sold until
1774, and Alexander Dobbin retained his lot on Corbin Street
until 1768, when he sold one-half of it to William Temple Coles,
an Irishman from Dublin.[49]

As early as 1754, the Catawbas and Cherokees had begun to
grow restive, and Captain Hugh Waddell, of Belmont, Bladen
County, North Carolina, was sent to the west with instructions to
hold the Indians in check.[50] On July 5, 1755, Waddell obtained lot

40. Worth S. Ray, *The Lost Tribes of North Carolina* (Austin, Tex.:
published by the author, 1947), pp. 520-23; see also p. 51 above.
41. Rowan Deeds, V, 534, VI, 112; *NCCR*, VI, 799, IV, 12.
42. McCubbins Collection (excerpts from court records, newspapers, correspondence, and miscellaneous items collected by Mrs. J. F. McCubbins of
Salisbury), filed alphabetically by families, Salisbury Public Library,
Salisbury, N.C., "Alexander" file (hereafter cited as McCubbins Collection).
43. *Ibid.*
44. *Ibid.*
45. Rowan Deeds, II, 45.
46. Rowan Deeds, IV, 493; VI, 254.
47. N.C. Land Grants, VI, 126.
48. Rowan Deeds, II, 48, 49; III, 537.
49. Rowan Deeds, VIII, 179; McCubbins Collection, "Dobbins" file; Rowan
Will Books, Clerk's Office, Rowan County Courthouse, Salisbury, N.C., A,
221 (hereafter cited as Rowan Wills).
50. Waddell was born in Lisburn, County Down, Ireland; *NCCR*, V, xxiii;
Rumple, *Rowan County*, p. 84.

number thirteen in the east square adjoining John Dunn and established headquarters in Salisbury.[51] It is not possible to ascertain whether Waddell's headquarters was among the seven or eight log houses observed by Governor Dobbs during his visit in July.

As has been noted, Arndt, Cusick, Ryle, and Montgomery operated public houses, or ordinaries. It may seem curious that a community of eight houses would include four inns, but it must be remembered that the process of settlement was in motion and that hundreds of newcomers were pouring into the region. These people sought food and lodging for themselves, and stables and grain for their animals. A public inn was therefore the source of considerable profit. As early as the fall of 1753, the court announced the following set of rules to be observed by ordinary keepers in the county (later to include the town):

... Rates as followeth for Liquors, etc., viz.: all Spirituous Liquors in proportion to Six Shillings per Gallon, 1 Quart of Loaf suggar punch and half a pint of Spirits therein Four Pence; Brown Sugar Do. Per quart; Small Beer One Penny Per Quart; Stewed spirits the Half pint the Same as Brown Sugar Punch. Each Dinner of Roast Boiled flesh 8 pence Brakefast and Supper four Pence Each Pasturing for Each for the first 24 hours 14 pence and for Each 24 hours afterwards 2 pence, Stableage each 24 hours with good hay or fodder 6 pence ... Lodging Each Night in a good Bed and Clean Sheets Two Pence.[52]

Many ordinary keepers were apparently as guilty of the attempt to avoid payment of fees as were their farming neighbors, for the court ordered in 1755 that no petition for a license to keep an inn was to be considered unless the necessary fees were paid at the time of presenting the petition.[53]

One of the first settlers to petition for an ordinary license in 1756 was a Pennsylvania German named Jacob Frank.[54] The author has been unable to determine the year in which Frank settled in Salisbury, and it is quite possible that he was one of the first settlers on the town site, perhaps antedating Alexander, Arndt, and Cusick. He never obtained legal title to land in Salis-

51. Rowan Deeds, IV, 200.
52. Rowan Court Minutes, I, 7.
53. Rowan Court Minutes, I, 21; *NCSR,* XXIII, 183. The fee charged for keeping an inn was £30 proclamation money.
54. Strassburger, *German Pioneers,* I, 130, 131, 133, 227, 265, 268, 271.

bury (a circumstance common to many of the early German settlers in Rowan), but his spring, still house, and dwelling house seem to have been located in the south portion of the east square,[55] possibly on James Carter's property.

Other settlers who obtained licenses for ordinaries in Salisbury in 1756 and 1757 included Archibald Craig, Thomas Bashford, James Bowers, John Verrell, Luke Dean, James Berry, and Henry Horah. Horah, originally from Cecil County, Maryland,[56] asked to keep a tavern "at his dwelling house where Deacon formerly lived."[57] The reference to James Deacon indicates that the inn may have been located on Second Creek, twelve miles west of Salisbury, for both Deacon and Horah possessed land along that creek.[58] On the other hand, Horah's inn (and Deacon's home) might have been in the town, for the former obtained title to four lots in 1757 and 1762. Horah operated a weaver's shop on one of his lots, probably one of the three which he obtained in the southwest square in 1762.[59] He also bought lot number nine in the north square from a tailor named Bostian Boise.[60]

Archibald Craig, his wife, Mary, and his son, James, purchased seventeen lots in the town before 1763. These tracts were in the east square, with the exception of one bought by Mary Craig after the death of her husband early in 1758.[61]

Thomas Bashford, who probably removed to Salisbury from Anne Arundel County, Maryland,[62] formed a partnership with Robert Gillespie for the purpose of speculating in town lots and county lands.[63] They obtained lot number two in the south square (already fraudulently granted to Theodore Feltmatt), and lots

55. Rowan Deeds, II, 156. For some reason, Frank was unable to prosper. He lost his property in 1756, and was declared "not worth forty shillings" by the court in 1758.

56. Cecil County Deed Books, Office of Registrar of Deeds, Cecil County Courthouse, Elkton, Md., VIII, 295.

57. McCubbins Collection, "Horah" file. See Appendix G.

58. N.C. Land Grants, XI, 8; Rowan Deeds, III, 17.

59. Rowan Deeds, VI, 19.

60. Ibid., II, 197. The author has no information on Boise. See Appendix G.

61. Rowan Deeds, II, 360, 334, 240, 241, 242, 407.

62. Testamentary Proceedings of Maryland, 1657-1777, Maryland Hall of Records, Annapolis, Md., liber 36, folio 274.

63. Rumple, Rowan County, p. 152. Gillespie originated in New Castle County, Delaware, or Cecil County, Maryland. He was probably a brother of Thomas Gillespie (see pp. 40-41 above). Maryland Calendar of Wills, VIII, 26; Rowan Deeds, IV, 382, XIII, 309, Will of James Gillespie, New Castle County Wills (identified by means of a card index), Hall of Records, Dover, Del.; Records of Augusta County, I, 315; Wilson, Tinkling Spring, p. 475.

three, eleven, and twelve in the east square.[64] On February 21, 1759, the following information was included in the description of a deed transferring lots three, eleven, and twelve from Bashford to Alexander Dobbins and Henry Horah:

. . . whereas William Brandon . . . died intestate and at the time of his death was possessed of a considerable personal estate, after whose death Ànne Brandon (now Anne Bashford) widow and relic of the said William Brandon administered on the said estate to secure the same for the use and benefit of the children of the said intestate, namely James Brandon and John Brandon, both infants, and whereas . . . Thomas Bashford having from many casualties in his business become greatly indebted to sundry persons, and having from part of the money arising from the sale of the said William Brandon made many purchases of lands, and the remainder applied to his own interest and advantage . . . [to] . . . Alexander Dobbins . . . are conveyed . . . certain lands to sell in order to meet the obligation to James and John Brandon.[65]

There can be no doubt that Bashford engaged in questionable enterprises. That Gillespie was also involved is not clear, for he had previously dissolved his partnership with Bashford.[66]

James Bowers, a tavern-keeper, of Baltimore County, Maryland, bought lot number one in the south square, lot number three in the west square, and lot number one in the east square.[67] Bowers lived in Salisbury in 1756[68] but returned to Maryland within seven years, for a deed of September, 1763, stated that James Bowers of Baltimore County, Maryland, sold lot number one in the south square of Salisbury to his son Bernard Bowers of Rowan County, North Carolina.[69]

John Verrell was an itinerant attorney who had one law practice in Salisbury and another in Sussex County, Virginia, two

64. Rowan Deeds, III, 533; II, 363-65.
65. William Brandon did not die intestate. His will was produced in 1799, causing an extended legal conflict among his heirs. Bashford evidently suppressed the will. Rowan County Minute Docket for the Court of Equity Begun March Term, 1799, Office of Clerk of Court, Rowan County Courthouse, Salisbury, N.C., pp. 173-78 (hereafter cited as Rowan Minute Dockets); Rowan Deeds, IV, 71.
66. James S. Brawley, *The Rowan Story: 1753-1953* (Salisbury, N.C.: Rowan Printing Co., 1954), p. 56.
67. Rowan Deeds, II, 406, 238, 237.
68. Rowan Court Minutes, I, 38.
69. Rowan Deeds, V, 446.

hundred miles to the northeast.[70] He traveled back and forth between the two, at least until 1771. Verrell bought no lot in the town land itself; his tavern and law office were probably located on a 640-acre tract adjoining the township on the west.[71]

An Indian trader named Luke Dean bought lot number five in the south square from William Alexander and twelve lots in the east square from Archibald Craig.[72] Dean lived on the Yadkin River in 1758 and emigrated to Georgia before 1766.[73]

James Berry, from Talbot County, Maryland,[74] was evidently a candlemaker. In 1756, he furnished candles for public use, receiving in payment 8s. 7d. "out of the public money raised in this county."[75]

Two prominent residents of North Carolina's east coast purchased lots in Salisbury during the period considered in this study. Charles Cogdell, Jr., of Carteret County, purchased a share of lot number one in the west square from Joseph Woods.[76] William Dry, of New Hanover County, was certainly the most celebrated of the North Carolinians who owned lots in the town without actually residing there. Dry was a member of the North Carolina Assembly in 1760 and became a member of Governor Dobbs's Council two years later.[77] With the outbreak of the French and Indian War, it was Dry who was commissioned to complete the construction of old Fort Johnston at the mouth of the Cape Fear, begun in 1747 as a defense against the Spanish.[78] Dry purchased from Conrad Michael fifty-nine acres in the northwest corner of

70. Williamsburg *Virginia Gazette,* October 3, 1771.

71. Rowan Deeds, III, 428; Rowan Court Minutes, I, 35.

72. By an act of the Assembly (Dec. 22, 1789), these twelve lots were transferred by escheat to the University of North Carolina. In 1796, Adlai Osborne, attorney for the university's trustees, sold the twelve lots to three citizens of Salisbury for £50. Rowan Deeds, VI, 253; II, 312; XIV, 701.

73. Rowan Court Minutes, I, 55; Rowan Deeds, VI, 253. Dean's departure may well have been a hurried and involuntary one. In July, 1767, he was presented by a grand jury in Georgia for "keeping a disorderly house, and entertaining horse-stealers, and other persons of ill-fame; and also for entertaining and harboring slaves." Hooker, *Carolina Backcountry,* p. 235.

74. *Maryland Calendar of Wills,* III, 205; Maryland Wills, 1635-1777, Maryland Hall of Records, Annapolis, Md., XXIV, 436, XXVII, 60.

75. Rowan Court Minutes, I, 34.

76. John Frohock was Cogdell's associate in the purchase. Cogdell's father was a member of the Assembly, where, in April, 1761, he was charged with contempt "for throwing a cat upon Mr. Charles Robinson." *NCCR,* II, 645, IV, 712, VI, 695; N.C. Land Grants, VI, 147; Rowan Deeds, III, 79.

77. *NCCR,* VI, 442, 831, 1077.

78. *Ibid.,* IV, 1255, xi.

Carter's old tract, including nearly one-half of the east and south squares of Salisbury![79]

Conrad Michael, a tanner, was one of three Germans from Pennsylvania who settled in Salisbury between 1756 and 1762. Michael was twenty-five years old when he arrived in Philadelphia in 1754.[80] Three years later, he bought from Peter Arndt the three lots which had been purchased by the latter in 1755.[81] Then, in June, 1757, Michael acquired James Carter's 350-acre tract in a rather strange transaction which furnishes insight into the character of the redoubtable Carter. Carter had earlier become involved in legal difficulties with Sabinah Rigby, the widow of William Rumsey. At a court held in Enfield, North Carolina, Sabinah Rigby recovered from Carter £200 currency of Maryland (valued at £150 sterling), a debt to be discharged upon Carter's payment of £100 (valued at £75 sterling) with interest, dating from 1738. Acting under orders from Justice Peter Henley of the Enfield Court, Sheriff David Jones of Rowan sold Carter's land at auction. And Michael bought it.[82] Michael did not remain long in Salisbury, however. In 1764, he expressed the desire to return to Germany, where he died before 1777.[83]

John Lewis Beard arrived in Philadelphia from Rotterdam aboard the ship "Patience" in 1749.[84] Six years later he was in Salisbury, where he acquired four lots in the east square "containing 576 square poles, including the spring, still house, and dwelling house where Jacob Frank now lives."[85] Beard was a butcher by trade[86] and may have operated a shop in the township. He was an unusually energetic man and, unlike most of his fellow Germans, assumed an active role in the affairs of the town.[87] He was naturalized in July, 1755.[88]

Henry Baker probably removed to North Carolina from Maryland.[89] He was a wagonmaker and married Barbara Bowers

79. Rowan Deeds, IV, 732.
80. Strassburger, *German Pioneers*, I, 609-12.
81. Rowan Deeds, III, 522.
82. Rowan Court Minutes, I, 47; Rowan Deeds, III, 538, II, 244.
83. Rowan Deeds, VI, 170; VIII, 550.
84. Strassburger, *German Pioneers*, I, 409; McCubbins Collection, "Beard" file. The name was originally Johann Ludwig Barth.
85. Rowan Deeds, II, 156.
86. *Ibid.*
87. Rumple, *Rowan County*, p. 67.
88. *Ibid.*; Rowan Court Minutes, I, 21.
89. Rowan Court Minutes, I, 151; Cecil County Judgments, S.K. no. 3 (1723-

in Rowan County in 1758.[90] In October, 1761, Baker obtained Bowers' lot number three at a public auction conducted by Sheriff Benjamin Milner.[91] A court ruling awarded Hugh Montgomery £8 19s. 10d. proclamation money "for damages incurred at the hands of James Bowers, Jr., hatter."[92] Bowers' lot, "also known as Bowers' shop,"[93] was sold to Baker as highest bidder. Bowers was placed in the sheriff's custody for his offense.[94]

In addition to the settlers already described, sixteen persons of English or Scotch-Irish origin obtained lots in the growing town between 1756 and 1762. There is evidence to indicate that nine of these actually lived in the town, while the other seven may or may not have been residents.

Those who owned lots in Salisbury but whose actual residence there cannot be established were Samuel Kirkpatrick, John Johnston, William Reed, William McKnight, John Howard, John Braly, and John Brevard.[95] A Samuel Kirkpatrick was living in Martic township, Lancaster County, Pennsylvania, in 1747.[96] His name did not appear on the Martic township tax lists for 1751, 1754, or 1759. Johnston, Reed, McKnight, Howard, Braly, and Brevard have previously been discussed.

The nine settlers who made their homes in Salisbury were Hugh and Mary Montgomery, James Huggen, William Williams, John Mitchell, Robert Johnston, William McConnell, Elizabeth Gillespie, and John Long. Hugh Montgomery, a merchant from Philadelphia, bought lot number two in the west square from William Montgomery in August, 1756.[97] Hugh Montgomery's eldest daughter, Mary, obtained twelve square poles of lot number one in the south square. This property had belonged to James Carter since 1753, but was purchased at auction in 1757 by one Andrew

---

30) and S.K. no. 4 (1730-32, 1736-41, 1741-43, 1746-47), Hall of Records, Annapolis, Md., S.K. no. 4 (1730-32), p. 134 (hereafter cited as Cecil Judgments).

90. Rowan Deeds, V, 274; Rowan County Marriage Records, Office of Registrar of Deeds, Rowan County Courthouse, Salisbury, N.C.

91. Rowan Court Minutes, I, 75; Rowan Deeds, IV, 399, X, 274.

92. Rowan Deeds, V, 274.

93. Ibid.

94. Rowan Court Minutes, I, 66.

95. Rowan Deeds, III, 518; II, 333; IV, 497, 57, 56, 412, 673; V, 183, 177.

96. Lancaster County Will Books, Clerk's Office, Lancaster County Courthouse, Lancaster, Pa., J-1, 114 (hereafter cited as Lancaster Wills).

97. Rowan Deeds, II, 385. Hugh Montgomery died in 1780. His tombstone may yet be seen in the "English" cemetery in Salisbury.

Cranston, a doctor.[98] Hugh Montgomery paid Cranston £10 for the land and presented it to Mary.[99]

As previously indicated, James Huggen, Robert Johnston, and John Long settled on plantations before moving to Salisbury. In July, 1758, Huggen purchased lot number one in the west square and made it his residence.[100] Johnston was a son of Robert Johnston, who died on Beaver Dam Branch of Fourth Creek in 1757. A hatter by trade, the younger Johnston acquired lots eighty-two and eighty-three in the east square and lots eighty-three and ninety-one in the north square.[101]

In 1758, John Long bought lot number three in the south square and also obtained lot number nine at an auction of certain of Robert Gillespie's holdings.[102] It is probable that Long built on at least one of these lots, although confirmation for this is lacking. According to tradition, Long was killed in the expedition against the Cherokees early in 1760,[103] but he later filed a claim for having provided a wagon to be used in that campaign.[104] In any case, he was dead by July, 1760, because at that time his wife Hester was referred to as his "relict."[105] William McConnell, a cousin or nephew of John McConnell of Davidson's Creek, was a merchant who acquired two lots in Salisbury from Hugh Montgomery in April, 1762.[106]

In 1751, two Welshmen named William Williams lived in Augusta County, Virginia. One of them moved to Orange County, North Carolina, in 1751 or 1752. The other, originally from the Appoquinimink Creek district,[107] purchased a lot in

98. Cranston appears to have originated in either Chester County, Pennsylvania, or Cecil County, Maryland. Cecil Judgments, S.K. no. 3 (1730-32), p. 249; Delaware Land Records, Hall of Records, Dover, Del.: New Castle County Reference C¹ no. 27 (hereafter cited as Delaware Land Records).

99. Rowan Deeds, II, 382; III, 558.

100. *Ibid.*, II, 394. It is probable that Huggen also maintained a residence on his Coddle Creek plantation.

101. *Ibid.*, V, 256, 257.

102. *Ibid.*, II, 359, 392.

103. Rumple, *Rowan County,* pp. 183-84.

104. *NCCR,* XXII, 821.

105. Rowan Court Minutes, I, 72.

106. "Anson Abstracts," p. 114; Lancaster Wills, B-1, 42, 81; Rowan Deeds, IV, 706, 709.

107. This William Williams, who obtained a 444-acre tract called Bachelor's Choice "on Sassafras Road near Appoquinimink Creek" in 1739, was undoubtedly the same man consulted in the boundary dispute between Pennsylvania and Maryland (See p. 26 above). Delaware Land Records: New Castle County Reference W³ no. 52; Rowan Wills, B, 136; *Records of Augusta County,* III, 334, 348.

Staunton, Virginia, in 1754. Four years later he made his way to Salisbury.[108]

Williams' brother, Henry, continued on to South Carolina. Williams purchased thirteen lots in Salisbury before 1763 and operated a hattery in the town until his death in 1783.[109] He was an independent and probably a lonely man. It is likely that he never married, as neither wife nor children are mentioned in his will. During the Revolution, Williams was called into court, where, "being suspected of disaffection to the independent government was required to take the oath."[110]

John Mitchell, probably from Cecil County, Maryland,[111] was a merchant who bought land in Salisbury from William Williams in July, 1760.[112] On November 30, 1767, he received from Hugh Forster lot number thirty-seven in the north square "to be appropriated to no other use than for the residence of a schoolmaster and the place for a school house, for the public use and benefit of the inhabitants now and hereafter of the town of Salisbury."[113] This is the first reference to any kind of educational institution in the township, indicating that there was no school in Salisbury during the period covered by this study. Mitchell left Rowan County in 1770 or 1771 and established himself in St. John's Parish, Colleton County, South Carolina.[114]

The story of Elizabeth Gillespie is an interesting one. Her husband, Robert Gillespie, the former business partner of Thomas Bashford, was scalped and killed by the Cherokees during the Indian uprising of 1759.[115] In June, 1760, the widow bought part of lot number two in the north square, which had previously been conveyed by John Ryle to William Williams.[116] She operated an inn on this lot, probably one built by Ryle in 1755.[117] In 1761, widow Gillespie acquired lot number eleven in the north square

108. Rowan Deeds, II, 396.
109. Rowan Wills, B, 136; Rowan Deeds, II, 396.
110. McCubbins Collection, "Williams" file.
111. "Colonial Militia, 1740-1748," *Maryland Historical Magazine*, 56 vols. (Baltimore: published under authority of Maryland Historical Society, 1906-61), VI, 47.
112. Rowan Deeds, IV, 251.
113. *Ibid.*, VI, 550.
114. *Ibid.*, VII, 312; McCubbins Collection, "Mitchell" file.
115. Brawley, *Rowan Story*, p. 27.
116. Rowan Deeds, IV, 241.
117. *Ibid.*, IV, 763.

and a 275-acre tract adjoining the town land on the north.[118] The following year, she bought the remaining portion of Ryle's old lot.[119] The extent and location of her purchases indicates that she was a shrewd, capable woman and that her husband had left her financially well established. In 1763, the widow married William Steele, of Lancaster County, Pennsylvania, who obtained sixteen lots in the north square of Salisbury "adjoining Elizabeth Gillespie."[120] Their son, John Steele, became a prominent figure in the early history of the state of North Carolina. In 1787, he entered the state legislature and, three years later, became a member of the first Congress of the United States under the Constitution.[121] He was appointed by Washington first Comptroller of the Treasury of the United States, a position which he held until 1802.[122] Margaret, daughter of the widow by her first husband Robert Gillespie, married Samuel Eusebius McCorkle, a co-founder of the University of North Carolina.[123]

Thus, it will be seen that the town of seven or eight buildings observed in 1755 by Governor Dobbs had grown to include at least thirty-five homes, inns, or shops. This would mean that there were more than 150 people living in the township by 1762. In addition, 24 persons had purchased lots in the town. As far as can be determined, these people were non-residents, although it is possible that well-to-do planters such as George Cathey, John Howard, William McKnight, John Brevard, Alexander Dobbin, and James Carson may have erected "town houses" on their lots. By 1762, 74 of the 256 original lots in the township had been purchased. In addition, 8 lots had been sold lying outside the limits of the town land.

At least fifteen of Salisbury's inhabitants were tradesmen. There was a candlemaker, a doctor, two lawyers, a potter, three

118. *Ibid.,* IV, 763; V, 307. Lot number eleven had been sold to George Cathey in 1756.

119. *Ibid.,* V, 308.

120. Rowan Deeds, VI, 160; C. L. Hunter, *Sketches of Western North Carolina, Historical and Biographical, Illustrating Principally the Revolutionary Period of Mecklenburg, Rowan, Lincoln and Adjoining Counties, Accompanied with Miscellaneous Information. Much of It Never Before Published* (Raleigh, N.C.: Raleigh News Steam Job Print, 1877), p. 185; Rumple, *Rowan County,* p. 189.

121. Rumple, *Rowan County,* p. 189.

122. *Ibid.*

123. Hunter, *Sketches of Western North Carolina,* p. 185; Blackwell P. Robinson, *William R. Davie* (Chapel Hill: University of North Carolina Press, 1957), pp. 224, 237, 240-44.

hatters, an Indian trader, a weaver, a tailor, a tanner, a butcher, two merchants, and a wagonmaker. Sixteen inns were licensed in Salisbury by the end of 1762.

The town had no newspaper, library, church, or school during the first ten years of its existence. The first newspaper was not established in Salisbury until 1799.[124] The Anglican inhabitants held religious services in private homes, but no church building was erected until the Lutheran residents built one in 1767.

124. Brawley, *Rowan Story,* p. 151. The paper was the *North Carolina Mercury and Salisbury Advertiser,* the only newspaper published in western North Carolina during the eighteenth century.

# XV

## THE ECONOMIC ORDER

The settlers of the northwest Carolina frontier were by no means a group of destitute encroachers. Most of those who avoided payments of taxes and quit rents seem to have been unwilling, rather than unable, to pay. At the time of the outbreak of the French and Indian War, Governor Dobbs stated that few poor persons dared take up lands in the west and that only rich planters from the north moved into the back country.[1] It has previously been noted that many of the pioneers were of prosperous Quaker background. Moreover, many of the Scotch-Irish settlers had prospered during twenty or thirty years sojourn in Pennsylvania and Maryland.

Tax collectors and elders in the various Presbyterian congregations of Pennsylvania were generally men of wealth and prominence, and a considerable number of these positions were occupied either by subsequent migrants to Carolina or by the fathers and uncles of those who sought homes in the Yadkin and Catawba valleys. Although it was inexpensive, land was not free in the southern piedmont; yet an overwhelming majority of the newcomers obtained legal grants.[2] The German immigrants customarily left Pennsylvania in the fall immediately after gathering their crops. By so doing they arrived in the Yadkin Valley just before cold weather, well-supplied with the means of obtaining land and passing the winter without excessive hardship.[3]

Communication and trade are two of the essential factors in

1. William Herman Gehrke, "The German Element in Rowan and Cabarrus Counties" (unpublished master's thesis, University of North Carolina, 1934), p. 43.

2. Land grants occupied such an overwhelming proportion of the desirable land by 1762 that the researcher is led to conclude that squatters were but few.

3. Carl Hammer, *Rhinelanders on the Yadkin: The Story of the Pennsylvania Germans in Rowan and Cabarrus* (Salisbury, N.C.: Rowan Printing Co., 1943), p. 28.

the growth of a frontier community. Both played a key role in the development of the Carolina frontier. The most important avenue was unquestionably the long wagon road, often called the "Carolina Road" or "Road to Yadkin River,"[4] which extended northward through the Shenandoah Valley into Pennsylvania.

Prior to 1740, the road followed a course from Lancaster northwestward to Harris' Ferry, thence southwestward through the Cumberland Valley by way of Falling Spring (modern Chambersburg) to the present site of Hagerstown, Maryland. Thence it continued southward through Winchester, Staunton, the present-day sites of Roanoke and Martinsville, and on through Wachovia and Salisbury to the Waxhaw settlement.

By 1745, in order to shorten the route, wagons began following a path which extended from Lancaster to Winchester by way of the present-day towns of York (crossing the Susquehanna at Wright's Ferry), Gettysburg (Marsh Creek settlement), Frederick, and Williamsport (Williams' Ferry).[5] South of Roanoke the road was probably nothing more than an Indian trail until 1746 or 1747.

As settlers streamed into the back country of Carolina, the number and importance of roads increased. In the spring of 1753, the Rowan County Court ordered "that the courthouse be erected at where the road to the settlement called the Irish Settlement forks to wit the one fork leading to John Brandons, Esquire, and the other over the place the old wagon road over Grants Creek formerly called Sill's path, and at the most convenient spring and other conveniences of the said court house."[6] It is obvious from this entry that the town originated at a crossroad. The road leading to John Brandon's plantation was the Indian trading path, which continued southward to the Waxhaw settlement. There, contact was made with roads which extended toward Charleston.

4. The roads were kept in good repair by the settlers themselves. In October, 1758, the Rowan County Court ordered that "James Carson be appointed Commissioner of the Road, from the Town to Anson Line." and that "Capn Evan Ellis, be appointed Commissioner of the Road from the Shallow ford into the Quaker Road leading to David Jones'." Minutes of Rowan County Court of Common Pleas and Quarter Sessions, 1753-1869, typed copy in 3 vols. (part of the original manuscript, torn, faded, and very difficult to read is in the State Department of Archives and History, Raleigh, N.C.), Salisbury Public Library, Salisbury, N.C., I, 61 (hereafter cited as Rowan Court Minutes).

5. Charles E. Kemper, "Historical Notes from the Records of Augusta County, Virginia, Part II," *Papers and Addresses of the Lancaster County Historical Society*, 65 vols. (Lancaster, Pa. 1897-1961), XXV, 151.

6. Rowan Court Minutes, I, 3.

In describing the people who had settled before 1750 on his own lands, Governor Dobbs stated that many of them "have gone into indigo with good success which they sell at Charles town having a wagon road to it, though 200 miles distant because our roads are not yet shortened and properly laid out, and from the many merchants there, they afford them English goods cheaper, than at present in this province, the trade being in few hands they take a much higher price."[7] In March, 1756, Governor Dobbs directed that a road be laid out from Salisbury to Charleston "by way of Cold Water at the end of Lord Granville's line."[8] It was "to pass by Mr. Martin Phifer's (formerly Arthur Patton's)," and was to be "as straight as possible."[9]

As early as the fall of 1756, a brisk trade had developed between Salisbury and Charleston. On October 18, William Glen and Charles Stevenson, of Charleston, South Carolina, "but now at Salisbury," named Thomas Bashford and John Cathey their attorneys for the purpose of collecting debts and dues. In 1758, two men were jailed in Salisbury "for passing bad South Carolina currency."[10]

The old wagon road over Grants Creek extended as far as Thyatira Church, thus connecting Salisbury with the inhabitants of western Rowan. The Indian trading path, which crossed the Yadkin River at the trading ford, linked the town with settlements along Deep River and the headwaters of the Cape Fear. Innes Street was continued southeastward as a road to the German settlement on lower Second Creek. Two ferries were established on the Yadkin by 1757 in order to afford dry transportation for heavily laden wagons. On September 18, 1753, Benjamin Rounsavill petitioned the court for a license to keep a public ferry over the Yadkin River "at his own plantation . . . rates man and horse four pence a footman wagon load on and four horses four shillings."[11] On July 19, 1757, it was ordered that "Archibald

7. *The Colonial Records of North Carolina*, 10 vols., ed. William L. Saunders (Raleigh, N.C.: Printers to the State, 1886-90), V, 356 (hereafter cited as *NCCR*). As Meriwether has pointed out, "economic improvement demanded access to capital and markets, which in the eighteenth century could be found only on the coast." R. L. Meriwether, *The Expansion of South Carolina, 1729-1765* (Kingsport, Tenn.: Southern Publishers, Inc., 1940), p. 182.

8. Rowan Court Minutes, I, 37.

9. Rowan County Deed Books, Office of Registrar of Deeds, Rowan County Courthouse, Salisbury, N.C., III, 395.

10. Rowan Court Minutes, I, 59.

11. *Ibid.*, I, 5. Rounsavill lived on the east bank of the river.

Craig keep a public ferry over the Yadkin River at the Trading Road, and to take the same fees allowed by the former license."[12] Craig died in 1758, and, due probably to his infirmity and inability to supervise the ferry, Luke Dean was licensed in April, 1758, to keep an ordinary and a ferry "at his dwelling house on Yadkin."[13]

A majority of the immigrants who streamed into western North Carolina in the 1750's crossed the Yadkin at this place, either on the ferries or by fording the stream. Another ferry was located twelve miles up the river in what is now Davie County. That there was considerable trading activity in that area is indicated by the fact that the "upper inhabitants" of Rowan petitioned in 1753 that "a road be cut from the ferry to the road called the Cape Fare road for the convenience of said settlement to trade of Cape Fare."[14]

How were these roads built and maintained? At periodic intervals, the court appointed prominent men living at widely separated points to serve as commissioners for the roads. It was the responsibility of each of these commissioners to obtain service for road construction and maintenance from the able-bodied men living in his particular district. Fines were levied upon commissioners and individual settlers for failure to meet this obligation.

In addition to indigo, the principal crops of the original settlers appear to have been wheat, rye, barley, spalce, and possibly hops and hemp. According to Rhoda Barber, many of the settlers along the Susquehanna before 1750 "were tradesmen, weavers, shoemakers etc. they were mostly paid for their work in grain, harvest wages us'd to be half a bushel of wheat or the price of it—raising grain did not appear the greatest object with the farmers, there was no great demand for it then. Hops and hemp was what they looked to for profit—"[15] Meat supplies were also plentiful in Pennsylvania, the market price for beef, pork or mutton being two and one-half pence a pound.[16]

Although there is little evidence that hops and hemp were grown on the Carolina frontier, the numerous references to

12. *Ibid.,* I, 45.
13. *Ibid.,* I, 55.
14. *Ibid.,* I, 2.
15. Journal of Rhoda Barber, 1726-82, Historical Society of Pennsylvania, Philadelphia.
16. Henry J. Ford, *The Scotch-Irish in America* (Princeton, N.J.: Princeton University Press, 1915), p. 270.

livestock in the wills and court minutes of Rowan County leave little doubt that meat products were as plentiful as in Pennsylvania. John Dickey's ledger[17] clearly reveals the fact that cereals were raised in quantity.

In 1746, four dollars Pennsylvania money was equivalent in value to three dollars Virginia currency[18]—a fact which may have encouraged many entering the valley of Virginia from the north to move on to Carolina. In 1753, salt (which sold at ten shillings a bushel) and rum (priced at ten shillings a gallon) were imported into the Shenandoah Valley from Lancaster County, Pennsylvania.[19] These products were also shipped to the Carolina frontier, for Dickey was selling both salt and "liquor" (which he distinguished from whiskey and brandy) to the settlers there as early as 1756.[20]

Faust has stated that the German farmers in Pennsylvania were superior to those of other nationalities. Entering upon the most fertile lands, they were chiefly responsible for the great quantities of wheat produced in Pennsylvania after 1740.[21] These facts are interesting, for they provide additional evidence that the Pennsylvania Germans did not migrate to Carolina in any numbers until other national groups had already done so. The Scotch-Irish, as previously indicated, obtained the best land located northwest, west, and southwest of Salisbury. The Germans settled largely on less productive soil in the southeastern portion of the county or in the forks of the Yadkin.

The county sheriff had many tasks of an economic nature. He collected the taxes; executed the orders and sentences of the courts and the assembly; made arrests; summoned jurors, principals, and witnesses to court; confiscated property and conducted auctions; and supervised the county jails.[22] The job was ap-

17. Store Account Book (1755-86) of John Dickey, merchant, in Duke University Library, Durham, N.C., p. 9. The item for September 5, 1757, indicates local hemp or flax production. (Hereafter cited as Dickey Ledger.)

18. *Chronicles of the Scotch-Irish Settlements in Virginia, Extracted from the Original Court Records of Augusta County, 1745-1800,* 3 vols., comp. and ed. Lyman Chalkley (Rosslyn, Va.: Commonwealth Printing Co., 1912) I, 21.

19. Kemper, "Historical Notes, Part II," XXV, 148.

20. Dickey Ledger, pp. 2, 3, 10, 14.

21. A. B. Faust, *The German Element in the United States, with Special Reference to Its Political, Moral, Social, and Educational Influence,* 2 vols. (New York: Steuben Society of America, 1927), I, 138.

22. For an excellent account of the role of the sheriff, see Julian P. Boyd, "The Sheriff in Colonial North Carolina," *The North Carolina Historical Review,* 39 vols. (Raleigh, N.C.: North Carolina Historical Commission and Department of Archives and History, 1924-62), V (no. 2), 151-80.

parently too difficult or too tempting for David Jones, who could
nor or would not collect the taxes. Legal proceedings were instituted against Jones by Robert Jones, the Junior Attorney-General
of North Carolina, who, in his report of December, 1758, stated
that

a suit against David Jones (suit has been continuing) sheriff of
Rowan, now amounting to £1355.8.7 proclamation money due for
balance of public taxes from the said county for the years 1753, 1754,
1755, 1756 and 1757 on which Jones has paid £150 proclamation
money in part thereof and judgment was rendered against him for
balance being £1205.8.7 proclamation money unless Jones produces
authenticated settlement with the county court entitling him to a dis-
count for insolvents.[23]

David Jones was relieved of his duties in 1758 and replaced by
Edward Hughes,[24] who was in turn succeeded in 1760 by
Benjamin Milner.[25] The last named seems to have been somewhat
more conscientious. A Provincial Court of Public Claims, meeting in April, 1762, declared that "Benjamin Milner, sheriff of
Rowan County, was allowed his claim of £20 for his salary as
sheriff for the years 1759 and 1760, having fully accounted with
the treasurer for those years."[26]

The settlers on the Carolina frontier owned a considerable
number of slaves. In 1768, according to the tax returns from six
of nineteen county districts, 1,123 settlers possessed 104 Negroes
and mulattoes over twelve years of age.[27] Of these slaves, 77 were
owned by pioneers mentioned in this study. The distribution was
as follows:[28]

Three sons of Morgan Bryan...........................7 Slaves
William Grant........................................2
Jonathan Hunt........................................4
William Linville.....................................1
John Davidson........................................2
Thomas Little........................................1
Francis Lock.........................................4

23. *NCCR*, V, 1083.
24. Rowan Court Minutes, I, 114.
25. *Ibid.*, I, 75.
26. *Ibid.*, I, 92.
27. Rowan County Tax Lists for 1768, Clerk's Office, Rowan County Courthouse, Salisbury, N.C., pp. 363-76.
28. *Ibid.*

John McConnell......................................3
Alexander McCulloch................................1
Andrew Neal........................................3
Robert Oliphant....................................3
Adam Sherrill......................................2
William Sherrill, Sr...............................1
John Braly.........................................2
John Brevard.......................................2
Robert Brevard.....................................2
James Carruth......................................2
Walter Carruth.....................................1
Thomas Cook........................................1
George Davidson....................................2
William Davidson...................................1
Patrick Hamilton...................................1
James Huggen.......................................1
Mary Houston.......................................1
David Kerr.........................................2
Hugh Lawson........................................4
Hugh McKnight......................................1
John McKnight......................................2
John McWhorter.....................................1
Alexander Osborne..................................4
Hugh Parks.........................................4
James Potts........................................1
William Reese......................................1
Moses White........................................2
Moses Winsley......................................3
William Denny......................................2

James Carter evidently owned slaves, for in July, 1756, he sold a Negro man and woman to Jonathan Boone, his son-in-law.[29]

John Frohock, probably the frontier's most prosperous citizen, named thirty-eight slaves in his will, dated 1768.[30] According to Frohock, one of these slaves had been bought from George Magoune.[31] Alexander Cathey's will indicates that he was possessor of two slaves by 1766.[32]

29. Rowan Court Minutes, I, 35.
30. Will of John Frohock, Rowan County Wills, State Department of Archives and History, State of North Carolina, Raleigh, N.C., vol. VIII, p. 49, folio 1.
31. *Ibid.*
32. Rowan County Will Books, Clerk's Office, Rowan County Courthouse, Salisbury, N.C., A, 39.

The sheriff disposed of unclaimed runaway slaves as provided by law,[33] and at least five cases involving Negroes were brought before the county court during the period considered in this study. In July, 1755, the court ordered that "a runaway Negro man be committed to the gaol of Salisbury and that the Sheriff hire him out."[34] In January of the following year, two Negroes "supposed to belong to Mary Webb" were required "to continue in the custody of the sheriff, and that he have liberty to hire them out to the best advantage."[35]

Several conclusions are apparent regarding the economic order on the frontier. In the first place, a considerable number of settlers were men of means if not affluence. Secondly, economic conditions were similar to those in the Susquehanna and Shenandoah valleys. Thirdly, a brisk trade was quickly developed with the coast at Charleston and Cape Fear. Finally, such matters as ferry privileges and tolls, road maintenance, tax collecting, and disposition of runaway slaves were controlled by law.

33. Rowan Court Minutes, I, 24.
34. *Ibid.*
35. *Ibid.,* I, 28.

# XVI

## *LIFE OF THE PEOPLE*

Perhaps the most interesting aspect of life on the northwest Carolina frontier is to be found in the way settlers of two centuries ago revealed the same human failings common among their descendants of today. Authors such as Rumple, Wilson, and Hunter have emphasized the devout, God-fearing qualities in the early settlers, qualities deemed necessary for a successful conquest of the frontier. There is considerable evidence to indicate that other characteristics distinguished many of the original inhabitants of the Yadkin-Catawba Valley.

In 1756, one Jean Wainwright complained to James Carter that Thomas Bashford and Robert Gillespie had "Bet and Battered and abused her without the least provocation."[1] Both were ordered by Carter to appear "before me or some other of his majesties [justices] of S$^d$ County."[2] Although the results of this case are not recorded, Bashford's illegal actions following the death of William Brandon (see page 163 above) would seem to indicate that he, at least, might well have been guilty of "battering" Jean Wainwright. In March of the previous year, a certain Henry Kingsbury brought a suit for trespass[3] against Edward Cusick. William Harrison, Kingsbury's attorney, began by pointing out that Cusick was a person of good character who "had not Only got Obtained and Enjoyed the good Esteem and Opinion as well of his Neighbours and Creditors as other Persons his Majesties Subjects and Persons of great Worth, Credit, and Reputation But also had Acquired and Obtained Great Profit and Gains by such his Trading and Dealing as

1. Rowan County Civil and Criminal Cases, 1753-64, 4 folders, State Department of Archives and History, Raleigh, N.C., folder no. 2 (1753-56) (hereafter cited as Rowan Cases).
2. *Ibid.*
3. Trespass cases were quite common in occurrence.

Afs$^d$."[4] Nevertheless, continued Harrison, on October 1, 1754, Cusick had twice called Kingsbury "a Rogue, a thief, and a villain,"[5] for which slander the latter was bringing suit.

It has already been noted that John Sill was among the first inhabitants of the Irish settlement and that the records reveal no deed for him.[6] Records of the Inferior Court of Common Pleas and Quarter Sessions for Rowan County reveal that Sill took Malcolm Campbell to court for nonpayment of debt dating from September 1, 1756. According to the description included in the case, Campbell wagered five pounds proclamation money that Sill could not prove that he had obtained warrant for a tract of land claimed by him. However, James Carter and Griffith Rutherford told Campbell that Sill had obtained a warrant and paid the survey money, whereupon (for reasons not given) Campbell refused to pay Sill the five pounds.[7]

The same court meeting in January, 1762, received notification from Edmund Fanning, King's attorney, that Adam Hall of Rowan County, "little regarding the laws of this province did . . . retail and sell 2 half Pints of Whiskey and one Quart of Beer contrary to an Act of Assembly of this Province . . ." and should as a consequence be fined ten pounds proclamation money.[8] Fanning requested that Hall be brought into court to answer the charge.

Bad blood seems to have existed in October, 1760, between Alexander Cathey and John McElwrath. John Oliphant, one of the justices of the peace, took the deposition of John Dobbin, James Carson, and Alexander Cathey to the effect that McElwrath was, as Cathey put it, "a Person of Lewd Life and Conversation and a Common Disturber of his Majestys Peace."[9] Dobbin, in his statement, testified that "John Mcklewrath was in his shop some time in September Last ye said Dobin & Mckellwrath being in Discors about Law bisnes between ye said Alexander and ye said Mckellwrath. Mcklwrath Swor by God if he could not

4. Rowan Cases, folder no. 2 (1753-56).
5. Ibid.
6. Minutes of Rowan County Court of Common Pleas and Quarter Sessions, 1753-1869, typed copy in 3 vols. (part of the original manuscript, torn, faded, and very difficult to read, is in the State Department of Archives and History, Raleigh, N. C.), Salisbury Public Library, Salisbury, N.C., I, 35 (hereafter cited as Rowan Court Minutes).
7. Rowan Cases, folder no. 4 (1760-69).
8. Ibid.
9. Rowan Cases, folder no. 3 (1758-59).

get Law he would turn as bad as Aney Chirch and would take it at his own hand."[10] Carson stated that "on the first of Septe 1760 . . . he saw John Mcwrath Standing near the Court house on the Main Street with a cut Lash in his Hand he was askt by some persons which this deponat doth not Remember who was he Raging agains he sd that damd Rogue Eleck Cathey had Robed him on the Kings Highways and further said that if he meaning said Eleck^r would come nigh he would cut him to peses."[11] Walter Carruth, another justice, issued a notice "to any Lawfull Officer" to summon Andrew Cathey and Peter Lawrance to appear before Carruth for the purpose of testifying "what they know concerning John McElrath's threatening to maim, wound, and Evil Intrate Alexander Cathey Esq^r."[12] Records in possession of the Knox family, after describing the "magnificent grazing country" up and down Third Creek, describe how "A man (semi-barbarian) by the name of Mclwrath owned a great amount of land on both sides of the creek probably and had large droves of horses. He forbade the original members of Third Creek Church from making roads through his land; had a law suit on it. Our church-going ancestors and other emigrants gained it on the grounds that it was their meeting and mill road."[13]

The numerous entries in John Dickey's ledger book indicate consumption by the settlers of a considerable quantity of brandy and other liquors. John Kerr purchased nearly two gallons of liquor from Dickey between September 26, 1758, and January 26, 1759.[14] James Graham and James Story were even more prolific in their alcoholic acquisitions. Story bought nothing but liquor between June 5, 1758, and March 24, 1759.[15] Quaintly, his very next purchase (April 16) was 8s.5d. worth of drugs, obtained by Dickey from an unidentified doctor.

10. *Ibid.* The misspellings in this and all subsequent quotations in this chapter are printed as they appear in the original manuscripts.

11. *Ibid.*

12. *Ibid.*

13. Hattie S. Goodman, *The Knox Family: A Genealogical and Biographical Sketch of the Descendants of John Knox of Rowan County, North Carolina, and Other Knoxes* (Richmond, Va.: Whittet and Shepperson, Printers and Publishers, 1905), p. 194. In addition to furnishing evidence regarding the character of John McElwrath, the above quotations provide an excellent illustration of the unreliability of frontier spelling. It will be noted that McElwrath's name is written seven times and spelled in six different ways.

14. Store Account Book (1755-86) of John Dickey, merchant, in Duke University Library, Durham, N.C., p. 3.

15. *Ibid.,* p. 10.

Just as is the case today, petty offenses were common, major crimes less so. During the period from 1753 to 1762, no one was executed for murder; but other types of crime were common and sometimes comical.

In June, 1753, John Baker petitioned the court that "whereas the said John Baker happened to be in a late affray with another person whereupon the person with whom he had the said affray . . . bit the under part of his ear off . . . he prays that his petition be recorded and granted and the court ordered the clerk to give him a certificate of the same."[16] Ear-cropping was common punishment for larceny, and Baker was anxious to have a certificate to show that he was not a thief. Later the same year, James Stewart was brought into court by order of Thomas Potts, one of the justices, on suspicion of stealing a pair of buckles. The court decided that the proceedings were illegal and the charges were dismissed—although Stewart was required to pay a fine of ten shillings for "his insulting of Thomas Potts, Esquire."[17]

Fines were commonly assessed for such offenses as cursing, drunkenness, and refusal to accept jury duty. Robert Tate, in 1754, was fined twenty shillings "for condemning the authority of the court and for two oathes also."[18] At the same time, he was forced to pay thirty shillings "for being drunk and incapable of attending as grand juror."[19] James Jones was fined five shillings for contempt of court and five shillings for swearing.[20] As already noted in an earlier chapter, James Bowers was jailed for an attack on Hugh Montgomery and certain of his property was auctioned to pay the fine incurred.

Not all of the settlers were guilty of wrongdoing. In 1755, the court ordered "that Henry Horah have and receive for his trouble with a certain sick man for whom he had provided meat, drink, and lodging the sum of three pounds proclamation money, and likewise Paul Beefle the some of one pound five shillings like money, and also Peter Arrand for his trouble likewise the sum of one pound ten shillings like money to be paid out of the public dues."[21]

16. Rowan Court Minutes, I, 1.
17. *Ibid.,* I, 9.
18. *Ibid.,* I, 15.
19. *Ibid.,* I, 16.
20. *Ibid.,* I, 60.
21. *Ibid.,* I, 26. Despite the general rolling character of the region, the

Perhaps the most serious social problem which confronted the growing community was that of illegitimate or orphaned children. The pages of the county court minutes are filled with accounts of the provisions made for these unfortunates. Usually, the court placed the orphan in the custody of a prominent citizen until the child should reach the age of twenty-one. The orphan's position was thus much the same as that of an indentured servant, except for the fact that the county court, rather than the orphan, made contract for the indenture. The case of James Fletcher may be used as an illustration of the procedure followed. In March, 1754,

James Carter, Esquire, produced an orphan boy named James Fletcher and prays that the said orphan may be bound to him until he arrives to age, the consideration of this court was that the said James Fletcher should be bound to James Carter until he arrive at the age of 21 years . . . the said Carter do oblige himself to pay the fees that may become due to my lords office for the clearance of two certain tracts and entrys of land in this county left to him [Fletcher] by William Bishop deceased and also to pay the quit rents which hereafter may grow due until ye servant come to the age aforesaid and also to teach or instruct him the said servant to read English and to write a legible hand.[22]

The orphan was not without recourse, however. The guardian was answerable to the court for his treatment of fatherless children instructed to this care. In April, 1755, Elizabeth Deason (or Deacon), widow of the James Deacon mentined earlier in this study, petitioned the court to grant her the guardianship of the orphans of Joseph Reed, "she being the mother of said children."[23] James Carter and James Carson presented themselves as her security, thereby making themselves equally liable with her for any ill treatment which should befall the children. The court ordered that "the said Elizabeth Deason have the guardianship of said orphans until complaint be given to this court against said guardian, setting forth that said orphans is not brought up in a Christianlike manner and provide sufficient clothing and apparel and meat and drink during her guardianship."[24] As the result

plethora of creeks imparted a marsh-like character to much of the land. Malaria and other types of fever were common.

22. *Ibid.,* I, 11.
23. *Ibid.,* I, 20.
24. *Ibid.*

of a complaint lodged by an orphan named Unity Cosby, she was transferred by the court from the guardianship of James Huggen to that of Alexander Osborne to serve "4 years . . . till she Attain the age of Eighteen yeares."[25]

Indentured servitude constituted another problem. Servants often ran away, and females sometimes made nuisances of themselves by having illegitimate children. In 1755, the court directed one Mathias Cramps to serve Edward Cusick one year beyond the expiration of his indenture because of the expenses incurred by Cusick as a result of the servant's "bad behavior and absenting himself from his master's service."[26] John Tassell, a servant of William Alexander, ran away and stayed for seven months. The court added six months to Tassell's original indenture of four years.[27] Thomas and Elinor Jordan were described as convicts and were required to serve Edward Cusick for a period of seven years, dating from June 6, 1756.[28]

Women indentures who had illegitimate children were usually required to add one year to the time of their indenture in order to compensate their masters for expenses incurred and time lost during the period of pregnancy. Six cases of this sort were recorded during the period covered in this study. It seems reasonable to assume that there were additional cases which were not brought into court.

Nor were the county officers themselves immune from the vicissitudes of frontier life. A multiple office-holder of James Carter's stature was rarely popular with the settlers, and his necessary duties as justice of the peace did not serve to increase his popularity. In October, 1756, Dr. Andrew Cranston "with force of arms to wit Swords Clubs etc in and ag[t] James Carter Esq[r] . . . in the execution of his [Carter's] office as his Majesties Justice of the Peace . . . comitted an assult did make and him the s[d] James Carter then & there did beat bruise wound & evily Intreat soe that of his life he was much dispaired and other Enormities in and ag[t] the s[d] James he offered."[29] In his capacity as surveyor, too, Carter did not always conduct himself in a manner calculated to win the affection of the frontiersmen. In December, 1758, it was

25. *Ibid.*, I, 65.
26. *Ibid.*, I, 26.
27. *Ibid.*
28. *Ibid.*, I, 36.
29. Rowan cases, folder no. 2 (1753-56).

resolved in the Assembly that "James Carter a Surveyor in the Earl's Office [Granville], under Pretence of receiving Entries and making Surveys, has at different times exacted and extorted considerable sums of Money from several Persons, without returning the same into the Office; by which they have been prevented getting their Deeds."[30]

John Edwards, Jr., reported how he and James MacManus, while engaged in surveying a tract of land in September, 1749, were set upon by a number of persons then living on the land. According to Edwards, after he and MacManus had finished the survey, "several of the Neighbours and Particularly [John] Withrow two of the Brandons and others came and hindered the s$^d$ James McManus from making any other Survey by drawing their Swords on him and threatening to shoot him with Rifles which they had with them."[31] It seems quite clear that frontier life involved considerably more than fighting Indians, attending church, and raising families.

It has already been seen that the settlers of Quaker origin exercised local political influence out of proportion to their numbers. Of those persons representing the northwest frontier in the North Carolina Assembly, however, two were Presbyterians (including one of dubious authenticity) and one was of Quaker origin. James Carter was a member of the Assembly by February 27, 1754, and (probably with the outbreak of the French and Indian War) was commissioned major in the colonial militia.[32] Eight days after becoming a member, he was appointed to a committee to prepare a bill for "granting an Aid to his Majesty for defence of the Frontier."[33] The following month Carter introduced a bill (which passed the Assembly) for inspecting indigo, rice, pork, beef, pitch, and tar.[34] In October, 1755, he and Cornelius Harnett brought up a bill for directing the method of selecting vestries of those parishes lacking legally constituted vestries.[35]

30. *The Colonial Records of North Carolina*, 10 vols., ed. William L. Saunders (Raleigh, N.C.: Printers to the State, 1886-90), V, 1052 (hereafter cited as *NCCR*).

31. Rowan Cases, folder no. 2 (1753-56).

32. *NCCR*, V, 182, 810.

33. *Ibid.*, V, 246.

34. *Ibid.*, V, 255.

35. *Ibid.*, V, 504.

John Brevard and John Brandon were the Presbyterian representatives. Brevard was a member of the Assembly by December 12, 1754.[36] One week later he was appointed to a House committee to prepare a bill for securing the payment of quit rents due the King and Granville, "for quieting the free-holders in the possession of their lands and for other purposes."[37] Brevard continued in membership, at least at intervals, until November, 1759.[38]

On February 26, 1754, John Brandon and Josiah Dixon brought up a bill for "stamping and emitting" a sum of money.[39] The following month Brandon assisted in the preparation of a resolution that the public treasurers pay for the expedition "against the French and Indians at Ohio" out of the money left over from the construction of forts. The resolution further stipulated that this money be replaced out of the £12,000 "to be stamped and emitted" by virtue of an act for "raising and subsisting the said forces."[40]

Religious life on the northwest frontier, as indicated in earlier chapters, revolved largely around the Presbyterian congregations at Thyatira and Centre. John Brandon, one of the leading figures in the Cathey settlement, lies buried in Thyatira churchyard; yet there is some doubt regarding Brandon's Presbyterian origins. The proceedings of the Donegal (Pennsylvania) Presbytery reveal that in 1733

. . . A supplication from Jo[h] Brandon being now presented ye Pby after consideration thereof approve of Mr. Thomson's conduct in refusing to baptise his child and Judge sd Jo[h] censurable for his sin and disorderly conduct in forsaking the ordinances of Xt dispensed by Mr. Thomson, & applying so abruptly . . . to y[e] church of England to have his child baptised. W[ch] being intimated to Jo[h] Brandon he acknowledged the same and professed his sorrow for it whereupon the Pby absolved him.[41]

The "Mr. Thomson" referred to was the Reverend John Thomson, the first minister of any denomination on the northwest

36. *Ibid.*, V, 232.
37. *Ibid.*, V, 243.
38. *Ibid.*, V, 689, 1007; VI, 132.
39. *Ibid.*, V, 181.
40. *Ibid.*, V, 190, 211.
41. Records of the Donegal Presbytery (typed copy), vols. 1A and 1B (Philadelphia: Presbyterian Historical Society, 1937), IA, 12-13.

frontier of Carolina. He was ordered by the Philadelphia Synod in May, 1744, to correspond with many people of "desolate condition" in North Carolina.[42] Thomson, who was well acquainted with many of the original settlers on the northwest frontier, welcomed the opportunity of associating with them. Until his death in 1753 or 1754, Thomson maintained preaching "stands" at William Morrison's, at Cathey's meetinghouse (Thyatira), at Osborne's meetinghouse (Centre), near what is now Fourth Creek Church, on Third Creek near Samuel Young's, and a few miles south of Davidson's Creek (near what is now Hopewell Church).[43]

In terms of colonial prominence, John Thomson was unquestionably the most celebrated of the early inhabitants of the Carolina frontier. After being twice elected moderator of the General Synod of the Presbyterian Church, Thomson became the first moderator of the new Presbytery of Donegal in 1732.[44] Two years later his pamphlet *The Poor Orphans Legacy* was published by Benjamin Franklin.[45] In 1744, Thomson was a member of the original board of trustees of a public school or "seminary of learning" which was established by the New Castle Presbytery and which later grew into the University of Delaware.[46] A visitor to Virginia many times between 1733 and 1744, Thomson finally settled in what is now Prince Edward (then Amelia) County where he remained until his removal to Carolina in 1750.[47] While living in Virginia, Thomson is believed to have established a school which served as a forerunner of Hampden-Sydney College.[48] In the "New" vs. "Old" Side controversy, Thomson was

42. *Records of the Presbyterian Church in the United States of America Embracing the Minutes of the General Presbytery and General Synod 1706-1788 Together with an Index and the Minutes of the General Convention for Religious Liberty 1766-1775* (Philadelphia: Presbyterian Board of Publication and Sabbath-School Work, 1904), p. 175. See also p. 55 above.

43. E. F. Rockwell, "The Gospel Pioneer in Western North Carolina," *The Historical Magazine, and Notes and Queries Concerning the Antiquities, History, and Biography of America*, 23 vols. in 3 ser. (Boston: C. Benjamin Richardson and others, 1857-75), XXIII (3rd ser., vol. III), 147.

44. J. G. Herndon, "The Reverend John Thomson," *Journal of the Presbyterian Historical Society*, 36 vols. (Philadelphia: Presbyterian Historical Society, 1901-58), XX, 121.

45. *Ibid.*, XX, 138-39. Thomson wrote the pamphlet shortly after the death of his wife as a reminder that his eleven children would be orphans if he should die.

46. *Ibid.*, XX, 150-52.

47. *Ibid.*, XXI, 34-35.

48. *Ibid.*, XXI, 42-43.

strongly opposed to Whitefield and Tennent.[49]   In 1741, he wrote
a pamphlet on church government and, in 1749, *An Explication
of the Shorter Catechism,* which apparently came to be widely used
in the Centre congregation.[50]

In 1755, the Reverend Hugh McAden of the New Castle
Presbytery set out on a missionary tour of the southern frontier.
He kept a journal of his travels which sheds considerable light
on the Carolina settlements.   On the morning of September 3,
1755, McAden wrote ". . . [I] came to Henry Sloan's, at the
Yadkin Ford, where I was kindly entertained 'till Sabbath day;
rode to the meeting house and preached to a small Congregation.
. . . Many adhere to the Baptists that were before wavering, and
several that professed themselves to be Presbyterians; so that very
few at present join heartily for our ministers."[51]   On Friday,
September 12, McAden crossed the Yadkin and rode "about 10
miles" to James Allison's.   On Saturday he proceeded "Three or
four miles to Mr. Brandon's [probably John Brandon]."   On
Sunday he preached "at the meeting house to a considerable congregation of professing people," and, the following day, he rode
to John Luckey's, "some 5 or 6 miles."   Three days later he visited
a man about to die from a fall from his horse.[52]   Then, McAden
continued, he "went home with John Andrew, a serious, good
man, I hope, with whom my soul was much refreshed by his warm
conversation about the things of God."   The next day he rode to
Walter Carruth's "about 8 miles" and stayed there until September 21, at which time he preached to a large congregation, "who
seemed pretty regular and discreet."   Then, while en route to
David Templeton's, "about 5 miles from Mr. Carruth's," he met a
group of settlers who had fled from the region of the Calfpasture
River in the valley of Virginia because of Indian depredations.
He rode on to William Denny's, "four miles further."   Denny
gave him "a pair of shoes, made of his own leather, which was
no small favor."   On Tuesday, September 23, he returned to

49. Rockwell, *Gospel Pioneer,* III, (no. 1), 145.
50. *Ibid.*
51. From the Journal of the Reverend Hugh McAden, April, 1755-May,
1756, quoted in William H. Foote, *Sketches of North Carolina, Historical and
Biographical, Illustrative of the Principles of a Portion of Her Early Settlers*
(New York: Robert Carter, 58 Canal Street, 1846), p. 167.
52. Foote, *North Carolina Sketches,* p. 168.   The dying man referred to by
McAden was probably William Brandon.   Rowan County Minute Docket for
Court of Equity Begun March Term, 1799, Office of Clerk of Court, Rowan
County Courthouse, Salisbury, N.C., pp. 173-74.   See also p. 163 above.

David Templeton's, and on Wednesday, "a day appointed for fasting and prayer," rode to the meetinghouse and preached. He then went home with Captain Alexander Osborne, "about six miles." After a week with Osborne, he visited William Reese, "about seven miles" and proceeded on Sunday, October 5, to the home of Captain Richard Lewis, "about three miles distant," and preached. On October 12 he rode seven miles to "justice [William] Alexander's." He remarked at the presence of a serious drought condition, noting that he had not seen "so much as one patch of wheat or rye on the ground."[53]

McAden then made his way into Anson (now Mecklenburg) County, evidently returning to Rowan in December. He noted that on December 28, Sunday, he preached at Cathey's meetinghouse to a large audience. The settlers urged him to remain, but he refused because the people were divided between the "Old" and "New" Sides. He preached at Captain John Hampton's on Second Creek, crossed the Yadkin, and lodged with Henry Sloan. He preached at the meetinghouse on January 11, 1756, "in company with Mr. Miller, The Baptist minister from Jersey."[54]

It is probably safe to assume that most of those with whom McAden lodged on his travels were individuals whom McAden would have described as "serious, good men." The Carolina frontier, like all communities then and now, consisted of individuals of every description. It has been said of James Stewart, who lived on Third Creek, that he "had much to hinder him in his Christian life. He lived when infidelity was rampant, not only in this region, but also in other parts of the world. There were those near akin to him who openly denied the Christian faith."[55] It is evident that the Reverend McAden would not have been welcome in every home.

The library of William McRae consisted of the Bible, *The Confession of Faith,* Vincent's Catechism, Boston's *Fourfold State of Man,* Allein's *Alarm to Sinners,* Baxter's *Call to the Unconverted,* and Baxter's *Saint's Rest.*[56] Each Sunday the elder McRae asked each member of the family questions from the Catechism; the young people who failed to repeat them were not

53. Foote, *North Carolina Sketches,* pp. 168-69.
54. *Ibid.,* pp. 170-71.
55. S. C. Alexander, *An Historical Address, Delivered at the Centennial Celebration of Thyatira Church, Rowan County, N. C., October 19, 1855* (Salisbury, N.C.: J. J. Bruner, 1855), p. 21.
56. Foote, *North Carolina Sketches,* pp. 434-35.

considered fit to hold a respectable place in society.[57] John Mc-
Whorter, whose home was in the Davidson's Creek settlement,
was a brother to Dr. Alexander McWhorter, who studied theology
at West Nottingham, Maryland, in company with Alexander
Martin, William Tennent, James Waddell, and Benjamin Rush.[58]

There seems to have been a small library in Thyatira Church
by 1765, containing among other works Mosheim's *Ecclesiastical
History,* Prideaux's *Connections,* and Butler's *Analogy of Natural
and Revealed Religion.*[59] There is nothing to indicate when this
library was established or whether these books were widely used.
John Sloan of Coddle Creek was the "possessor of many books,"[60]
while Samuel Young's library consisted of over one hundred
volumes.[61]

According to Rumple, a classical school was established about
1760 near Alexander Osborne's house.[62] At this "Crowfield
Academy" were educated (or prepared for college) Adlai Osborne
(son of Alexander), Samuel Eusebius McCorkle (son of Alexander), James Hall (son of James) and Ephraim Brevard (son
of John).[63] According to Hunter, both Robert Brevard and
James Alexander (son of William) were teachers in Rowan
County before the Revolution.[64]

57. *Ibid.*

58. Alexander McWhorter Papers, Southern Historical Collection University
of North Carolina, Chapel Hill, N.C.; Henry J. Ford, *The Scotch-Irish in
America* (Princeton, N.J.: Princeton University Press 1915), p. 419.

59. Alexander, *Historical Address,* p. 17.

60. Rowan County Will Books, Clerk's Office, Rowan County Courthouse,
Salisbury, N.C., C, 212 (hereafter cited as Rowan Wills). Sloan's will also
referred to "the Grammer School and the New Fourth Creek Library."

61. Rowan Wills, D, 250.

62. Jethro Rumple, *A History of Rowan County, North Carolina, Containing
Sketches of Prominent Families and Distinguished Men* (Salisbury, N.C.: J. J.
Bruner, 1881), p. 86. It may be noted in support of Rumple's statement that
Henry Hendry, John Braly, and Robert Steel, all schoolmasters, lived at the
time within ten miles of Osborne's House. Rowan County Deed Books, Office of
Registrar of Deeds, Rowan County Courthouse, Salisbury, N.C., V, 183, VI, 81;
Harold B. Carruth, *Carruth Family: Brief Background and Genealogical Data
of Twenty Branches in America* (Ascutney, Vt., 1952), pp. 164, 178-79; tomb-
stone of John Braly, cemetery of Centre Presbyterian Church; Chalmers G.
Davidson, *Major John Davidson of Rural Hill, Mecklenburg County, N.C.,
Pioneer, Industrialist, Planter* (Charlotte, N.C.: Lassiter Press, Inc., 1943),
p. 3.

63. Rumple, *Rowan County,* pp. 86-87.

64. C. L. Hunter, *Sketches of Western North Carolina, Historical and Bio-
graphical, Illustrating Principally the Revolutionary Period of Mecklenburg,
Rowan, Lincoln and Adjoining Counties, Accompanied with Miscellaneous
Information, Much of It Never Before Published* (Raleigh, N.C.: Raleigh News

There is little to indicate the existence of an established German congregation during the period considered in this study, although there may have been one in the forks of the Yadkin and another on lower Second Creek. According to James Brawley,

The oldest church organization known in Davie [County] was that of the "Dutch Meeting House" founded by the early German settlers on the east side of Dutchman's Creek between Mocksville and the Yadkin. . . . The . . . meeting house . . . [came to be known] as Heidelberg Church after the name of the German settlement there. The first records are incomplete but the first entry stated that Christina Buhe (Booe) was baptised there in 1766. . . . The Indians burned the old log church in 1765.[65]

There is a tradition among the Germans of Rowan County that a meetinghouse existed in the region of Dutch Second Creek prior to 1750, but it is not substantiated by the records.[66] It is perhaps of significance that only two[67] of the German settlers known to have been on the frontier prior to 1763 were among those taking part in construction of the Organ Church, begun in 1774.[68] This may well reflect the presence south of Salisbury before 1763 of many more Germans than the records indicate. It so, an earlier meetinghouse might have existed.

Georg Henrich Berger (or Birrer) and Johann Ludwig Barth were the most prominent of the early German settlers. Both became town commissioners, trustees for the Salisbury Academy, and members of the Committee of Safety in 1775.[69]

According to McLanahan, the Scotch-Irish migrated as families, and the Germans traveled both individually and as families. He contrasted this with the English of seventeenth-century Virginia, many of whom removed to America as single men, and with the Puritans, "who came as part of a colony already formed."[70]

Steam Job Print, 1877), p. 61. It is not clear from Hunter's remarks whether or not Brevard and Alexander were teaching prior to 1762.

65. James S. Brawley, "Davie Is Wealthy in Land, History," *Salisbury Post* (March 18, 1956), p. 4.

66. See p. 150 above.

67. Carl Hammer, *Rhinelanders on the Yadkin: The Story of the Pennsylvania Germans in Rowan and Cabarrus* (Salisbury, N.C.: Rowan Printing Co., 1943), pp. 31-32. The two were Georg Henrich Berger (Birrer) and Wendel Miller. It is probable that Johannes Rintelmann was also present before 1763.

68. *Ibid.*

69. *Ibid.*, pp. 29, 31.

70. Samuel McLanahan, "Scotch-Irish Family Life a Prime Factor in the

While it is true that many single individuals—Scotch-Irish, German, English, Welsh, and Huguenot—migrated to the Carolina frontier, there is no question that the overwhelming majority, regardless of national origin, arrived as families—and in many cases as closely-knit groups of families. Indeed, many family groupings (such as the Cathey-Brandon-Locke, Brevard-McWhorter, Carruth-Huggen, Bryan-Linville, Boone-Carter-Frohock, Van Pool-Hampton, and Craig-Howard) reflected associations involving a generation or more.

A final significant feature of frontier life may be noted in the location of the sites chosen for settlement. During the seventeenth century, when communication with England was essential and most traveling was done by water, immigrants to America usually established themselves on the banks of navigable rivers. A century later, with the settlement of the back country, most travel in America was overland; the rivers of the piedmont had little significance as transportation routes. Accordingly, home sites were located not on the rivers but along the upper reaches of the numerous creeks. Each home place nearly always included a fresh-water spring, thereby providing the settler with one source of water for himself and his family and another (the creek itself) for his animals.

Achievements of the Race," *The Scotch-Irish in America: Proceedings and Addresses,* 10 vols. (published by the Society, 1889-1901), X, 143-44.

# XVII

# THE FRENCH AND
# INDIAN WAR

Insofar as the people of the Carolina frontier were concerned, the French and Indian War began in 1753 and ended in 1760. In November, 1753, acting Governor Matthew Rowan wrote the Earl of Holdernesse that "three French and five Northward Indians came down to kill some of the Catawba Indians but were met by 13 of the Catawbas who killed two French and three of the Northward Indians . . . this action was within less than two miles of Rowan County Court House during the sitting of the court."[1] From 1754 to 1758, heavy Indian attacks occurred in the Shenandoah Valley in Virginia and along the Catawba River.[2] These assaults had a considerable effect upon the southward movement. From October, 1754, to the end of 1756 at least 68 persons were killed by the Shawnees and Delawares in the Shenandoah Valley.[3] During the same period, 13 were wounded and an additional 75 taken prisoner.[4] In the Shenandoah Valley in 1757 and 1758, 49 settlers were slain, five wounded, and 86 taken prisoners.[5] The number of taxable persons in Rowan County was an estimated 1,531 in 1756.[6] Three years later there were fewer than 800, the remainder having fled for safety east of the Yadkin.[7]

1. *The Colonial Records of North Carolina*, 10 vols., ed. William L. Saunders (Raleigh, N.C.: Printers to the State, 1886-90), V, 25 (hereafter cited as *NCCR*).
2. William H. Gehrke, "The German Element in Rowan and Cabarrus Counties" (unpublished master's thesis, University of North Carolina, 1934), pp. 43-44.
3. *Chronicles of the Scotch-Irish Settlements in Virginia, Extracted from the Original Court Records of Augusta County, 1745-1800*, 3 vols., comp. and ed. Lyman Chalkley (Rosslyn, Va.: Commonwealth Printing Co., 1912), II, 510-12.
4. *Ibid.*
5. *Ibid.*
6. E. B. Greene and Virginia D. Harrington, *American Population Before the Census of 1790* (New York: Columbia University Press, 1932), pp. 160-61.
7. *Records of the Moravians in North Carolina*, 7 vols., ed. Adelaide Fries (Raleigh, N.C.: Edwards and Broughton Printing Co., 1922-47), I, 205-33; Greene and Harrington, *American Population*, pp. 160-61.

Even the Catawba Indians, previously friendly toward the whites, were aroused to acts of violence. In 1754, William Morrison reported to the court that several Catawbas "came to him at his mill and attempted to throw a pail of water into his meal trough, and when he would prevent them they made many attempts to strike him with their guns over his head."[8] Other settlers complained that the Indians were stealing bread, meat, meal, and clothing. It was also charged that the red men had attempted to abduct children and to stab any man or woman who attempted to stop them.[9]

By 1755, Governor Dobbs became seriously concerned. Having originated in Antrim County, Ireland, he had a personal interest in the welfare of the western settlers, many of whom had migrated from Antrim County.[10] Moreover, Dobbs owned more than two hundred thousand acres of land situated on Rocky River and its branches.[11] Should the settlers on his lands be driven off, he would suffer heavy financial loss.

Consequently, Fort Dobbs was constructed approximately twenty-seven miles west of Salisbury.[12] It was described in December, 1756, by Francis Brown, one of the commissioners appointed by the governor to inspect the frontier defenses:

... a good and substantial building ... the oblong square fifty-three feet by forty, the opposite angles twenty-four and twenty-two; in height twenty-four and a half feet ... the thickness of the walls which are made of oak logs regularly diminished from sixteen inches to six; it contains three floors and there may be discharged from each floor at one and the same about a hundred muskets ... found under command of Captain Hugh Waddell forty-six effective officers and soldiers appearing well and in good spirits.[13]

In August, 1755, the governor sent the Board of Trade an account of his western trip, remarking that "Before I returned from the Frontier I gave directions to put the Frontier in the best state of defence against the Indian incursions, by having 100 select men

8. *NCCR*, V, 141.
9. *Ibid.*, V, 142.
10. Among those from Antrim County were Walter Carruth, Alexander and John Dobbin, Thomas Bashford, James and John Huggen, and John Biggs.
11. Minnie Hampton Eliason, *Fort Dobbs: Historical Sketch* (Statesville, N.C.: Brady Printing Co., 1915), p. 9.
12. See p. 100 above.
13. *NCCR*, V, 849.

in readiness to joyn [sic] our Frontier company.[14] These measures apparently discouraged the Cherokees—if only temporarily. Acting in conjunction with Peyton Randolph and William Byrd of Virginia, Waddell concluded a temporary peace with the Cherokees in February, 1756.[15]

The Catawbas, however, continued to annoy the settlers. In May, 1756, a conference was held with the Catawba chiefs at the house of Peter Arndt.[16] Following the meeting, Chief Justice Peter Henley stated that he supposed "there will soon be a war," and asked Governor Dobbs "to send us some ammunition as soon as possible, and . . . build us a fort for securing our old men, women and children when we turn out to fight the enemy on their coming."[17] Dobbs wrote the Board of Trade in August, 1757, that a party of Catawbas had insulted Chief Justice Henley at a sitting of the Supreme Court in Salisbury. The Indians then proceeded northward, reported Dobbs, and "upon their return after doing little or nothing in Virginia having robbed a waggon and tied up a waggoner with his own chain and upon their being followed and the goods retaken they returned loaded their guns and insulted the court."[18] Dobbs apparently felt that the government of South Carolina was chiefly responsible for the trouble with the Catawbas. As early as 1755, he complained of special favors granted the Catawbas by Governor Glen in an effort to win Indian support in the boundary dispute with North Carolina, a dispute which affected Dobbs's own lands.[19] In his report to the Board of Trade in 1757, he stated that the Catawbas had been "Spirited up . . . to insult our planters."[20]

It was at this time that one of the frontier's most illustrious citizens yielded—at the wrong time—to temptation. On May 17, 1757, it was announced in the Assembly that

Mr. James Carter one of the members thereof for Rowan County having been intrusted together with Mr. John Brandon with the sum of Five Hundred pounds proclamation money to be by them applied

14. *Ibid.,* V, 419-20.
15. James S. Brawley, *The Rowan Story, 1753-1953* (Salisbury, N.C.: Rowan Printing Co., 1954), pp. 24-25.
16. *NCCR.,* V, 579-81.
17. *Ibid.*
18. *Ibid.,* V, 784.
19. Hugh T. Lefler and A. R. Newsome, *North Carolina: The History of a Southern State* (Chapel Hill: University of North Carolina Press, 1954), pp. 150-51.
20. *NCCR,* V, 784.

in purchasing arms and ammunition for the defense of the frontier province of Rowan and have neglected to apply the said money for the purpose aforesaid and also have hitherto neglected to account for the same and further moved that the said James Carter may be called by this House to answer for his neglect.[21]

As a result of this misappropriation of public money, Carter was relieved of his position as a justice of the peace for Rowan. He was forced to resign his major's commission in the county militia and was expelled from his seat in the Assembly.[22]

Legal action was also instituted in October, 1755, against John Brandon, John Nisbet, and Edward Hughes for similar misuse of public funds.[23] Nisbet died a month later, however, and Brandon passed away in May, 1756;[24] so proceedings against them were dropped. Hughes was appointed sheriff "about the time judgment was rendered against him," and legal action was suspended until he was out of office.[25]

In 1758, with the Cherokee threat in temporary abeyance, Hugh Waddell left Fort Dobbs and went to Pennsylvania for service against the French and Indians.[26] Members of the frontier militia began returning to their homes. Between June and November, 1758, only Jacob Frank and one assistant were present at Fort Dobbs. Their services were recognized by the Assembly, which awarded them £20 9s. 8d. proclamation money at the conclusion of their sojourn at the fort.[27]

Peace on the frontier did not last long. Late in 1758, urged on by the French, the Cherokees resumed their attacks upon the settlers. John and William Ireland, Andrew Morrison, and John Oliphant were among the inhabitants of the Catawba Valley who were "forced from their lands."[28] The following year the Indians

21. *Ibid.*, V, 846, 1082-83. In 1754, Carter had been member of a committee to investigate "Indian outrages" and to prepare a bill for "granting an aid to his Majesty for defense of the frontier of their Province and other purposes." *NCCR*, V, 175-76, 246.

22. *Ibid.*, V, 810, 892.

23. *Ibid.*, V, 1082-83.

24. Both have clearly decipherable tombstones in Thyatira churchyard.

25. *NCCR*, V, 1083.

26. Eliason, *Fort Dobbs*, p. 3.

27. *NCCR*, V, 977; Eliason, *Fort Dobbs*, pp. 13-14.

28. Minutes of Rowan County Court of Common Pleas and Quarter Sessions, 1753-1869, typed copy in 3 vols. (part of the original manuscript, torn, faded, and very difficult to read, is in the State Department of Archives and History, Raleigh, N.C.), Salisbury Public Library, Salisbury, N.C., I, 71 (hereafter cited as Rowan Court Minutes).

killed Robert Gillespie and the fourteen-year-old son of Richard Lewis.[29] They then attacked Fort Dobbs—but without success.[30] Hugh Waddell, who returned to Carolina early in 1759, provided a graphic description of the attack in a letter to Governor Dobbs dated February 29, 1760:

In return for your excellency's news I shall give you a little nigher home for several days I observed that a small party of Indians were constantly about the fort, I sent out several small parties after them to no purpose, the evening before last between 8 and 9 o'clock I found by the dogs making an uncommon noise there must be a party nigh a spring which we sometimes use. As my garrison is but small, and I was apprehensive it might be a scheme to draw out the garrison, I took out Captain Bailie who with myself and party made up ten; we had not marched 300 yards from the fort when we were attacked by at least 60 or 70 Indians. I had given my party orders not to fire until I gave the word, which they punctually observed: we received the Indians fire: when I perceived they had almost all fired, I ordered my party to fire which we did not further than 12 steps each loaded with a bullet and seven buck shot, they had nothing to cover them as they were advancing either to tomahawk or make us prisoners: they found the fire very hot from so small a number which a good deal confused them; I then ordered my party to retreat, as I found the instant our skirmish began another party had attacked the fort, upon our reinforcing the garrison the Indians were soon repulsed with I am sure a considerable loss, from what I myself saw as well as those I can confide in they could not have had less than 10 or 12 killed or wounded, and I believe they have taken six of my horses to carry off their wounded . . . On my side I had 2 men wounded one of whom I am afraid will die as he is scalped, the other is in a way of recovery and one boy killed near the fort whom they durst not advance to scalp. I expected they would have paid me another visit last night, as they attack all fortifications by night, but find they did not like their reception.[31]

Following the fight at Fort Dobbs, Waddell determined to carry the war to the Cherokees. Expeditions were conducted under Hugh Montgomery of Salisbury, Griffith Rutherford, and James Grant. More than fifteen Indian villages were destroyed,

29. Brawley, *Rowan Story*, p. 27.
30. *Ibid.*
31. *NCCR*, VI, 229-30. The scalped man and slain boy are probably references to Gillespie and young Lewis.

and the frontier was pushed westward to the foothills of the Appalachians.[32]

Among the militia officers who took part in the campaign were Colonel Alexander Osborne, Captain Martin Pfeiffer, Captain Conrad Michael, and Captain John Kerr.[33] The company commanders who had charge of patrolling the area between the Yadkin and Catawba during the campaign included Colonel Nathaniel Alexander, Captain Thomas Allison, and Lieutenants William Luckie, John McWhorter, Hugh Parks, and William Neill.[34] Major John Dunn and his company saw service in 1759 and 1760,[35] while Hugh Montgomery and John Oliphant supervised the provisioning of the expedition.[36]

The part played by frontier settlers in the Cherokee War is indicated in the following table:[37]

## PUBLIC CLAIMS ALLOWED
### 1 May, 1760

| POUNDS | SHILLINGS | PENCE | NAME | SERVICE | DATE |
|---|---|---|---|---|---|
| 24 | 0 | 0 | Moses Alexander | Waggoning | 1760 |
| 45 | 4 | 0 | Col. Nathaniel Alexander and Company | Ranging | 1760 |
| 182 | 16 | 0 | Lt. Alexander Dobbin and Company | Ranging | 1759 |
| 117 | 14 | 8 | Capt. Conrad Michael and Company | Expedition | 1760 |
| 112 | 2 | 2 | Capt. James McManus and Company | Ranging | 1759-60 |
| 33 | 15 | 0 | Capt. Conrad Michael | Waggoning the Expedition | 1760 |
| 27 | 0 | 0 | Henry Horah | Waggoning the Expedition | 1760 |
| 59 | 7 | 6 | Capt. Conrad Michael and Company | Ranging | 1759-60 |
| 108 | 15 | 0 | John Long | Waggoning the Expedition | 1760 |
| 45 | 15 | 0 | John Dunn | Waggoning the Expedition | 1760 |

32. Brawley, *Rowan Story*, p. 27.
33. Eliason, *Fort Dobbs*, p. 17.
34. *Ibid.*
35. *The State Records of North Carolina*, 16 vols. (XI through XXVI), ed. Walter Clark (Winston, N.C.: M. I. and J. C. Stewart, Printers to the State, 1895-96; Goldsboro, N.C.: Nash Brothers, Book and Job Printers, 1898-1905), XXII, 826 (hereafter cited as *NCSR*).
36. Eliason, *Fort Dobbs*, p. 17.
37. *NCSR*, XXII, 820-23.

| POUNDS | SHILLINGS | PENCE | NAME | SERVICE | DATE |
|---|---|---|---|---|---|
| 42 | 0 | 0 | Thomas Parker | Waggoning the Expedition | 1760 |
| 45 | 15 | 0 | Hugh Montgomery | Waggoning the Expedition | 1760 |
| 26 | 5 | 0 | John Ryle | Waggoning the Expedition | 1760 |
| 2 | 4 | 8 | Thomas Bashford | Provisions to the Cherokee Indians | 1757-58 |
| 9 | 17 | 2 | Charles Cogdell | Disbursements to the Cherokee nation | No date |

In addition, the committee recommended to the Assembly that "a proper allowance be made for the taking of ten Indian scalps (produced by Col. Hugh Waddell and Mr. John Frohock), taken by a party of volunteers who went out at their own expense, and has not brought any charge against the public for the same."[38] This request was allowed by the House in the form of £100, with the stipulation that the sum was to be "equally divided among the adventurers in proportion to the number of scalps taken by each respective company."[39]

The fighting in 1760 virtually destroyed the power of the Cherokees to make war, and peace resulted the following year.[40] Waddell, having done his duty, returned to Wilmington in 1762.[41] The role of the Carolina frontier in the war with France had ended. Indeed, the frontier line itself had been pushed westward to the foothills of the Blue Ridge. A new era in the colonial history of North Carolina was about to begin.

38. *Ibid.*, XXII, 823.
39. *Ibid.*
40. Jethro Rumple, *A History of Rowan County, North Carolina, Containing Sketches of Prominent Families and Distinguished Men* (Salisbury, N.C.: J. J. Bruner, 1881), p. 85.
41. Eliason, *Fort Dobbs*, p. 17.

# XVIII

## CONCLUSION

The settlement of the northwest Carolina frontier was an historical process involving two interrelated elements: land and people. As has been seen, the region extending in a giant, gentle curve from the Delaware Valley and the "head of Chesapeake" to west-central Carolina was actually a continuous, undulating, well-watered plain of savannah grass, differing in no important way at its northern and southern extremities. Flanked by the Alleghenies to the northwest and the Blue Ridge to the southeast, this fertile belt (inhabited only by Indians west of the Susquehanna) provided a place of abode and at the same time a sheltered avenue for any who wished to push on to the south. As the central portions of Virginia, Maryland, and North Carolina were virtually uninhabited as late as 1740, the western piedmont region provided cheap, fertile land which would be virtually free of competitive immigration from the east for many years to come.

The influx of thousands of families into this natural avenue began before 1730 and continued until the outbreak of war with the Shawnees and Cherokees in 1754. The chief reason for this movement of population was undoubtedly economic, stemming from the depletion of the soil on Maryland's Eastern Shore and the rapidly rising price of land in Pennsylvania—the latter due in large measure to the immigration of Ulster Scots following the economic dislocation in northern Ireland.

A second important cause of the southward movement may be described as politico-military. The revocation of the Edict of Nantes (1685) and the destructive wars of Louis XIV, culminating in the Treaty of Utrecht (1715), disrupted the lives of thousands of French Huguenots and Rhenish Germans and resulted in a wave of migration to Pennsylvania contemporaneous with that of the Ulster Scots. The border war between Pennsylvania and Maryland and the outbreak of King George's War

(1739), combined with the reluctance of Quaker authorities to extend either political equality or aid against Indian assaults along the frontier, caused a sharp increase in the southward movement after 1740.

There were also religious motives for the settlement of western Carolina. The clash of a half-dozen antithetical religious beliefs at the "head of Chesapeake" during the 1730's undoubtedly inspired the departure of many, as did the extreme rigidity of Quaker doctrine from East Jersey to Maryland's western shore. It is of interest that the Welsh (and some Irish), clearly identifiable among the English Baptists and Quakers in Pennsylvania, were absorbed by the English majority by the time they reached the Carolina frontier. Much the same statement can be made concerning the numerous Huguenots among the Presbyterians, though the former had largely lost their separate identity in Ulster before migrating to America.

In the case of individual families, an important reason for migration was the death of the patriarch, or head of the family. As illustrated many times in the present study, a man with several teen-aged sons would settle in Maryland, Delaware, or Pennsylvania and live there until his death. As the migration to America first became heavy during the period 1717-30, hundreds of these men died in the 1730's and 1740's. As their sons had not the means to start a life of their own until disposition had been made of the estate, it would seem fair to conclude that thousands of men in their twenties and thirties were literally freed after 1735.

R. D. W. Connor and Samuel A'Court Ashe have stated that western North Carolina was settled chiefly by Scotch-Irish and German pioneers from Pennsylvania.[1] The evidence with regard to the area considered in this study[2] clearly indicates that the majority of the first settlers were indeed Scotch-Irish or German.[3] The evidence does *not* clearly indicate that a majority originated

1. Robert D. W. Connor, *North Carolina, Rebuilding an Ancient Commonwealth, 1584-1925*, 4 vols. (Chicago and New York: American Historical Society, Inc., 1929), I, 155-60; Samuel A'Court Ashe, *History of North Carolina*, 2 vols. (Greensboro, N.C.: Charles L. Van Noppen, 1908), I, 276-77.

2. Approximately nine hundred square miles.

3. Of the 70 known German settlers, at least 40 landed at Philadelphia. Virtually all the Scotch-Irish settlers were inhabitants of the Fourth Creek, Davidson's Creek, or Irish settlements. By the end of 1762, these three congregations comprised at least 305 identifiable families. There were, in addition, at least 165 non-German, non-Presbyterian families. This gives a total of 540 families, or approximately 3,000 persons.

in Pennsylvania.[4] It should not be forgotten that Maryland was settled fifty years before Pennsylvania and that a surplus population had developed on the Eastern Shore by 1730. Because of the fact that both occurred simultaneously, historians have inadvertently linked the movement of persons westward from Maryland, Delaware, and New Jersey with the direct influx from the British Isles after 1720. A majority of the earliest settlers in northwestern Carolina originated in established settlements elsewhere in America or had themselves been in the colonies at least thirty years. Most of the later, and less well-to-do, pioneers appear to have settled *originally* in Lancaster County, indicating a much more recent arrival in America. This is of significance in view of the fact that the earlier group dominated the economic, political, religious, and social life of the settlement. Moreover, a higher proportion of the Quaker, Baptist, or Anglican settlers originated among older American families than was the case with the Presbyterians.

The evidence indicates that the English-speaking settlers entered the Yadkin-Catawba basin somewhat earlier than the German. Occupation of the best land by the Scotch-Irish, the small number of Germans appearing in the court records, and the absence of a Lutheran or Reformed church all indicate the later arrival of the Germans. It is possible, however, that the *small number* of Germans,[5] rather than their belated arrival, may provide the true explanation.

Irrespective of origin, the settlers invariably located as close to the sources of the larger creeks as possible, thereby insuring adequate water and the most fertile soil. Close examination of the location of land grants produces the conclusion that there was very little squatting after 1752. Virtually all the desirable land was covered by legally authorized land warrants.[6]

4. That is, exclusive of present-day Delaware. In addition to the 40 German families, 179 of the settlers considered in this study are known to have originated in Pennsylvania, while 62 others probably did so. In computing "probable" origin the author divided each "possible" category (see Appendix H) by two, since there are approximately twice as many possible origins (due to contradictory evidence) as there are individuals involved. In adding the total number of Presbyterians considered in the study, the author arrived at a figure of 305. By using the method indicated above, the total figure ("certains" plus one-half the "possibles") came to 309. Much the same result followed when the method was applied to the non-Presbyterian settlers. (See map inside back cover).

5. Quite unlike the situation in Pennsylvania.

6. The average amount of land legally possessed by each settler was approxi-

Consideration of the character and institutions of the pioneers on the northwest Carolina frontier provides valuable insight into the process of frontier settlement. Despite the Presbyterian majority, there is little evidence that the pioneers were inordinately religious. The background and activities of such pioneers as Morgan Bryan, Israel Boone, David Jones, James Carter, John Frohock, James Story, Robert Tate, Thomas Bashford, John Brandon, John Nisbet, John McElwrath, Andrew Cranston, Abraham Cresson, Edward Hughes, Luke Dean, Alexander Cathey, Hugh Forster, Archibald Hamilton, Elizabeth Deacon, Adam Hall, Griffith Rutherford, Silas Enyart, William Roberts, Edward Cusick, John Newman Oglethorpe, and James Bowers indicate that there was a geniune need for the admonitions of John Thomson and the preaching of Hugh McAden and Benjamin Miller. There is no record that those pioneers of Quaker, Anglican, Lutheran, or Reformed origin even established a church during the period covered by this study.

Necessity for the establishment and maintenance of central authority appears to have been clearly recognized by the inhabitants of Rowan County. In 1761, Sheriff Milner was able to report collection of taxes from 1,373 persons out of a possible 1,486. Petitions for such property as town lots, inns, and ferries were dutifully made; roads were built and maintained; warrants and surveys were made with surprising efficiency and accuracy; and the rights of orphaned children and indentured servants were effectively protected.

Another fact revealed by the study is the surprising ease with which people traveled great distances in a region so recently wrested from the Indians. The freedom of movement exercised by such persons as John Verrell, John Dunn, Conrad Michael, James Bowers, Luke Dean, Charles Cogdell, Benjamin Milner, and John Frohock raises some question concerning the inadequacy of frontier communications.

It can be stated that the township of Salisbury was essentially an administrative, rather than a social, center. Lacking a school, library, newspaper, or church, the village was essentially a place where the court met and where weary immigrants sought food and repose. Rowan County, it must be remembered, was an agri-

---

mately one square mile. It is interesting to note how little overlapping occurred in the land surveys. This was in large measure due to the fact that the chain-carriers for the surveyors were local residents.

cultural region. The incoming settlers sought cheap land, not town lots—and yet Salisbury grew.

The climate and the soil, said U. B. Phillips, are what have made the South distinctive. To these ingredients should be added the people—not the Negro, as Phillips thought, but the white people. One cannot help but conclude, in view of the evidence contained in the present study, that any assessment of southern history should emphasize exploitation of the land and the eighteenth-century evolution of family relationships, clan loyalties, and a cultural homogeneity which in countless cases spanned at least three generations, two continents, and a half-dozen American colonies! Perhaps the truest understanding of the history of western North Carolina, the South, and the nation, is to be found in careful study of the process by which they were settled. Who were the initial inhabitants? Why did they settle and under what circumstances? That there is need for detailed investigation of these questions is perhaps the most important conclusion to be derived from this study.

For in spite of the enormous amount of work which has been done, Frederick Jackson Turner's central thesis—that the American frontier was fundamental in determining the American character—stands in need of documentation. American historians must still ask themselves this question: What was the American frontier?

# APPENDICES

## Appendix A

### Prominent Officials of Rowan County, 1753-1762

| Clerks of the Court | | Sheriffs | |
|---|---|---|---|
| John Dunn | 1753-55 | David Jones | 1753-57 |
| Thomas Parker | 1755-60 | Edward Hughes | 1758 |
| John Frohock | 1760-62 | Benjamin Milner | 1759-62 |

### Trustees for Town Land of Salisbury
James Carter 1753-62
Hugh Forster 1753-62

## Appendix B

A Partial List of Quakers Appearing (1675-1747) in the Records of the Monthly Meetings at Burlington, New Jersey; Middletown (Bucks County), Pennsylvania; New Garden (Chester County), Pennsylvania; and Nottingham (on the Border Between Chester County, Pennsylvania, and Cecil County, Maryland) [From records in Friends Library, Swarthmore College, Swarthmore, Pennsylvania]

### Burlington

Abbott, Ann
Abbott, John
Abbott, Mary
Barton, Aaron
Barton, Edward
Barton, John
Barton, Mary
Barton, Thomas
Barton, William
Borden, Jonathan
Borden, Joseph
Borden, Obadiah
Bryan, Benjamin
Bryan, Daniel
Bryan, Elizabeth
Bryan, John
Bryan, Mary
Bryan, Rebecca
Bryan, Thomas

Carter, Henry
Carter, William
Deacon, George
Deacon, Isaac
Deacon, John
Dunn, Mary
Edwards, John
Ellis, Rowland
Ellis, Sarah
Evans, Rebecca
Forster, William
Gant, Zebulon
Gardner, John
Harford, Charles
Hunt, Margaret
Hunt, Sarah
Hunt, William
Jones, John
Jones, Joseph

Lambert, Thomas
Parker, Richard
Potts, Thomas
Roberts, Edward
Roberts, John
Roberts, Mary
Shinn, Abigail

Shinn, Elizabeth
Shinn, George
Shinn, James
Shinn, Levi
Shinn, Samuel
Shinn, Thomas
Willcockson, George

*Middletown*

Abbott, Ann
Abbott, John
Abbott, Mary
Barton, Edward
Barton, Obadiah
Boone, Deborah
Borden, Francis
Borden, Mary
Brock, Ruth
Brock, Stephen
Bryan, Rebecca
Carter, Elizabeth
Carter, Isabel
Deacon, George
Dunn, Ralph
Dunn, Sarah
Dunn, William
Ellis, Rowland
Ellis, Thomas
Fletcher, Elizabeth
Fletcher, Robert
Frost, John
Gamble, Elizabeth
Gamble, Joseph

Harrison, Peter
Harrison, Richard
Harrison, Sarah
Harrison, Thomas
Harrison, William
Hill, James
Hill, Thomas
Iredell, Thomas
Jones, David
Milner, Edward
Parker, John
Parsons, John
Potts, David
Potts, Daniel
Potts, John
Potts, Jonathan
Potts, Sarah
Potts, Thomas
Turner, Edward
Welch, Joseph
Whitaker, James
Whitaker, John
Yates, James
Yates, John

*New Garden-Nottingham*

Andrew, Moses
Barton, Elizabeth
Blunston, Samuel
Bryan, Elinor
Bryan, Martha
Bryan, Morgan
Bryan, Thomas
Carter, Catherine
Carter, Robert
Carter, Hanna
Cartledge, Mary
Fincher, Elizabeth
Fincher, Francis
Fincher, John
Fincher, Jonathan
Fincher, Mary
Fincher, Sarah
Forster, Francis
Giles, John

Giles, Jacob
Giles, Nathaniel
Hanby, Elizabeth
Hanby, Mary
Hanby, William
Hendricks, John
Hendricks, Rebecca
Hendricks, Tobias
Hunter, Ann
Hunter, William
Parsons, Henry
Parsons, Margaret
Pennington, Isaac
Reece, John
Rigbie, Elizabeth
Rigbie, James
Rigbie, Nathan
Rigbie, Susannah
Robinson, George

Ross, Alexander
Ruddell, Anne
Ruddell, Cornelius
Ruddell, John
Toole, Garret
Underhill, Elizabeth
Underhill, Ester
Underhill, John
Underhill, Joseph
Underhill, Thomas
Whitaker, James
Whitaker, Joseph
Whitaker, Peter
Winsley, Benjamin
Winsley, Mary
Wright, Elizabeth
Wright, John

## Appendix C

A Partial List of Quakers Arriving in Philadelphia, 1682-1729 (From *Quaker Arrivals at Philadelphia, 1682-1750: Being a List of Certificates of Removal Received at Philadelphia Monthly Meeting of Friends,* ed. Albert C. Myers [Baltimore: Southern Book Co., 1957], pp. 5-85.)

| NAME | DATE OF ARRIVAL | FROM |
|---|---|---|
| Abbott, William | 1701 | Ireland |
| Barton, Isaac | 1714 | Ireland |
| Barton, James | 1699 | England |
| Bryan, Benjamin | 1714 | Burlington, N.J. |
| Bryan, Thomas | 1707 | Burlington, N.J. |
| Carter, Elizabeth | 1686 | Barbadoes |
| Chambers, Benjamin | 1682 | England |
| Chambers, John | 1713 | England |
| Crawford, James | 1709 | Duck Creek, Del. |
| Davies, David | 1713 | Wales |
| Davies, John | 1713 | Wales |
| Dunn, William | 1711 | England |
| Ellis, Mary | 1720 | Chesterfield, N.J. |
| Ellis, Thomas | 1683 | Wales |
| Evans, John | 1682 | England |
| Fincher, Francis | 1683 | England |
| Gamble, Francis | 1687 | Barbadoes |
| Gardner, John | 1682 | England |
| Goforth, Aaron | 1711 | England |
| Harper, John | 1682 | England |
| Harrison, Richard | 1716 | West River, Md. |
| Harrison, William | 1705 | The Clifts, Md. |
| Hurford, John | 1700 | England |
| Osborne, Peter | 1711 | England |
| Parker, George | 1709 | Burlington, N.J. |
| Parker, Richard | 1701 | England |
| Parsons, Henry | 1716 | ? |
| Parsons, Thomas | 1699 | England |
| Robinson, Richard | 1703 | London |
| Robinson, William | 1703 | England |
| Scott, Abraham | 1699 | London |
| Steel, James | 1702 | England |
| Steel, James | 1711 | Duck Creek, Del. |
| Storey, Thomas | 1699 | England |
| Streator, James | 1699 | England |

Turner, Edward          1686          Chester County, Pa.
Williams, William      1729          Gwynedd, Pa.
Wood, Joseph           1727          Bucks County, Pa.

## Appendix D

### From Index to Philadelphia Wills, 1682-1900
(Historical Society of Pennsylvania, Philadelphia)

| Name | Date | Name | Date |
|------|------|------|------|
| Bell, William | 1744 | Holmes, John | 1741 |
| Best, Mary | 1692 | Hugh[e]s, Edward | 1720 |
| Carter, Elizabeth | 1744 | Hugh[e]s, Edward | 1721 |
| Carter, Henry | 1709 | Hugh[e]s, John | 1736 |
| Carter, John | 1710 | Jones, David | 1717 |
| Carter, Mary | 1748 | Jones, David | 1725 |
| Carter, Thomas | 1743 | Jones, David | 1733 |
| Carter, William | 1738 | Jones, Henry | 1687 |
| Cresson, James | 1746 | Jones, Henry | 1688 |
| Cresson, Mary | 1710 | Jones, Henry | 1727 |
| Cresson, Sarah | 1752 | Jones, Henry | 1732 |
| Cresson, Solomon | 1746 | Lindsay, Alexander | 1729 |
| Davis, Samuel | 1759 | Morgan, William | 1727 |
| Deacon, John | 1698 | Potts, Thomas | 1719 |
| Dunn, James | 1764 | Potts, Thomas | 1726 |
| Dunn, William | 1725 | Robinson, Richard | 1745 |
| Elliot, Peter | 1688 | Scott, Thomas | 1703 |
| Evans, Thomas | 1710 | Turner, Edward | 1687 |
| Evans, Thomas | 1748 | Thompson, Moses | 1748 |
| Fincher, William | 1731 | Thompson, Samuel | 1746 |
| Forster, Thomas | 1750 | Thompson, Thomas | 1734 |
| George, Edward (of Radnor, | | Walton, Richard | 1776 |
| Chester County) | 1737 | Williams, Henry | 1723 |
| George, Thomas | 1739 | Williams, William | 1742 |
| Grant, William | 1756 | | |

## Appendix E

### Occupations of Settlers on the Northwest Carolina Frontier, 1747-1762

Adam, Johannes          potter
Arndt, Peter            tavern keeper
Baker, Henry            wagonmaker

| | |
|---|---|
| Baker, Samuel | miller |
| Barth, Johann Ludwig | butcher, tavern keeper |
| Bashford, Thomas | innkeeper |
| Beard, John Lewis | butcher, tavern keeper |
| Berry, James | candlemaker |
| Boise, Bostian | tailor |
| Boone, Jonathan | spinner |
| Boone, Squire (senior) | weaver |
| Bowers, James | tavern keeper |
| Braly, John | schoolmaster |
| Brandon, James | miller |
| Brandon, John | tailor |
| Brünner, Georg | gunsmith |
| Bunting, John | weaver |
| Carson, James | tanner |
| Carter, James | millwright, surveyor |
| Cathey, Andrew | shoemaker |
| Cathey, George | miller |
| Craig, Archibald | innkeeper, ferry operator |
| Cranston, Andrew | doctor |
| Cusick, Edward | innkeeper |
| Deane, Luke | Indian trader, innkeeper, ferry operator |
| Dickey, John | gunsmith, merchant and store keeper |
| Dickson, Michael | weaver |
| Douglass, Alexander | stonemason |
| Dunn, John | attorney |
| Feree, Isaac | ferry operator |
| Forster, Hugh | saddler |
| Franck, Jacob | innkeeper, distiller |
| Frohock, John | miller |
| Gillespie, Elizabeth | innkeeper |
| Gillespie, Matthew | cordwainer |
| Graham, James | stiller |
| Grob, Henrich | millwright |
| Hall, David | blacksmith |
| Harrison, William | attorney, innkeeper |
| Hendry, Henry | schoolmaster |
| Hickey, John | merchant |
| Horah, Henry | weaver, innkeeper |
| Hughes, Edward | tavern keeper |
| Huggen, James | tavern keeper |
| Johnston, Robert (junior) | hatter |
| Jones, David | weaver |
| King, Richard | clothier |

| | |
|---|---|
| Lock, Francis | carpenter |
| Long, John | tavern keeper, planter-merchant |
| Luckie, Robert | wheelwright |
| Lynn, James | architect |
| Lynn, John | doctor |
| McConnell, William | merchant |
| McDowell, David | joiner |
| McGuire, John | Indian trader |
| McHenry, Henry | tailor |
| McKnight, William | malster |
| McManus, James | merchant |
| Magoune, George | innkeeper |
| Michael, Conrad | tanner |
| Miller, James | tailor |
| Mitchell, John | merchant |
| Montgomery, Hugh | merchant, tavern keeper |
| Montgomery, William | tavern keeper |
| Morrison, William | miller |
| Oglethorpe, John Newman | surgeon |
| Oliphant, John | miller |
| Parker, John | doctor |
| Patton, John | blacksmith |
| Reed, Samuel | cordwainer |
| Rintelmann, Christopher | weaver |
| Rounsavill, Benjamin | ferry operator |
| Ryle, John | innkeeper |
| Shinn, Samuel | mason |
| Sleven, William | weaver |
| Steel, Robert | schoolmaster |
| Strayhorn, Gilbert | tailor |
| Thompson, John | cooper |
| Thomson, John | Presbyterian minister |
| Verrell, John | attorney, tavern keeper |
| Walton, Richard | tanner |
| Whitesides, John | miller |
| Williams, William | hatter |
| Woods, Robert | carpenter |

Appendix F

German Settlers on the Northwest Carolina Frontier, 1747-1762

| Name As It Appears in Rowan Records | Name As It Appears in Strassburger's Compilation | Date of Arrival From Rotterdam (where known) | Age on Arrival (where known) | Name of Vessel (where known) |
|---|---|---|---|---|
| Aaron, Conrad | Conrad Arndt | | | |
| Aaron, Jacob | Jacob Arndt | | | |
| Aaron, Peter | Peter Arndt | 1733 | | |
| Aaronhart, Killen | Killen Ernhardt[1] | | | |
| Aaronhart, Philip | Philip Ernhardt | | | |
| Adams, John | Johannes Adam[1] | | | |
| Agender, Henry | Henrich Agader | 1731 | 10 | Restauration |
| Akinder, John | Johannes Agader | 1731 | 33 | |
| Barringer, Michael | Michael Behringer[1] | | | |
| Beam, Peter | Peter Böhm | 1738 | | Pink Plaisance |
| Beard, John Lewis | Johann Ludwig Barth | 1749 | | |
| Beefle, Paul | Paulus Buffell (Biefel) | 1738 | | Patience and Margaret |
| Berrier, George Henry | Georg Henrich Birrer[1] | | | |
| Bonacher, Michael | | | | |
| Booe, Stophel | Christopher Buhe | 1738 | 25 | Hope |
| Brock, Paul | Paul Brack | 1738 | 21 | |
| Brinegar, Adam | Adam Bruninger | 1731 | 5 | |
| Brown, Jacob | Jacob Braun[1] | | | |
| Brown, Michael | Michael Braun | 1737 | | Britannia |

| Name As It Appears in Rowan Records | Name As It Appears in Strassburger's Compilation | Date of Arrival From Rotterdam (where known) | Age on Arrival (where known) | Name of Vessel (where known) |
|---|---|---|---|---|
| Brown, Stephen | Stephen Braun | | | Britannia |
| Bruner, George | Georg Brünner | 1739 | 19 | St. Andrew Galley |
| Bruner, Henry | Henrich Brünner | 1739 | 20 | Patience |
| Bullen, Conrad | | | | Robert and Alice |
| Butner, Adam | Adam Büttner[1] | | | |
| Butner, Peter | Peter Büttner | | | |
| Clingman, Alexander[2] | | | | |
| Eary, Peter | | | | |
| Eller, Christian | Christian Eller (Öhler) | 1747 | | Snow Fox |
| Eller, Jacob | Jacob Eller (Öhler) | | | Winter Galley |
| Eller, Peter | Peter Eller (Öhler) | | | Britannia |
| Felker, Jacob | Jacob Völcker[3] | 1732 | 17 | St. Andrew Galley |
| Feltmatt, Theodore | | | | |
| Fisher, Frederick | Friedrich Fischer[1] | 1748 | | Jamaica Galley |
| Fite, Peter | Peter Veit | | 23 | Jamaica Galley |
| Fraley, Frederick | Friedrich Fröhlich | | | |
| Fraley, Henry | Heinrich Fröhlich | 1740 | 25 | Samuel |
| Frank, Jacob | Jacob Franck[1] | | | |
| Fullwider, Jacob | Jacob Volenweider | 1749 | | Priscilla |
| Gatshe, John | Johann Gets (Götz) | 1733 | 40 | Pennsylvania Merchant |
| Grubb, Henry | Heinrich Grob[4] | 1743 | | Francis and Elizabeth |
| Hartman, Harmon | Herman Hartmann | | | |

| Name As It Appears in Rowan Records | Name As It Appears in Strassburger's Compilation | Date of Arrival From Rotterdam (where known) | Age on Arrival (where known) | Name of Vessel (where known) |
|---|---|---|---|---|
| Heller, Henry | Heinrich Heller[1] | 1737 | | Samuel |
| Hinkle, Jacob | | | | |
| Hinkle, Peter | Pietter Henckels | | | |
| Kern, Conrad | Conrad Kern | 1735 | 21 | Billender Oliver |
| Lingle, Lawrence | Lorentz Lingel[1] | 1754 | | Phoenix |
| Lemley, George | Jerg Lembgen | | | |
| Litsler, Frederick | Friedrich Litzlehr | 1748 | | Hampshire |
| Lovewater, Joseph (Jacob) | Joseph Lobwasser | 1749 | | Crown |
| March, Rudolph | Rudolf Mertz | 1747 | | Restauration |
| Michael, Conrad | Conrad Michael | 1743 | 20 | Francis and Elizabeth |
| Miller, Wendell | Wendel Müller[1] | 1754 | 25 | Brothers |
| Peasinger, John | Johannes Bösinger | | | |
| Peeler, Anthony | Anthony Biehler | 1736 | 25 | Harle |
| Pheagley, Peter | Peter Vögeli | 1738 | | Robert and Alice |
| Phifer, Martin | Martin Pfeiffer[1] | 1736 | 18 | Harle |
| Raiblen, Martin | | | | |
| Rendleman, Christopher | Christopher Rintelmann | 1754 | 36 | Neptune |
| Roan, Henry | Henrich Rohn | 1753 | | Halifax |
| Saltz, Anthony | Anthony Salz[1] | | | |
| Shore, Frederick | Fried Schor | 1750 | | Sandwich |
| Smith, George | Georg Schmidt[1] | | | |
| Smith, Michael | Michael Schmidt | | | |

| Name As It Appears in Rowan Records | Name As It Appears in Strassburger's Compilation | Date of Arrival From Rotterdam (where known) | Age on Arrival (where known) | Name of Vessel (where known) |
|---|---|---|---|---|
| Smith, Peter | Peter Schmidt | | | |
| Snap, Lawrence | Lorentz Schnepp | 1733 | 21 | Samuel |
| Stagnor, John Barnett | Johann Bernhardt Steigner | 1738 | 24 | Billender Thistle |
| Strozer, Peter | Peter Ströher | 1751 | | Patience |
| Thompson, Claus | Nicklaus Thommen[5] | 1736 | 24 | Princess Augusta |
| Verble, Philip | Philip Wirbel | 1741 | | Europa |
| Wolfsgill, Joseph | Joseph Wolfskehl | 1743 | 14 | Loyal Judith |
| Ziverly, Henry | Henrich Zobeli | 1748 | 18 | Patience |

1. Examination of Strassburger's work produces the conclusion that these were probably the original spellings

2. Probably a German.

3. A Johan Jacob Felker (Völcker), aged seventeen (and sick), arrived at Philadelphia aboard the "Pink Plaisance" in 1732. This is the only Jacob Felker to land at Philadelphia after 1727. Daniel, a son of Jacob Völcker of Tulpehocken, Pennsylvania, was baptized March 17, 1744. *Pennsylvania German Pioneers. A Publication of the Original Lists of Arrivals in the Port of Philadelphia from 1727 to 1808,* 3 vols., comp. and ed. Ralph Beaver Strassburger (Norristown, Pa.: Pennsylvania German Society, 1934), I, 79; *Notes and Queries, Historical, Biographical and Genealogical, Relating Chiefly to Interior Pennsylvania,* annual vols., ed. William H. Egle (Harrisburg: Harrisburg PublishingCo., 1896), p. 36.

4. See p. 128.

5. See p. 130

## Appendix G

### Settlers on the Northwest Carolina Frontier Whose Names Indicate French Origin[1]

As Commonly Spelled in
Colonial Records | Original French Spelling
--- | ---
Boise | Bouisset (Bouysset, Bouisse)
Brevard (Bravard) | Bravard
Braly | Bralier, Braley
Bunting[2] | Bonnetain, Bonton
Cathey | Cattier (Catheau)
Cavin | Cavin
Feree | Féry, Ferry
Gracy | Graciet
Hardin | Hardin
Horah | Horie
Huey | Houy (Huet, Hui)
Jack | Jack (from Jäckel)
Jetton | Giton (Gitton)
Lambert | Lambert
Laurence | Laurents (Laurence)
Luckey | Lucké
Marlin | Marlin
Oliphant | Oliphant
Pendry | Pentray
Rambo | Rambeau
Rounsavill | Ronce[ville], Ronce[valle]
Sherrill | Chérel
Simonton | Simoneton

1. Including Alsace-Lorraine; based on Albert Dauzat, *Dictionnaire étymologique des noms de famille et prénoms de France* (Paris: Libraire Larousse, 1951.)

2. Often spelled "Buntin" in Rowan County records.

Appendix H

Chart Indicating Origins of Non-German Settlers
on the Northwest Carolina Frontier[1]

| | | Eastern Shore of Maryland | Western Shore of Maryland | Cecil-New Castle area | Eastern Chester County | Western Chester County | Eastern Lancaster County | Western Lancaster County | Bucks County | Phila-delphia County | New Jersey | Virginia | Southern Delaware | North Carolina |
|---|---|---|---|---|---|---|---|---|---|---|---|---|---|---|
| Presbyterians (Scotch-Irish and Huguenots) | Certain | 24 | 14 | 39 | 29 | 39 | 17 | 47 | 1 | 0 | 11 | 1 | 0 | 0 |
| | Possible[2] | 16 | 9 | 19 | 14 | 21 | 30 | 28 | 0 | 0 | 1 | 0 | 3 | 6 |
| Non-Presbyterians (English, Welsh, Irish, French) | Certain | 9 | 18 | 19 | 7 | 2 | 16 | 0 | 11 | 10 | 7 | 3 | 0 | 0 |
| | Possible[2] | 19 | 6 | 12 | 14 | 4 | 3 | 0 | 6 | 4 | 7 | 0 | | |

1. Does not include thirty-two persons (sixteen of them Presbyterians) whose origins remain obscure.
2. Persons concerning whose origins contradictory evidence exists.

# Appendix I

## PARTIAL LIST OF ELDERS SERVING IN PENNSYLVANIA, DELAWARE, AND MARYLAND PRESBYTERIAN CONGREGATIONS, 1713-1745

| NAME | CONGREGATION | PRESBYTERY | DATE |
|------|--------------|------------|------|
| George Gillespie (Minister) | White Clay Creek | New Castle | 1713 |
| David Evans (Minister) | ? | New Castle | ? |
| John Steel | Head of Christiana | New Castle | 1731 |
| William Williams | ? | New Castle | ? |
| John Hall | ? | New Castle | 1725 |
| John McDowell | Upper Elk | New Castle | 1726 |
| Roger Lawson | Upper Elk | New Castle | 1726 |
| David Alexander | Upper Elk | New Castle | 1726 |
| John Brevard | Upper Elk | New Castle | 1726 |
| John Kilpatrick | Octoraro | New Castle | 1727 |
| James Alexander | Octoraro | New Castle | 1727 |
| Patrick Campbell | Octoraro | New Castle | 1727 |
| Samuel Cavin | ? | Donegal | 1732 |
| William McDowell | Head of Christiana | New Castle | 1731 |
| Arthur Patterson | Middle Octoraro | Donegal | 1732 |
| Hugh Kirkpatrick | Middle Octoraro | Donegal | 1733 |
| John Kirkpatrick | Nottingham | Donegal | 1733 |
| John Luckie | Nottingham | Donegal | 1733 |
| James Cook | Pequea | Donegal | 1733 |
| William Whitesides | Pequea | Donegal | 1733 |
| Alexander Davidson | Octoraro | Donegal | 1734 |
| John Mordah | Octoraro | Donegal | 1734 |
| Andrew Cochran | Chesnut Level | Donegal | 1735 |
| Alexander Robertson | Chesnut Level | Donegal | 1735 |
| Walter Carruth | Paxtang | Donegal | 1738 |
| James Cook | Paxtang | Donegal | 1738 |
| Robert King | Donegal | Donegal | 1740 |
| William Stevenson | Donegal | Donegal | 1740 |
| John Graham | Donegal | Donegal | 1740 |
| James Crawford | Donegal | Donegal | 1740 |
| John McEwen | Forks of Brandywine | Donegal | 1740 |
| John Andrew | Middle Octoraro | Donegal | 1740 |
| James Alexander | Middle Octoraro | Donegal | 1740 |
| Samuel Young (Minister) | Drawyers | New Castle | 1720 |
| John Thompson | Rock | New Castle | 1742 |
| Robert Mackey | Rock | New Castle | 1745 |
| Matthew Woods (Minister) | New Hanover | Donegal | ? |

PARTIAL LIST OF TAX ASSESSORS SERVING IN LANCASTER
COUNTY, PENNSYLVANIA, 1737-1753

| NAME | TOWNSHIP | DATE |
|------|----------|------|
| Hugh Hall | Derry | 1737 |
| James Allison | Donegal | 1736 |
| David Templeton | Harmony Ridge | 1742 |
| Robert King | Little Brittain | 1742 |
| John Hugan | Manchester | 1744 |
| John Mitchell | West Pennsborough | 1744 |
| John Mitchell | Drumore | 1744 |
| John Barclay | Colerain | 1744 |
| James McKee | Derry | 1746 |
| John Cowan | Hanover | 1746 |
| William Morrison | Colerain | 1746 |
| James Kerr | Donegal | 1746 |
| Moses White | Rapho | 1747 |
| Hugh Barclay | Colerain | 1749 |
| John Cowan | Salsbury | 1750 |
| John Potts | Rapho | 1750 |
| John Watt | Paxtang | 1753 |
| Martin Pfeiffer | Manheim | 1752 |

# BIBLIOGRAPHY

I. PRIMARY SOURCES

A. Manuscripts

Rhoda, Barber, Handwritten Journal, 1726-82. Historical Society of Pennsylvania, Philadelphia.

Blanche-Baker Papers. Include pamphlets and genealogical data relating to seven families considered in this study. Southern Historical Collection, University of North Carolina, Chapel Hill, N.C.

The Blunston Licenses (original), 1734-35. Land Office, Capitol Building, Harrisburg, Pa.

Bucks County, Pennsylvania, Miscellaneous Papers, 1682-1850. 2 volumes. A collection of letters and land records. Historical Society of Pennsylvania, Philadelphia.

Buffington and Marshall Papers, 1705-80. 6 volumes. Contains letters from and to persons in Rowan County, N.C. Chester County Historical Society, West Chester, Pa.

Henry A. Chambers, "The Chambers Family of Iredell County, N.C., A.D. 1754-1912." Manuscript in Chambers Papers, Southern Historical Collection, University of North Carolina, Chapel Hill, N.C.

Chester County Miscellaneous Papers, 1684-1847. Historical Society of Pennsylvania, Philadelphia.

Chester County Tavern License Papers, 1700-54. 10 volumes. Chester County Historical Society, West Chester, Pa.

Chester County Tax Lists for 1722-27, 1735, 1737, 1738, 1740, 1741, 1747, and 1753 (unpaginated manuscript). Chester County Historical Society, West Chester, Pa.

Commissioner's Minute Book, 1729-70. Office of the County Commissioner, Lancaster, Pa.

Gilbert Cope Collection. Genealogical data on eighteenth-century Pennsylvania families. Collections of the Genealogical Society of Pennsylvania, Historical Society of Pennsylvania, Philadelphia.

Curry Collection. Consists in part of files of data concerning a number of North Carolina families, including forty-two family names considered in this study. Southern Historical Collection, University of North Carolina, Chapel Hill, N.C.

George F. Davidson Collection, 1748-1887. 1,660 items in 5 boxes. Material relating to the Davidson family considered in the present study. Duke University Library, Durham, N.C.

Derry and Paxtang Tax Lists for 1750 (unpaginated manuscripts). Office of the County Commissioner, Lancaster County Courthouse, Lancaster, Pa.

Dobbs Papers. Papers of Arthur Dobbs, Governor of North Carolina, 1754-65. Southern Historical Collection, University of North Carolina, Chapel Hill, N.C.

James King Hall Collection. Includes data on King and Hall families of Iredell and Rowan Counties. Southern Historical Collection, University of North Carolina, Chapel Hill, N.C.

Hanover Township Tax Lists (unpaginated manuscripts, 1750-51, no date, 1756). Office of the County Commissioner, Lancaster County Courthouse, Lancaster, Pa.

John Abner Harris Papers. Include two volumes of genealogical data pertaining to ten of the families considered in this study. Southern Historical Collection, University of North Carolina, Chapel Hill, N.C.

Index to the Will Books of Philadelphia City and County, 1682-1900. Historical Society of Pennsylvania, Philadelphia.

Alfred R. Justice Collection. Genealogical data on eighteenth-century Pennsylvania families. Collections of the Genealogical Society of Pennsylvania, Historical Society of Pennsylvania, Philadelphia.

Lancaster County Appearance Dockets, 1747-52 (unpaginated manuscripts). Office of the County Commissioner, Lancaster County Courthouse, Lancaster, Pa.

Lancaster County Common Pleas Dockets, 1729-51. These documents are collected in twenty-three chronological listings of cases in pamphlet form (for the most part unpaginated), each one containing cases for approximately two years. Office of the County Commissioner, Lancaster County Courthouse, Lancaster, Pa.

Lancaster County Land Warrants, 1733-61 (unpaginated manuscripts, arranged alphabetically). Office of the County Commissioner, Lancaster County Courthouse, Lancaster, Pa.

Lancaster County Miscellaneous Papers, 1724-1816. Historical Society of Pennsylvania, Philadelphia.

Lancaster County Tax Lists for 1750, 1751, 1754, 1756, 1758, and 1759 (manuscripts, identified by date and township). Office of the County Commissioner, Lancaster County Courthouse, Lancaster, Pa.

Lightfoot Papers, 1733-1816. Contain miscellaneous warrants and surveys of lands in Lancaster, Chester, Berks, and other counties. Historical Society of Pennsylvania, Philadelphia.

Macay-McNeely Papers. Include lawyer's account book (1759-74) containing data relevant to the present study. Southern Historical Collection, University of North Carolina, Chapel Hill, N.C.

McCubbins Collection. Excerpts from court records, newspaper, correspondence, and miscellaneous items collected by Mrs. J. F. McCubbins of Salisbury; filed alphabetically by families. Salisbury Public Library, Salisbury, N.C.

Henry Eustace McCulloh Survey Book. Surveys and plats of lands in Rowan County, North Carolina. Southern Historical Collection, University of North Carolina, Chapel Hill, N.C.

Alexander McWhorter Papers. Southern Historical Collection, University of North Carolina, Chapel Hill, N.C.

New Castle County Assessment Lists (Brandywine Hundred, 1739). Hall of Records, Dover, Del.

New Castle County Court of Common Pleas, 1703-17, 1727-40. The original lists are in folders, undesignated save by a penciled number on the outside cover. Hall of Records, Dover, Del.

Nisbet Papers. Included are ninety eighteenth-century items concerning various families considered in this study. Southern Historical Collection, University of North Carolina, Chapel Hill, N.C.

Northampton County, Pennsylvania, Miscellaneous Manuscripts, 1727-58. Contain land warrants, letters, and surveys. Historical Society of Pennsylvania, Philadelphia.

Court of Philadelphia County, Paper, 1697-1749. 3 volumes (unpaginated). Historical Society of Pennsylvania, Philadelphia.

Philadelphia Landholders, 1734 (unpaginated manuscript). Historical Society of Pennsylvania, Philadelphia.

A Plan of 16,500 Acres of Land Lying on the Great or West River of the Calfpasture, in the *Preston and Virginia Papers of the Draper Collection of Manuscripts.* Publications of the State Historical Society of Wisconsin, Calendar Series, volume I. Madison, Wisconsin: published by the Society, 1915.

Record of Births (unpaginated), St. Paul's Parish Register, Kent County, Maryland. Hall of Records, Annapolis, Md.

Rowan County Civil and Criminal Cases, 1753-64. 4 folders. State Department of Archives and History, Raleigh, N.C.

Rowan County Tax Lists for 1768 (typed from manuscripts). Clerk's Office, Rowan County Courthouse, Salisbury, N.C.

Rowan County Wills (original). State Department of Archives and History, Raleigh, N.C.

Rumsey Family Papers, 1662-1870. 1,250 items in 7 boxes. Papers of one of the largest landholders in Cecil County, Maryland, in the 1730's. Library of Congress.

Store Account Book (1755-86) of John Dickey, merchant. Duke University Library, Durham, N.C.

The Taylor Papers: Being a Collection of Warrants, Surveys, Letters, &C., Relating to the Early Settlement of Pennsylvania (including correspondence for the period 1723-50 and scattered miscellaneous items for the period 1672-1775 in unmarked volumes). 10 volumes. Historical Society of Pennsylvania, Philadelphia.

Alexander H. Torrence Letters and Papers, 1754-1915. 559 items in two boxes. Southern Historical Collection, University of North Carolina, Chapel Hill, N.C.


B. Public or Official Documents

Anson County Deed Books. Office of the Registrar of Deeds, Anson County Courthouse, Wadesboro, N.C.

Augusta County Deed Books. Office of the Registrar of Deeds, Augusta County Courthouse, Staunton, Va.

Augusta County Will Books. Clerk's Office, Augusta County Courthouse, Staunton, Va.

The Black Books: Calendar of Maryland State Papers. Annapolis, Md.: Hall of Records Commission, 1943.

Bucks County Administration Dockets. Clerk's Office, Bucks County Courthouse, Doylestown, Pa.

Bucks County Will Books. Office of the Registrar of Wills, Bucks County Courthouse, Doylestown, Pa.

Calendar of New Jersey Wills, in Documents Relating to the Colonial History of the State of New Jersey, first series, volumes XXX and XXXIII. A. Van Doren Honeyman (volume XXX) and William Nelson (volume XXXIII), eds. Somerville, N.J.: The Unionist Gazette Association, 1918 (volume XXX), and Paterson, N.J.: The Press Printing and Publishing Company, 1901 (volume XXXIII).

Cecil County Deed Books. Office of the Registrar of Deeds, Cecil County Courthouse, Elkton, Md.

Cecil County Judgments. S.K. no. 3 (1723-30) and S.K. no. 4 (1730-32, 1736-41, 1741-43, 1746-47), Hall of Records, Annapolis, Md.

Chester County Administration Dockets. Office of the Registrar of Wills, Chester County Courthouse, West Chester, Pa.

Chester County Deed Books. Office of the Registrar of Deeds, Chester County Courthouse, West Chester, Pa.

Chester County Orphans' Court Dockets, Minors' Estates. Office of the Registrar of Wills and Clerk of Orphans' Court, Chester County Courthouse, West Chester, Pa.

Chester County Will Books. Clerk's Office, Chester County Courthouse, West Chester, Pa.

Clark, Walter, ed. *The State Records of North Carolina*. 16 volumes (XI through XXVI). Winston, N.C.: M. I. and J. C. Stewart, Printers to the State, 1895-96; Goldsboro, N. C.: Nash Brothers, Book and Job Printers, 1898-1905.

Colonial Land Grant Records of North Carolina. State Library, Raleigh, N.C.

Cumberland County Register's Dockets. Clerk's Office, Cumberland County Courthouse, Carlisle, Pa.

Cumberland County Wills. Office of the Clerk, Cumberland County Courthouse, Carlisle, Pa.

Delaware Land Records. Hall of Records, Dover, Del.

Dorchester County Deed Books. Office of the Registrar of Deeds, Dorchester County Courthouse, Cambridge, Md.

Egle, William H., and John B. Linn, eds. *Pennsylvania Archives,* Second Series, 19 volumes. Harrisburg: State Printers, 1877-96.

Egle, William H., ed. *Pennsylvania Archives,* Third Series, 30 volumes. Harrisburg: State Printers, 1894-99.

Frederick County Court Judgments, 1748-59. Hall of Records, Annapolis, Md.

Granville County Deed Books. Office of the Registrar of Deeds, Granville County Courthouse, Oxford, N.C.

Halifax County Deed Books. Office of the Registrar of Deeds, Halifax County Courthouse, Halifax, N.C.

Hazard, Samuel, ed. *Pennsylvania Archives,* first series, 12 volumes. Philadelphia: printed by Joseph Severns and Company, 1852-56.

*Heads of Families: First Census of the United States, 1790; State of Pennsylvania.* Dept. of Commerce and Labor, Bureau of the Census, S. N. D. North, Director. Washington: Government Printing Office, 1908.

Hunterdon County Court Minutes. Volume I-VII (1713-56). Hall of Records, Flemington, N.J.

Iredell County Deed Books. Office of the Registrar of Deeds, Iredell County Courthouse, Statesville, N.C.

Iredell County Will Books. Clerk's Office, Iredell County Courthouse, Statesville, N.C.

Kent County Deed Books. Office of the Registrar of Deeds, Chestertown, Md.

Kent County Wills. Office of the Registrar of Wills, Kent County Courthouse, Chestertown, Md.

Lancaster County Deed Books. Office of the Registrar of Deeds, Lancaster County Courthouse, Lancaster, Pa.

Lancaster County Will Books. Clerk's Office, Lancaster County Courthouse, Lancaster, Pa.

Lunenburg County Deed Books. Office of the Registrar of Deeds, Lunenburg County Courthouse, Lunenburg, Va.

Maryland County Land Warrants. State Land Office, Annapolis, Md.

Maryland Wills, 1635-1777. Maryland Hall of Records, Annapolis, Md.

Minutes of Burlington (New Jersey) Monthly Meeting of Friends, 1675-1926. Records of births, deaths, marriages, membership, and removals. Friends Library, Swarthmore College, Swarthmore, Pa.

Minutes of the Cecil (Maryland) Monthly Meeting of Friends, 1698-1913. Records of births, deaths, and marriages; minutes of proceedings to 1779. Friends Library, Swarthmore College, Swarthmore, Pa.

Minutes of Chesterfield (New Jersey) Monthly Meeting of Friends, 1675-1847. Records of births, deaths, and marriages. Friends Library, Swarthmore College, Swarthmore, Pa.

Minutes of the Middletown Monthly Meeting of Friends (Langhorne, Pennsylvania), 1682-1947. Records of births, deaths, marriages, removals, condemnations, and acknowledgments. Friends Library, Swarthmore College, Swarthmore, Pa.

Minutes of the New Garden (Pennsylvania) Monthly Meeting of Friends 1685-1903. Records of births, deaths, removals, and marriages. Friends Library, Swarthmore College, Swarthmore, Pa.

Minutes of the Nottingham Monthly Meeting of Friends (western Cecil County, Maryland), 1691-1889. Records of births, deaths, marriages, and removals. Friends Library, Swarthmore College, Swarthmore, Pa.

*Minutes of the Provincial Council of Pennsylvania, From the Organization to the Termination of the Proprietary Government.* 16 volumes. Philadelphia: Jo. Severns and Company (and other printers), 1851-53.

Minutes of Rowan County Court of Pleas and Quarterly Sessions, 1753-1869. Typed copy in three volumes (part of the original manuscript, torn, faded, and very difficult to read, is in the State Department of Archives and History, Raleigh, N.C.), Salisbury Public Library, Salisbury, N.C.

Montgomery County Deed Books. Office of the Registrar of Deeds, Montgomery County Courthouse, Norristown, Pa.

New Castle County Wills (identified by means of a card index). Hall of Records, Dover, Del.

Northampton County Deed Books. Office of the Registrar of Deeds, Northampton County Courthouse, Jackson, N.C.

Northampton County Will Books. Office of the Clerk of the Court, Northampton County Courthouse, Jackson, N.C.

Orange County Deed Books. Office of the Registrar of Deeds, Orange County Courthouse, Orange, Va.

Prince Georges County Deeds. Hall of Records, Annapolis, Md.

Prince Georges County Judgments, 1731, 1732, 1738-40, 1747. Hall of Records, Annapolis, Md.

Probate Records of Maryland, 1635-1776. Maryland Hall of Records, Annapolis, Md.

*Proceedings and Acts of the General Assembly of Maryland, 1737-1744*, in the *Archives of Maryland*. Volumes XL and XLII. Bernard Christian Steiner, ed. Baltimore: Maryland Historical Society, 1921 and 1923.

Queen Annes County Deed Books. Office of the Registrar of Deeds, Queen Annes County Courthouse, Centreville, Md.

Rowan County Deed Books, Office of the Registrar of Deeds, Rowan County Courthouse, Salisbury, N.C.

Rowan County Marriage Records. Office of Registrar of Deeds, Rowan County Courthouse, Salisbury, N.C.

Rowan County Minute Docket for the Court of Equity Begun March Term, 1799. Office of the Clerk of the Court, Rowan County Courthouse, Salisbury, N.C.

Rowan County Will Books. Clerk's Office, Rowan County Courthouse, Salisbury, N.C.

Saunders, William L., ed. *The Colonial Records of North Carolina.* 10 volumes. Raleigh, N.C.: Printers to the State, 1886-90.

Somerset County Deed Books. Office of the Registrar of Deeds, Somerset County Courthouse, Princess Anne, Maryland.

Somerset County Will Books. Clerk's Office, Somerset County Courthouse, Princess Anne, Maryland.

Surry County Deed Books. Office of the Registrar of Deeds, Surry County Courthouse, Dobson, N.C.

Surry County Will Books. Clerk's Office, Surry County Courthouse, Dobson, N.C.

Sussex County Will Books. Office of the Registrar of Wills, Sussex County Courthouse, Georgetown, Del.

Talbot County Will Books. Clerk's Office, Talbot County Courthouse, Easton, Md.

Testamentary Proceedings of Maryland, 1657-1777. Maryland Hall of Records, Annapolis, Md.

York County Deed Books. Office of Registrar of Deeds, York County Courthouse, York, Pa.

York County Will Books. Office of the Clerk of the Court, York County Courthouse, York, Pa.

C. Newspaper

Williamsburg *Virginia Gazette*, 1736-1780.

D. Periodical Articles

"Abstracts of New Jersey Commissions, Civil and Military, from Liber A.A.A. of Commissions in the Secretary of State's Office at Trenton." *Publications of the Genealogical Society of Pennsylvania*, IX, no. 3 (1926), 227-35.

"Colonial Militia, 1740, 1748," *Maryland Historical Magazine*, VI (1911), 44-59.

Eshleman, H. Frank. "Assessment Lists and Other Manuscript Documents of Lancaster County Prior to 1729," *Papers and Addresses of the Lancaster County Historical Society*, XX (1916), 155-94.

Hinke, William J., "Church Record of Neshaminy and Bensalem, Bucks County, 1710-1738," *Journal of the Presbyterian Historical Society*, I (1901-02), 111-34.

———, "Reformed Church Records of Eastern Pennsylvania Arranged Chronologically and According to Counties," *Publications of the Genealogical Society of Pennsylvania*, XIII, nos. 1 and 2 (1936-37), 90-92.

"Landholders of Philadelphia County, 1734; A List of the Names of the Inhabitants of the County of Philadelphia, With the Quantity of Land They Respectively Held Therein, According to the Uncertaine Returns of the Constables," *Publications of the Genealogical Society of Pennsylvania*, I, no. 4 (1898), 166-83.

McBee, May Wilson, ed. "Anson County, North Carolina, Abstracts of Early Records," *The May Wilson McBee Collection*, Greenwood, Miss.: May Wilson McBee, 1950.

"Records of Holy Trinity (Old Swedes) Church, Wilmington, Delaware, from 1697 to 1773." Translated from the original Swedish by Horace Burr, with an abstract of the English records from 1773 to 1810. *Papers of the Historical Society of Delaware*, IX (1890), 365.

"Records of the Presbytery of New Castle Upon Delaware," *Journal of the Presbyterian Historical Society*, XIV, no. 7 (September, 1931), 289-308; XIV, no. 8 (December, 1931), 377-84; XV, no. 2 (June, 1932), 73-120; XV, no. 3 (September, 1932), 159-68; XV, no. 4 (December, 1932), 174-207.

"Records of the Welsh Tract Baptist Meeting, Pencader Hundred,

New Castle County, Delaware, 1701 to 1828. Copied from the Original Records in the Possession of the Meeting Officials," *Papers of the Historical Society of Delaware,* XLII (1904), 42-43.

"Register of Baptisms, 1701-1746, First Presbyterian Church of Philadelphia," *Publications of the Genealogical Society of Pennsylvania,* XIX, no. 3 (1952-54), 277-308.

### E. Other Printed Sources

Abstracts of Bucks County Wills, 1685-1795, in Collections of the Genealogical Society of Pennsylvania. Pennsylvania Historical Society, Philadelphia.

*Calendar of Delaware Wills: New Castle County, 1682-1800.* Abstracted and compiled by the Historical Research Committee of the Colonial Dames of Delaware. New York: Frederick H. Hitchcock, 1911.

*Catalogue and Errata of the Records of Holy Trinity (Old Swedes) Church as translated by Horace Burr.* Published by the Historical Society of Delaware. Wilmington: Press of Charles L. Story Company, 1919.

Chalkley, Lyman, ed. *Chronicles of the Scotch-Irish Settlements in Virginia, Extracted from the Original Court Records of Augusta County, 1745-1800,* 3 volumes. Rosslyn, Va.: The Commonwealth Printing Co., 1912.

Cotton, Jane [Baldwin], ed. *Maryland Calendar of Wills.* 8 volumes. Baltimore: Kohn and Pollock, Inc., 1904-28.

Fries, Adelaide, ed. *Records of the Moravians in North Carolina.* 7 volumes. Raleigh, N.C.: Edwards and Broughton Printing Company, 1922-47.

*Genealogical Data Relating to the German Settlers of Pennsylvania and Adjacent Territory from Advertisements in German Newspapers Published in Philadelphia and Germantown 1743-1800.* Compiled by Edward W. Hocker. Germantown and Philadelphia, 1935.

Grimes, J. Bryan, ed. *Abstract of North Carolina Wills, Compiled from Original and Recorded Wills in the Office of the Secretary of State.* Raleigh, N.C.: E. M. Uzzell and Company, State Printers and Binders, 1910.

Hinshaw, William Wade. *Encyclopedia of American Quaker Genealogy,* 6 volumes. Ann Arbor, Mich.: Edwards Brothers, Inc., 1936.

*Hopewell Friends History, 1734-1934, Frederick County, Virginia: Records of Hopewell Monthly Meetings and Meetings Reporting to Hopewell.* Compiled from official records and published by a joint committee of Hopewell Friends assisted by John W. Wayland. Strasburg, Va.: Shenandoah Publishing House, Inc., 1936.

*Index to Calendar of Maryland State Papers.* Compiled under the direction of John Henry Alexander. Baltimore: James S. Waters, 1861.

*An Index of the Source Records of Maryland, Genealogical, Biographical, Historical.* Compiled by Eleanor Phillips Passano. Baltimore: Waverly Press, Inc., 1940.

Index to Sussex County Deed Books, 1682-1842. Office of the Registrar of Deeds, Sussex County Courthouse, Georgetown, Del.

*An Index to the Will Books and Intestate Records of Lancaster Co., Pennsylvania, 1729-1850.* Prepared by Eleanor Jane Fulton and Barbara Kendig Mylin. Lancaster, Pa.: Intelligencer Printing Company, 1936.

Jones, Hugh, *The Present State of Virginia.* Richard L. Morton, ed. Chapel Hill: University of North Carolina Press, 1956.

Lawson, John. *The History of North Carolina, Containing the Exact Description and Natural History of that Country Together with the Present State Thereof and a Journal of a Thousand Miles Traveled through Several Nations of Indians, Giving a Particular Account of their Customs, Manners, etc.* London: printed for W. Taylor at the Ship, and F. Baker at the Black Boy in Pater Noster Row, 1714; and Raleigh, N.C.: Printed by Strother and Marcom at their Book and Job Office, 1860.

Michener, Ezra, ed. *A Restrospect of Early Quakerism: Being Extracts from the Records of Philadelphia Yearly Meeting and the Meetings Composing It. To Which is Prefixed an Account of Their First Establishment.* Philadelphia: T. Ellwood Zell, 1860.

Myers, Albert Cook, ed. *Narratives of Early Pennsylvania, West New Jersey and Delaware, 1630-1707.* New York: Barnes and Noble, Inc., 1959 (reprint).

———, *Quaker Arrivals at Philadelphia, 1682-1750: Being a List of Certificates of Removal Received at Philadelphia Monthly Meeting of Friends.* Baltimore: Southern Book Company, 1957.

Philadelphia Wills. 10 volumes. In Collections of the Genealogical Society of Pennsylvania, Historical Society of Pennsylvania, Philadelphia.

Records of the Donegal Presbytery (typed copy), volumes 1A and 1B. Philadelphia: Presbyterian Historical Society, 1937.

*Records of the Presbyterian Church in the United States of America Embracing the Minutes of the General Presbytery and General Synod 1706-1788 Together With an Index and the Minutes of the General Convention for Religious Liberty 1766-1775.* Philadelphia: Presbyterian Board of Publication and Sabbath-School Work, 1904.

Stock, Leo F., ed. *Proceedings and Debates of the British Parliaments Respecting North America.* 5 volumes. Washington, D.C.: Carnegie Institute of Washington, 1924.

Stoever, Casper. *Records of Reverend John Casper Stoever, Baptismal and Marriage, 1730-1779.* Harrisburg: Harrisburg Publishing Company, 1896.

Strassburger, Ralph Beaver, ed. *Pennsylvania German Pioneers: A Publication of the Original Lists of Arrivals in the Port of Philadelphia from 1727 to 1808.* 3 volumes. Norristown, Pa.: Pennsylvania German Society, 1934.

The Vestry Book and Register of St. Peter's Parish, New Kent and James City counties, Virginia, 1684-1786. Transcribed and edited by C. G. Chamberlayne. Richmond, Va.: Division of Purchase and Printing, 1937.

Waddell, Joseph A. *Annals of Augusta County, Virginia, From 1726-to 1871.* Staunton, Va.: C. Russell Caldwell, Publisher, 1902.

### F. Maps

Map of the Town of Salisbury, N.C., drawn by W. Moore, surveyor, August 7, 1823. North Carolina Room, University of North Carolina Library, Chapel Hill, N.C.

Tracy, A. G. Tract Map of Washington County, Maryland. Hall of Records, Annapolis, Md.

Transcript of a Map of Fourth Creek Congregation Drawn by William Sharp, 1773. Rowan County Courthouse, Salisbury, N.C.

## II. SECONDARY SOURCES

### A. Books

Adams, James Truslow, ed. *The Dictionary of American History.* 5 volumes. Second edition, revised. New York: Charles Scribner's Sons, 1940.

Alexander, S. C. *An Historical Address, Delivered at the Centennial Celebration of Thyatira Church, Rowan County, N. C., October 19, 1855.* Salisbury, N.C.: J. J. Bruner, Printer, 1855.

Arthur, John Preston. *Western North Carolina, A History.* Raleigh, N.C.: Edwards and Broughton Printing Company, 1914.

Ashe, Samuel A'Court. *History of North Carolina.* 2 volumes. Greensboro, N.C.: Charles L. Van Noppen, 1908.

Bailey, Kenneth P. *The Ohio Company of Virginia and the Westward Movement, 1748-1792: A Chapter in the History of the Colonial Frontier.* Glendale, Calif.: The Arthur H. Clark Company, 1939.

Bernheim, G. D. *History of the German Settlements and of the Lutheran Church in North and South Carolina, From the Earliest Period of the Colonization of the Dutch, German and Swiss Settlers to the Close of the First Half of the Present Century.* Philadelphia: The Lutheran Book Store, 1872.

Bisbee, Henry H. *Place Names in Burlington County in New Jersey.* Riverside, N.J.: The Burlington County Publishing Company. 1955.

Blackwelder, Ruth. *The Age of Orange.* Charlotte, N.C.: William Loftin, Publisher, 1961.

Bolton, C. K. *Scotch-Irish Pioneers in Ulster and America.* Boston: Bacon and Brown, 1910.

Bowden, James. *History of the Society of Friends in America.* 2 volumes. London: Charles Gilpin and W. & F. G. Cash, 1850-54.

Brawley, James S. *Old Rowan, Views and Sketches.* Salisbury, N.C.: Rowan Printing Company, 1959.

———. *The Rowan Story, 1753-1953: A Narrative History of Rowan County, North Carolina.* Salisbury, N.C.: Rowan Printing Company, 1953.

Brown, Richard L. *A History of the Michael Brown Family of Rowan County, North Carolina, Tracing Its Line of Posterity from the Original Michael Brown to the Present Generation and Giving Something of The Times One Hundred and Fifty Years Ago Together with Many Historic Facts of Local and National Interest.* Published under the auspices of the Michael Brown Family Association, 1921.

Carruth, Harold B. *Carruth Family: Brief Background and Genealogical Data of Twenty Branches in America.* Ascutney, Vt., 1952.

Chambers, T. F. *The Early Germans of New Jersey: Their History, Churches and Genealogies.* Dover, N.J.: Dover Printing Co., 1895.

Connor, Robert D. W. *North Carolina, Rebuilding an Ancient Commonwealth, 1584-1925.* 4 volumes. Chicago and New York: The American Historical Society, Inc., 1929.

Corbitt, David Leroy. *The Formation of the North Carolina Counties, 1663-1943.* Raleigh, N.C.: State Department of Archives and History, 1950.

Cunz, Dieter. *The Maryland Germans, A History.* Princeton, N.J.: Princeton University Press, 1948.

Dauzat, Albert. *Dictionnaire étymologique des noms de famille et prénoms de France.* Paris: Librairie Larousse, 1951.

Davidson, Chalmers G. *Major John Davidson of Rural Hill, Meck-*

*lenburg County, N.C., Pioneer, Industrialist, Planter.* Charlotte, N.C.: Lassiter Press, Inc., 1943.

Davis, Julia. *The Shenandoah.* New York and Toronto: Farrar and Rinehart, Inc., 1945.

Dixon, M. C. D., and E. C. D. Vann. *Denny Genealogy.* 3 volumes. New York: The National Historical Society, 1944.

*The Donegal Presbyterian Church: The Donegal People, Their History, and Other Historical Documents.* Harrisburg: The Evangelical Press, 1935.

Donehoo, George Patterson. *A History of the Cumberland Valley in Pennsylvania.* 2 volumes. Harrisburg: The Susquehanna History Association, 1930.

————. *A History of the Indian Villages and Place Names in Pennsylvania with Numerous Historical Notes and References.* Harrisburg: The Telegraph Press, 1928.

Dunaway, Wayland F. *The Scotch-Irish of Colonial Pennsylvania.* Chapel Hill: The University of North Carolina Press, 1944.

Egle, William H. *History of the Commonwealth of Pennsylvania, Civil, Political, and Military, From Its Earliest Settlement to the Present Time, Including Historical Descriptions of Each County in the State, Their Towns, and Industrial Resources.* Philadelphia: E. M. Gardner, 1883.

————, ed. *Notes and Queries, Historical, Biographical and Genealogical, Relating Chiefly to Interior Pennsylvania.* 3 series (12 volumes). Harrisburg: Harrisburg Publishing Company (reprinted from *Harrisburg Daily Telegraph*), 1878-1901.

Eliason, Minnie Hampton. *Fort Dobbs: Historical Sketch.* Statesville, N.C.: Brady Printing Company, 1915.

Faust, A. B. *The German Element in the United States, With Special Reference to Its Political, Moral, Social, and Educational Influence.* 2 volumes. New York: The Steuben Society of America. 1927.

Fisher, Sydney George. *The Making of Pennsylvania: An Analysis of the Elements of the Population and the Formative Influences that Created One of the Greatest of the American States.* Philadelphia: J. B. Lippincott Company, 1909.

Fleming, John K. *In Freedom's Cause: Samuel Young of Rowan County, N.C.* Salisbury, N.C.: The Rowan Printing Company, 1958.

Foote, William Henry. *Sketches of North Carolina, Historical and Biographical, Illustrative of the Principles of a Portion of Her Early Settlers.* New York: Robert Carter, 58 Canal Street, 1846.

Ford, Henry Jones. *The Scotch-Irish in America.* Princeton, N.J.: Princeton University Press, 1915.

Futhey, J. Smith, and Gilbert Cope. *History of Chester County, Pennsylvania, with Genealogical and Biographical Sketches.* 2 volumes. Philadelphia: Press of J. B. Lippincott and Company, 1881.

Goodman, Hattie S. *The Knox Family: A Genealogical and Biographical Sketch of the Descendants of John Knox of Rowan County, North Carolina, and Other Knoxes.* Richmond, Va.: Whittet and Shepperson, Printers and Publishers, 1905.

Greene, E. B., and Virginia D. Harrington. *American Population Before the Census of 1790.* New York: Columbia University Press. 1932.

*Guide to the Manuscript Collections of the Historical Society of Pennsylvania.* Second edition. Philadelphia: The Historical Society of Pennsylvania, 1949.

Hammer, Carl. *Rhinelanders on the Yadkin: The Story of the Pennsylvania Germans in Rowan and Cabarrus.* Salisbury, N.C.: Rowan Printing Company, 1943.

Hanna, Charles A. *The Scotch-Irish, Or the Scot in North Britain, North Ireland, and North America.* 2 volumes. New York: The Knickerbocker Press, 1902.

————. *The Wilderness Trail: Or, The Ventures and Adventures of the Pennsylvania Traders on the Allegheny Path, With Some New Annals of the Old West, and The Records of Some Strong Men and Some Bad Ones.* 2 volumes. New York and London: G. P. Putnam's Sons, The Knickerbocker Press, 1911.

Hansen, Harry, ed. *The World Almanac and Book of Facts for 1958.* New York: New York World Telegram Corporation, 1958.

Hardison, R. B., and R. C. Jurney. *Soil Survey of Rowan County North Carolina.* Washington, D.C.: Government Printing Office, 1915.

Hook, James W. *George Michael Eller and Descendants of His in America.* New Haven, Conn., n.d.

Hooker, Richard J. *The Carolina Back Country on the Eve of the Revolution.* Chapel Hill: The University of North Carolina Press, 1953.

Hunter, C. L. *Sketches of Western North Carolina, Historical and Biographical; Illustrating Principally the Revolutionary Period of Mecklenburg, Rowan, Lincoln, and Adjoining Counties, Accompanied with Miscellaneous Information, Much of It Never Before Published.* Raleigh, N.C.: The Raleigh News Steam Job Print, 1877.

James, Alfred P. *The Ohio Company: Its Inner History.* Pittsburgh: University of Pittsburgh Press, 1959.

Jernegan, Marcus W. *The American Colonies, 1492-1750.* New York: Frederick Ungar Publishing Company, 1959 (reprint).

Johnston, George. *History of Cecil County, Maryland, and the Early Settlements around the Head of Chesapeake Bay and on the Delaware River With Sketches of Some of the Old Families of Cecil County.* Elkton, Md.: published by the author, 1881.

Jones, Rufus, M. *Quakers in the American Colonies.* New York: Russell and Russell, Inc., 1962 (reprint).

Kegley, Frederick Bittle. *Kegley's Virginia Frontier: The Beginning of the Southwest; the Roanoke of Colonial Days, 1740-1783.* Roanoke, Va: The Southwest Virginia Historical Society, 1938.

Kercheval, Samuel. *A History of the Valley of Virginia.* Third edition. Woodstock, Va.: W. N. Grabill, 1902.

Klees, Fredric. *The Pennsylvania Dutch.* New York: The MacMillan Company, 1951.

Klein, H. M. J., ed. *Lancaster County, Pennsylvania: A History.* 3 volumes. New York and Chicago: Lewis Historical Publishing Company, Inc., 1924.

Lazenby, Mary Elinor. *Lewis Graveyard, With Mention of Some Early Settlers Along Fifth Creek, Iredell County, N.C.* Statesville, N.C., n.d.

Klett, Guy S. *Presbyterians in Colonial Pennsylvania.* Philadelphia: University of Pennsylvania Press, 1937.

Kuhns, Oscar. *The German and Swiss Settlements of Colonial Pennsylvania: A Study of the So-Called Pennsylvania Dutch.* New York: Holt and Company, 1901.

Lefler, Hugh T., and Albert R. Newsome. *North Carolina: The History of a Southern State.* Chapel Hill: The University of North Carolina Press, 1954.

Leyburn, James G. *The Scotch-Irish: A Social History.* Chapel Hill: The University of North Carolina Press, 1962.

Lingle, Walter L. *Thyatira Presbyterian Church, Rowan County, North Carolina (1753-1948).* Statesville, N.C.: Brady Publishing Company, n.d.

Long, Minnie R. H. *General Griffith Rutherford and Allied Families: Harsh, Graham, Cathey, Locke, Holeman, Johnson, Chambers.* Milwaukee, Wis.: Wisconsin Cuneo Press, 1942.

Lore, Adelaide, and Eugenia and Robert Hall Morrison. *The Morrison Family of the Rocky River Settlement of North Carolina: History and Genealogy.* Charlotte, N.C.: The Observer Printing House, 1950.

Mackey, William D. *White Clay Creek Presbyterian Church, Presbytery of New Castle.* Wilmington, Del.: James and Webb, Printers, 1876.

McDowell, John Hugh. *History of the McDowells, Erwins, Irwins and Connections.* Memphis, Tenn.: C. B. Johnston and Company, 1918.

McReynolds, George. *Place Names in Bucks County, Pennsylvania, Alphabetically Arranged in an Historical Narrative.* Doylestown, Pa.: Bucks County Historical Society, 1955.

Meriwether, Robert L. *The Expansion of South Carolina, 1729-1765.* Kingsport, Tenn.: Southern Publishers, Inc., 1940.

Murphy, Raymond E., and Marion Murphy. *Pennsylvania, A Regional Geography.* Harrisburg: The Pennsylvania Book Service, 1937.

Myers, Albert C. *Immigration of the Irish Quakers into Pennsylvania, 1682-1750, With their Early History in Ireland.* Swarthmore, Pa.: published by the author, 1902.

Nevin, Alfred. *Churches of the Valley: Or, an Historical Sketch of the Old Presbyterian Congregations of Cumberland and Franklin Counties in Pennsylvania.* Philadelphia: Joseph M. Wilson, 1852.

Newman, Harry Wright. *Anne Arundel Gentry.* n.p., n.d.

Paschal, George W. *History of North Carolina Baptists.* Volume I, 1663-1805. Raleigh, N.C.: The General Board, North Carolina Baptist State Convention, 1930.

Phifer, Charles H. *Genealogy and History of the Phifer Family.* Charlotte, N.C.: George E. Wilson, 1910.

Phillips, Ulrich B. *Life and Labor in the Old South.* Boston: Little, Brown and Company, 1948.

Ramsay, John Graham. *Historical Sketch of Third Creek Church in Rowan County, North Carolina.* Concord, N.C.: The Times Book and Job Presses, 1892.

Ray, Worth S. *The Lost Tribes of North Carolina.* Austin, Tex.: published by the author, 1947.

Robinson, Blackwell P. *William R. Davie.* Chapel Hill: The University of North Carolina Press, 1957.

Robinson, Thomas H. *Historical Sketch of Old Hanover Church, with Notes Relating to the Church at Conewago, and the New-Site Grave-Yard in Lower Paxtang Township,* by A. Boyd Hamilton. [Harrisburg]: Dauphin County Historical Society, 1878.

Rumple, Jethro. *A History of Rowan County, North Carolina, Containing Sketches of Prominent Families and Distinguished Men.* Salisbury, N.C.: J. J. Bruner, 1881.

Rupp, Daniel I. *The History and Topography of Dauphin, Cumberland, Franklin, Bedford, Adams, and Perry Counties: Containing a Brief History of the First Settlers, Notices of the Leading Events, Incidents and Interesting Facts, Both General and Local, in the History of these Counties, General and Statistical Descrip-*

*tions of all the Principal Boroughs, Towns, Villages, etc.* Lancaster, Pa.: Gilbert Hills, Proprietor and Publisher, 1846.

Russell, Elbert. *The History of Quakerism.* New York: The Macmillan Company, 1943.

Scharf, J. Thomas. *History of Delaware, 1609-1888.* 2 volumes. Philadelphia: L. J. Richards and Company, 1888.

————, and Thompson Westcott. *History of Philadelphia, 1609-1884.* 3 volumes. Philadelphia: L. H. Everts and Company, 1884.

Schmidt, Hubert G. *Rural Hunterdon, An Agricultural History.* New Brunswick, N.J.: Rutgers University Press, 1946.

Spraker, Hazel A. *The Boone Family, A Genealogical History of the Descendants of George and Mary Boone Who Came to America in 1717, Containing Many Unpublished Bits of Early Kentucky History, Also a Biographical Sketch of Daniel Boone, the Pioneer by One of his Descendants.* Rutland, Vt: The Tuttle Company, 1922.

Stephen, Sir Leslie, and Sir Sidney Lee. *The Dictionary of National Biography.* 30 volumes. London: Oxford University Press, 1937-38.

Stevens, S. K., and Donald H. Kent, eds. *Bibliography of Pennsylvania History.* Comp. Norman B. Wilkinson. Harrisburg: Pennsylvania Historical and Museum Commission, 1957.

Sutherland, S. H. *Population Distribution in Colonial America.* New York: Columbia University Press, 1936.

Tolles, Frederick B. *Quakers and the Atlantic Culture.* New York: The Macmillan Company, 1960.

Van Etten, Henry. *George Fox and the Quakers.* Trans. and rev. E. Kelvin Osborn. London: Longmans, Green and Company, 1959.

Wayland, John W. *The German Element of the Shenandoah Valley of Virginia.* Charlottesville, Va.: published by the author, 1907.

————, *A History of Shenandoah County.* Strasburg, Va.: Shenandoah Publishing House, 1927.

Wilson, Howard McKnight. *The Tinkling Spring, Headwater of Freedom: A Study of the Church and Her People.* Richmond, Va.: Garrett and Massie, Inc., 1954.

*Writings on Pennsylvania History, A Bibliography.* Comp. Arthur C. Bining, Robert L. Brunhouse, and Norman B. Wilkinson. Harrisburg: Pennsylvania Historical and Museum Commission, 1946.


B. Periodical Articles

Boyd, Julian P., "The Sheriff in Colonial North Carolina," *The North Carolina Historical Review*, V, no. 2 (1928), 151-80.

Brawley, James S., "Davie Is Wealthy in Land, History," *Salisbury Post* (March 18, 1956), p. 4.

Browning, Charles H., "Francis Campbell," *Pennsylvania Magazine of History and Biography,* XXVIII (1904), 62-70.

Connor, R. D. W., "Race Elements in the White Population of North Carolina," *North Carolina State Normal and Industrial College Historical Publications,* no. 1. Raleigh, N.C.: Edwards and Broughton Printing Co., 1920.

Futhey, J. Smith, "The Scotch-Irish," *Papers and Addresses of the Lancaster County Historical Society,* XI (1907), 220-31.

Glenn, Thomas A., "Genealogical Gleanings of the Wilsons, or Willsons, of Ulster," *Pennsylvania Magazine of History and Biography,* XXXVIII (1914), 346-54.

Heitman, Mary J., "The Bryan Family of Rowan Prominent in Early Days," *Mocksville Enterprise* (Feb. 10, 1938), p. 4.

Herndon, John Goodwin, "John McKnitt (ca. 1660-1714) and Some of His Kinfolk: Alexanders-Brevards-Dales," *Publications of the Genealogical Society of Pennsylvania,* XVI, (1948), 75-97.

———, "The Reverend John Thomson," *Journal of the Presbyterian Historical Society,* XX (1942), 116-58; XXI (1943), 34-59.

High, James, "Henry McCulloh: Progenitor of the Stamp Act," *North Carolina Historical Review,* XXIX, no. 1 (1952), 24-38.

Johnson, Christopher, "The Todd Family of Anne Arundel County," *The Maryland Historical Magazine,* IX (1914), 298-305.

Kemper, Charles E., "Historical Notes from the Records of Augusta County, Virginia, Part One," *Papers and Addresses of the Lancaster County Historical Society,* XXV (1921), 89-92 [Part I], 147-55 [Part II].

———, "Valley of Virginia Notes," *The Virginia Magazine of History and Biography,* XXXI (1923), 245-52.

———, "Valley of Virginia Notes," *The Virginia Magazine of History and Biography,* XXXIV (1926), 138-40.

McLanahan, Samuel, "Scotch-Irish Family Life a Prime Factor in the Achievements of the Race," *The Scotch-Irish in America: Proceedings and Addresses,* X (1901), 143-45.

McNeely, Robert Ney, "Union County and the Old Waxhaw Settlement," *The North Carolina Booklet: Great Events in North Carolina History,* XII, no. 1 (July, 1912), 6-20.

Magee, D. F., "The Whitesides of Colerain: The Revolutionary Captain and the Congressman," *Papers and Addresses of the Lancaster County Historical Society,* XVII, no. 8 (1913), 227-33.

Mervine, William M., "The Scotch Settlers in Raphoe, County Donegal, Ireland," *The Pennsylvania Magazine of History and Biography,* XXVI (1912), 257-72.

"The Pennsylvania Germans in Loudoun County, Virginia," *Pennsylvania German Magazine,* IX, No. 3 (1908), 125-33.

Powell, William S., "Notes for a Tour of Iredell County Conducted on September 12, 1948, for the North Carolina Society of County Historians." Mimeographed. North Carolina Room, University of North Carolina, Chapel Hill, N.C.

Rockwell, E. F., "The Gospel Pioneer in Western North Carolina," *The Historical Magazine, and Notes and Queries Concerning the Antiquities, History, and Biography of America,* XXIII (third series, volume III), 144-48.

Sachse, Julius F., "Benjamin Furly," *The Pennsylvania Magazine of History and Biography,* XIX (1895), 277-306.

Sellers, Charles G., Jr., "Private Profits and British Colonial Policy," *William and Mary Quarterly,* third series, VIII (1951), 535-51.

Spence, Mrs. A. K., "Heinrich Grobb (Henry Grubb), Swiss Emigrant to Virginia," *Virginia Magazine of History and Biography,* L (1942), 69-74.

Stewart, John, "Scotch-Irish Occupancy and Exodus," *Papers Read Before the Kittochtinny Historical Society,* II (1903), 17-23.

Stoudt, John J., "Daniel and Squire Boone," *Berks County Historical Review,* I, no. 4 (1936), 108-12.

Williams, David G., "The Lower Jordan Valley Pennsylvania German Settlement," *Proceedings and Papers Read Before the Lehigh County Historical Society,* XVIII (1950), 181 pp.

C. Periodicals

*Bulletin of Friends Historical Association of Philadelphia.* 51 volumes. Philadelphia, 1906-61.

*A Collection of Papers Read Before the Bucks County Historical Society.* 5 volumes. Riegelsville, Pa., 1908-26.

*The Historical Review of Berks County.* 27 volumes. Reading, Pa., 1935-61.

*Journal of the Presbyterian Historical Society.* 39 volumes. Philadelphia, 1901-61.

*Maryland Historical Magazine.* 56 volumes. Baltimore, 1906-61.

*North Carolina Historical Review.* 39 volumes. Raleigh, N.C., 1924-62.

*Papers and Addresses of the Lancaster County Historical Society.* 65 volumes. Lancaster, Pa., 1897-1961.

*Papers Read Before the Kittochtinny Historical Society.* 10 volumes. Chambersburg, Pa., 1900-22.

*The Pennsylvania German: A Popular Magazine of Biography, History, Genealogy, Folklore, Literature, etc.* 15 volumes. Lebanon, Pa., 1900-14.

*The Pennsylvania Magazine of History and Biography.* 85 volumes. Philadelphia, 1877-1961.

*Proceedings and Papers Read Before the Lehigh County Historical Society.* 24 volumes. Allentown, Pa., 1908-61.

*Publications of the Genealogical Society of Pennsylvania.* 22 volumes. Philadelphia, 1895-1961.

*The Scotch-Irish in America, Proceedings and Addresses.* 10 volumes. No place of publication, 1889-1901.

*Virginia Magazine of History and Biography.* 69 volumes. Richmond, Va., 1894-1961.

*William and Mary Quarterly.* Second series, 41 volumes. Williamsburg, Va., 1921-61.

*The Woodstock Letters: A Record of Current Events and Historical Notes Connected with the Colleges and Missions of the Society of Jesus in North and South America.* 90 volumes. Woodstock, Md., 1872-1961.

D. Unpublished Master's Thesis

Gehrke, William Herman. "The German Element in Rowan and Cabarrus Counties." Unpublished master's thesis, University of North Carolina, Chapel Hill, N.C., 1934.

# INDEX

Acrelius, Israel, 8
Adam, Johannes, in Salisbury, 158
Adams, Robert, 105
Ägader, Heinrich, 90n
Ägader, Johannes, 90, 92
Alexander, Allen, 94
Alexander, David, elder at "head of Christiana," 51
Alexander, James, Rowan County court meets at his house, 152; schoolmaster, 190; mentioned, 51-52, 157
Alexander, Moses, has lot in Salisbury, 159; serves against Cherokees, 198; mentioned, 51
Alexander, Nathaniel, has lot in Salisbury, 159; operates mill, 160; serves against Cherokees, 198; mentioned, 51
Alexander, William, mentioned, 33n, 51-52, 58, 157-58, 189
Alexander family, in Cecil County militia, 51; mentioned, 55
Allison, Andrew, justice of peace for Rowan County, 82n; mentioned, 52-53, 65-66
Allison, James, justice of peace for Rowan County, 82n; mentioned, 52, 99, 106, 188
Allison, John, 99
Allison, Mary, 52
Allison, Robert, 64-65
Allison, Samuel, 101
Allison, Thomas, serves against Cherokees, 198
Andrew, David, 96-97
Andrew, James, 97, 128
Andrew, John, elder in Middle Octoraro congregation, 97; characterized, 188
Andrew, Moses, 103, 130

Anglicans, at the "head of Chesapeake," 27; on northwest Carolina frontier, 131; small number of, 131
Anson County, justice of peace for, 50n; mentioned, 23, 24
Archibald, John, in Cecil County militia, 96
Archibald, William, 97
Armstrong, Abel, 118
Armstrong, James, 117-18, 119n
Armstrong, Mary, 118
Armstrong, William, 118
Arndt, Conrad, 92
Arndt family, 58
Arndt, Jacob, 92
Arndt, Peter, Rowan County court meets at his house, 152; operates public house, 161; mentioned, 55, 57-58, 87, 92, 129, 157, 195
Arndt family, 58

Baker, Henry, wagonmaker, 165; acquires Bowers' shop, 166; mentioned, 86
Baker, Samuel, operates public mill, 53
Bailey, Andrew, 78
Bailey, David, 78, 131
Bailey, William, 76, 78, 121, 131
Baptists, on northwest Carolina frontier, 130, 188; identified, 130-31
Barclay, Margaret, 126
Barclay, Robert, 120
Barkley (Barclay), Henry, 127-28
Barry, Andrew, court commissioner for Cecil County, 96; mentioned, 100
Barry, Catherine, 103
Barth, Johann Ludwig (Beard, John Lewis), acquires Jacob Franck's place, 165; mentioned, 191
Barton, Benjamin, in a case of debt, 76; mentioned, 130